TIME, PLACE AND MUSIC

SOURCE MATERIALS AND
STUDIES IN ETHNOMUSICOLOGY

I

FRITS KNUF AMSTERDAM

1973

TIME, PLACE AND MUSIC

AN ANTHOLOGY OF
ETHNOMUSICOLOGICAL OBSERVATION c. 1550 TO c. 1800

BY

FRANK HARRISON

Professor of Ethnomusicology in
the University of Amsterdam

FRITS KNUF 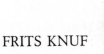 AMSTERDAM

1973

First published in 1973
by Uitgeverij Frits Knuf Amsterdam/Netherlands

Printed in The Netherlands

ISBN 90 602724 2

CONTENTS

MUSIC–NOTATIONS

ILLUSTRATIONS

PREFACE

Under the title *Time, Place and Music*, the author's inaugural oration as Professor of Ethnomusicology in the University of Amsterdam was published in June, 1971 in a small edition for private circulation. References in that print to an Appendix A and an Appendix B were explained there as indicating sections in a book containing ethnomusicological material whose publication was planned for some time during the succeeding months. This book is the fulfilment of that intention, with the modification that the publication of a reprint of Alexander Ellis's article 'On the musical scales of various nations', referred to in the 1971 print as Appendix B, has been postponed to a later date. The anthology planned as Appendix A, which has grown in the meantime to its present size, is limited for reasons of practicality and coherence to the time from *c.* 1550 to *c.* 1800 A.D. The series title *Source Materials and Studies in Ethnomusicology* conveys the intention, which it is hoped to realise, of reprinting material of various kinds, including not only further anthologies of observation and other documentary writings, but also theoretical, systematic and methodological works, and of printing original monographs.

The words 'Source Materials' and the plan of the present book may recall to English-speaking musicologists Oliver Strunk's *Source Readings in Music History*. This book resembles Professor Strunk's in consisting largely of writings that have previously existed in printed form, but which have mostly been difficult of access, and often in a language other than English, whose translation, when it existed, has in many cases been unsatisfactory or incomplete. However, while the materials in *Source Readings in Music History* are an integral part of their subject, the written and visual documentation of ethnomusicological observation in the less recent past has not hitherto been regarded as an essential part of the university study of ethnomusicology. In that respect this book is a symptom of a new tendency in being a selective contribution to the documentation of some two and a half centuries of observation by Europeans of music practices in continents other than Europe.

Present-day ethnomusicologists are accustomed to adopting, and to assuming in their colleagues, a *soi-disant* objective and scientific attitude to the acquisition and assessment of ethnomusicological evidence. If they are academics they are also frequently concerned with inculcating such an attitude in their disciples. While excessively subjective involvement is certainly undesirable, academic 'objectivity' may not always be complemented by the degree of positive intellectual engagement and penetration that is necessary for unbiassed understanding and non-assumptive exposition. The kinds of bias that may be exercised, particularly in current academic-centred observations of music-practices, are no less in need of a cool, hard look than those of the writers of the extracts printed here. Bias may be involved not only through social, intellectual and technical pre-suppositions, for example, irrelevant concepts of 'purity' or 'progress', but also in project-stereotypes geared to the current academic routines and career-structures, and in the selection and ordering of the information acquired. Such bias, where it exists, is quickly apparent if present-day academic motivations are frankly compared with those of earlier, non-academic observers.

Recorded sound is at present the primary documentation for ethnomusicological information, though video-tape, hopefully, may soon replace it in current field-work. All documentation before the use of sound recording is secondary, and consists of verbal description, or of the hand-drawn or photographic depiction of a musical event or artifact. Criteria for the evaluation of descriptive music-evidence from past, as from present sources must involve judgements about the observer's motives, opportunities, qualifications and methods, about the pertinence and perspicacity of his comment on contextual matters and about the technical *niveau* of his music-information. A long-dead observer's competence to record adequately each of the interdependent elements in a total situation may be gauged partly from available biographical sources and partly from the content and balance of his exposition. Elucidation of his motives generally needs a closer examination than such evidences afford to the place of his occupation in the society and career-structure of his time, and of any determinable personal and psychological factors which may have been relevant to his motivation.

A cursory inspection of these extracts shows that the overt motivations of their writers may roughly be classed as those of professional and proselytising Christians reporting or retailing others' reports (nos. 1, 2, 3, 7, 10, 11, 16), of a non-professional Christian with nevertheless predominantly Christian interests (no.6), or of travellers seeking information for one of three main purposes: settlement and colonisation (nos. 4 and 19), diplomacy with a view to trade (nos. 5, 8, 13, 14, 17), or exploration and/or exploitation (nos. 9, 15, 18). This broad motivation-grouping reveals common elements and comparable experiences that may be of considerable interest to social anthropologists as well as to musicologists. A closer assessment of the musical material in these reports depends, however, on as precise an examination as possible of the psychological and technical factors involved. Since all musical manifestations are the result of definite processes in specific situations, all are ultimately unique. And since an observer's mental outlook and the means of communication he uses are the products of similar processes and situations, every musical experience, if not every attitude to it, is also unique. Assessment of the value of music-information, from whatever time or place and assisted by whatever apparatus, is still ultimately an exercise in the assessment of individual perception and communication. The development of techniques of assessment is part of an ethnomusicologist's task. One of the purposes of this anthology, apart from the general human interest of its contents, is to make more easily available comparative materials for such assessment.

With five exceptions, the reports in this anthology were made from first-hand observation -- 'they heard it happen'. Of the exceptions, the reports of Juan de Torquemada, Nicholao Godinho, Pierre de Charlevoix and Jean-Baptiste Du Halde were compiled from official records of religious orders, and all three presumably unimpeded access to first-hand material. Charles de Rochefort, in the preface to the French original of item 4, emphasised his entire and faithful dependence on unnamed 'nobles Voyageurs'. The majority of the items were not originally written in English. For eight items (nos. 1, 2, 3, 11b, 12, 13, 17e, 17f) a complete English translation has been provided as well as the original text. In three instances where the items themselves are nearly contemporary translations (nos. 6, 7, and 10) the original text has not been given. In others short passages or phrases of the original are quoted in the course of the translation (nos. 4, 5, 8, 15, 16) or an extensive extract from the original is given separately (no. 11a). The translations are not intended as literary specimens, but as essays in transferring meaning; their critical examination may be one of the exercises in the assessment of evidence referred to in the previous paragraph. The bibliographical headings, and the bibliographical information given in some of the introductions, are aimed only at the immediate purpose of the anthology, and are not meant to be either comprehensive or critical.

Since none of the items in this anthology was written by a professional musician, there is only indirect evidence here of the attitudes of European musicians to non-European musics. Jean de Léry, who could sing Calvinist metrical psalms, was so captivated by the sound of indigenous Brazilians singing a dance-song that he remembered it long after 'with beating heart'. Though Engelbert Kaempfer, feeling called on to give an opinion of Persian court music, said it was noise rather than music, he added that it was neither confused nor disagreeable, but caressing to the ears and spirit. The song he sang for the Emperor of Japan was composed by himself, presumably both words and music. Gotifredo Ferrari's setting of a poem based on an experience of Mungo Park seems to have no extra-European element in the music. When Karl Kambra incorporated in *The Peyho Boatmen* the tune of the Chinese boatmen's refrain, in a form similar to that notated in John Barrow's account, he put it in a current European framework, while the tune and text of his

Moo-Lee-Chwa differ significantly from Barrow's *Moo-Lee-Wha.* To the editors of the Weimar periodical in which it was printed, Kampra's *The Peyho Boatmen* could provide their readers with an intriguing tea-party novelty —— an evocation of a song to whose sounds the tea they were drinking had been conveyed to the English merchants in Canton. When Johann Hüttner, who sent Kambra's song to the *Journal des Luxus und der Moden*, remarked on what he considered 'certain similarities between Chinese and ancient Greek music', the editors commented that any classical scholar who could publish a collection of ancient work-songs would earn the gratitude of contemporary music-lovers. The Kambra kind of setting, however, offended the ethnologist in Barrow, who took pains to obtain illustrations of Chinese instruments (Illustration N), and gave his music-notations (one taken down, he noted, by 'mr. Hittner', the others given to him by an English instrument-collector in Canton) in their 'unadorned state'. The English collector, who also 'made the drawings of their musical instruments', was presumably Mr. Matthew Raper (see p.169 and Illustration M). Father Du Halde's purpose in including notated tunes in his account of Chinese music was the modest one merely of giving his readers 'some Idea' of their character. Four tunes in the group that Barrow called 'Chinese Popular Airs' had previously been printed by Du Halde. A shorter version of one of the four was printed in 1926 by George Soulié de Morant and André Gailhard in their *Théâtre et musique modernes en Chine*, in a group of five tunes said to be themes used in the theatre for certain standard situations or feelings (the tunes are called *yeadi*, literally 'elegant flute'; see Lawrence Picken in *The New Oxford History of Music*, I, 1957, pp. 116-117) and to be earlier than the thirteenth century A.D. The *yeadi* in question is headed 'joy, pleasure, drinking'; it is given on p. 205 The music-notations published by Amédée Frézier are one evidence among many of the wide scope of his observations. He used them to give sharper focus to his descriptions of indigenous communal dancing and Spanish colonial dancing and to rebut the South-American Spaniards' pretensions to superior Christianity by exposing the 'singular', and even scripturally misconceived language of one of their religious songs. The music-notations given by Simon de la Loubère and Sir John Chardin are reproduced here in Illustrations D and E.

One of the illustrations in Frézier's book shows, among other things, three musical instruments. whose indigenous names he gave (Illustration H). it is sometimes difficult to judge the value of visual evidence, even when it is associated with a first-hand report. Since Frézier was an engineer and chartmaker, it can probably be assumed that he, or one of his staff, made the original drawings for the illustrations in his book. John Scheffer, Sir John Chardin and John Barrow were explicit about the sources of their drawings (Illustrations C, E, K and N), whose general accuracy there seems no reason to doubt. It has been possible to trace the drawings from which the engraving of Illustration N was done, and these are reproduced as Illustration M. Kaempfer said that his drawings of Japanese instruments (Illustration G) were taken from Japanese books. His fine plate of Persian instruments (Illustration F) and his detailed description of them seem thoroughly well observed. Most of the originals for the drawings in the embassy report by Olearius (possibly including Illustration B) were done by Olearius himself (see p. 60). There seems to be no indication in La Loubère's account of his embassy to Siam of the authorship of the drawings of musical instruments and of the notation of a song which he included, nor does Dr.John Francis Gemelli Careri's narrative of his Chinese visit identify the original executant of Illustrations J1-2. Most of the visual records connected with the Macartney embassy were the firsthand work of William Alexander. However, he was not present at the arrival of the Chinese Emperor at Jehol, and his watercolour of that occasion (Illustration L) was based on sketches made by Lieutenant Henry Parish.

Since this is an anthology of sources, there is neither explanation nor dicussion of terminology, and supplementary material and editorial footnotes have been kept to a minimum. Material inserted by the editor is enclosed in double brackets. All translations are the work of the compiler and editor, who wishes to thank his wife Joan Rimmer for posing many questions and suggesting some answers, Robert Pring-Mill for inspecting and suggesting emendations of the translation of Torquemada's chapter on the teaching of music to the Indians of Mexico, Simin Yusefzadeh for modernising the transcripts of Persian words in nos. 12 and 13, and for other help with those items, and Desmond Conacher for providing an Aristophanes reference.

Universiteit van Amsterdam
Etnomusicologisch Centrum "Jaap Kunst"   March 1st, 1973

1 JEAN DE LÉRY

Jean de Léry (1534-1611) studied theology at Geneva, and at the age of twenty-two set sail with a group of Calvinist companions for South America. Arriving at the Bay of Rio de Janeiro, they landed on the tall island then called *l'île aux François* on March 10th, 1557. Admiral Nicolas Durand de Villegagnon, who had come there in November, 1555, was building a fort and organising a French settlement, and sent to Calvin, who had been a fellow-student in theology, for ministers. Villegagnon put the group to work at building the fort, and after a month's quarreling with him, some, including Léry, left the fort and lived on the mainland until they could leave for France in January, 1558.

Léry's *Histoire d'un voyage faict en la terre du Brésil* was first published in 1578 in La Rochelle. Neither the first nor the second edition (1580) has music-notations; these first appeared in the third edition, from which the extracts printed here have been taken. Léry translated his book into Latin for the Geneva print of 1586, and it was published in a German translation in 1593 in Frankfurt. Both of these had the music-notations. A few extracts done into English from the Latin by Ed. Aston were included in the translation of Joannes Boemus's *The Manners, Lawes and Customes of all Nations* (London, 1611; originally in Latin, London, 1556). Samuel Purchas had ready a complete translation (which internal evidence shows was also done from the Latin) for his series *Haklytus Posthumus or Purchas His Pilgrimes* (London, 4 parts, 1625; reprinted, Glasgow, 1905-07), but, as he said, 'the most of it I have omitted' (reprint, XVI, 1906,p.518). Aston's extracts did not include any passage with music-notation; Purchas printed the three in Léry's Chapter XII. Léry's book has been edited with an Introduction by M.-R. Mayeux (Paris, 1957) under the title *Journal de bord de Jean de Léry en la terre de Brésil 1557,* while an abbreviated version was edited, with an Introduction, by Charly Clerc (Paris, 1927), under the original title. Both editors considerably modernised Léry's text; it is printed here exactly as it stands in the third edition, except that the letters u and v are distinguished, whereas in the original both are printed as u.

Léry had the printer enclose within asterisks (not always completed, as Léry remarked in a note to his readers) the new material in the third edition, for which he must have provided the tunes, whether notated by him or another. He could sing well, in the judgement of an indigenous South American, for he relates that he was given a gift of an *agoutti,* a little animal of the size of a month-old piglet, after he had sung a metrical psalm. With smiling face the Indian said: 'Truly you have sung marvellously well, and your splendid song reminded me of that of a nation which is our neighbour and ally, and I was extremely happy to hear it' (ed. Mayeux, p.345).

Five editions of Léry's book have been consulted for the transcriptions given here (Music-Notation I a-e). These are indicated as 1585 (3rd French edition), 1586 (1st Latin edition), 1593 (German translation), 1605 (Latin text published in Frankfurt) and 1625 (three tunes in Purchas). In a few cases smudging in the print has made white minims look like black semiminims; this has been specially noted here only in one case where it is possibly a real difference (footnote 4 to the Music-Notation). It may be useful to add here (Music-Notation If) the notation of three of these tunes as given by Marin Mersenne in his *Harmonie Universelle* (Paris, 1636; reprint, Paris, 1963) in the section *Livre Troisième des Genres de la Musique* (1963, II, p. 148 of that section). Jean Jacques Rousseau printed these tunes, with acknowledgement to Mersenne, at the end of his *Dictionnaire de Musique* (Paris, 1768) as a single barred tune with the title *Chanson des Sauvages du Canada* (here Music-Notation Ig.) The item following this, called *Danse Canadienne,* was also from Mersenne, who credited it to 'one of the Captains that the King has sent there'. In the same group of notations Rousseau printed an *Air Chinois* taken from Du Halde; this is the first tune in Du Halde's series of five (see item no. 16 below) with the notes in the second measure changed to *a"f"f"d"b"d"d"g"*, all eighth-notes. Rousseau's last item, called *Chanson Persane,* was taken from Chardin (given here in Illustration E). In the course of the entry *Musique* in the *Dictionnaire,* Rousseau commented on these tunes of non-European peoples:

> On trouvera dans tous ces morceaux une conformité de Modulation avec notre Musique, qui pourra faire admirer aux uns la bonté & l'universalité de nos règles, et peut-être rendre suspecte à d'autres l'intelligence ou la fidélité de ceux qui nous ont transmis ces Airs. (One will find in all these pieces a conformity of style with our music, which could make some people admire the soundness and the universality of our rules, and perhaps render suspect to other people the intelligence or the accuracy of those who have transmitted to us these tunes.

Histoire d'un voyage faict en la terre du Bresil, autrement dite Amerique.... avec les figures, reveue, corrigee & bien augmentee de discours notables, en ceste troisieme Edition. Le tout recueilli sur les lieux par JEAN DE LERY, natif de la Margelle, terre de sainct Sene, au Duché de Bourgogne, Pour Antoine Chuppin, ((La Rochelle)), MDLXXXV

....

Chap. VIII: *Du naturel, force, stature, nudite, disposition & ornemens du corps, tant des hommes que des femmes Sauvages, Bresilliens, habitans en l'Amerique: entre lesquels i'ay frequenté environ un an.*

p. 109

QUE s'il est question de sauter, boire & *Caouiner*, qui est presque leur mestier ordinaire, afin qu'outre le chant & la voix, dont ils usent coustumierement en leur danses, ils ayent encor quelques choses pour leur resveiller l'esprit, apres qu'ils ont cueilli un certain fruict qui est de la grosseur, & aucunement approchant de la forme d'une chastagne d'eau, lequel a la peau asses ferme: bien sec qu'il est, le noyau osté, & au lieu d'iceluy mettans de petites pierres dedans, en enfilant plusieurs ensemble, ils en font des iambieres, lesquelles liees à leurs iambes, font autant de bruit que feroyent des coquilles d'escargots ainsi disposees, voire presque que les sonnettes de par deça, desquelles aussi ils sont fort convoiteux quand on leur en porte.

Sonnettes composees de fruits

OUTREPLUS, y ayant en ce pays-la une sorte d'arbre qui porte son fruict aussi gros qu'un oeuf d'Austruche, & de mesme figure, les sauvages l'ayant percé par le milieu (ainsi que vous voyez en France les enfans percer de grosses noix pour faire des molinets) puis creusé & mis dans iceluy de petites pierres rondes, ou bien des grains de leur gros mil, duquel il sera parlè ailleurs, passant puis apres un baston d'environ un pied et demi de long à travers, ils en font un instrument qu'ils nomment *Maraca*: lequel bruyant plus fort qu'une vessie de pourceau pleine de pois, nos Bresiliens ont ordinairement en la main. Quand je traiterai de leur religion, ie diray l'opinion qu'ils ont tant de ce *Maraca*, que de sa sonnerie, apres que par eux il a esté enrichi de belles plumes, & dedié à l'usage que nous verrons là....

Maraca instrument bruyant fait d'un gros fruict.

. . . .

p.114

FINALEMENT adioustant aux choses susdites l'instrument nommé *Maraca* en sa main, & le pannache de plume qu'ils appellent *Arroroye* sur les reins, & ses sonnettes composees de fruicts à l'entour de ses iambes, vous le verrez lors, ainsi que ie le representeray encor en autre lieu, equippé en la facon qu'il est, quand il danse, saute, boit, & gambade.

Equippage des Sauvages beuvans & dansans.

....

Chap. IX: *Des grosses racines & gros mil, dont les Sauvages font farines qu'ils mangent au lieu de pain: & de leur bruvage qu'ils nomment* Caou-in.

....

p. 131

OR nos femmes Bresiliennes, faisans semblablement bouillir, & maschans aussi puis apres dans leur bouche de ce gros mil, nommé *Avati* en leur langage, en font encor du bruvage de la mesme sorte que vous

Bruvage fait de mil.

avez entendu qu'elles font celuy des racines sus mentionnees... Les
Sauvages appellent ce bruvage *Caou-in*, lequel estant trouble & epais
comme lie, a presque goust de laict aigre: & en ont de rouge & de blanc
comme nous avons de vin.

*Caou-in
bruvage ai-
gre.*

....

p. 136

SEMBLABLEMENT aussi, soit qu'ils boivent peu ou prou, outre ce que i'ay dit, qu'eux n'engendrans iamais melancolie, ont ceste
coustume de s'assembler tous les iours pour danser & s'esiouir en leurs
villages, encor les ieunes hommes à marier ont cela de particulier,
qu'avec chacun un de ces grans pennaches qu'ils nomment *Araroye*, lié
sur leurs reins, & quelques fois le *Maraca* en la main, & les fruicts secs
(desquels i'ay parlé cy dessus) sonnans comme coquilles d'escargots, liez
& arrengez à l'entour de leurs iambes, ils ne font presque autre chose
toutes les nuicts qu'en tel equippage aller & venir, sautans & dansans de
maison en maison: tellement que les voyant & oyant si souvent faire ce
mestier, il me resouvenoit de ceux qu'en certains lieux par-deçà on
appelle valets de la feste, lesquels és temps de leurs vogues & festes
qu'ils font des saincts & patrons de chacune parroisse, s'en vont aussi en
habits de fols, avec des marottes au poing, & des sonnettes aux iambes,
bagnenaudans & dansant la Morisque parmi les maisons & les places.

*Sauvages
grands dan-
seurs iour
& nuict.*

MAIS il faut noter en ceste endroit, qu'en toutes les danses de
nos Sauvages, soit qu'ils se suyvent l'un l'autre, ou, comme ie diray,
parlant de leur religion, qu'ils soyent disposez en rond, les femmes ny
les filles, n'estant iamais meslees parmi les hommes, si elles veulent
danser cela ce fera à part elles.

*Femmes &
filles separees
és danses des
Sauvages.*

....

Chap. XI: *De la varieté des oyseaux de l'Amerique, tous differens de
nostres: ensemble des grosses chauve-souris, abeilles, mousches, mou-
chillons & autres vermines estranges de ce pays-la.*

....

p. 158

L'AUTRE nommé *Canidé*, ayant tout le plumage sous le ventre
& à l'entour du col aussi iaune que fin or: le dessus du dos, les aisles &
la queuë, d'un bleu si naif qu'il n'est pas possible de plus, estant advis
qu'il soit vestu d'une toile d'or par dessous, & emmantelé de damas
violet figuré par dessus, on est ravi de telle beauté.

*Canidé,
oyseau de plu-
mage azuré.*

LES Sauvages en leurs chansons, font communément mention
de ce dernier, disans & repetans souvent selon ceste musique: ((Music-
Notation Ia)): c'est à dire, un oyseau iaune, un oyseau iaune, &c. car
iouue, ou *ioup* veut dire iaune en leur langage....

....

Chap. XII: *D'aucuns poissons plus communs entre les Sauvages de l'Amerique: & de leur maniere de pescher.*

....

p. 173

CAMOUROUPOUY-OU ASSOU, est un bien grand poisson (car aussi *Ouassou* en langue Bresilienne veut dire grand ou gros, selon l'accent qu'on luy donne) duquel nos *Tououpinambaoults* dansans & chantans, font ordinairement mention, disans, & repetans souvent ceste chantrerie, ((Music-Notation Ib)) & est fort bon à manger.

....

Chap. XIIII: *De la guerre, combats, hardiesse & armes des Sauvages Bresiliens.*

....

p. 215

AU surplus, tant au desloger de leur pays, qu'au departir de chacun lieu où ils s'arrestent & seiournent: à fin d'advertir & tenir les autres en cervelle, il y en a tousiours quelques-uns, qui avec des cornets, qu'ils nomment *Inubia*, de la grosseur & longueur d'une demie pique, mais par le bout d'embas large d'environ demi pied comme un Haubois, sonnent au milieu des troupes. Mesmes aucuns ont des fifres & fleutes faites des os des bras & des cuisses de ceux qui auparavant ont esté par eux tuez & mangez, desquelles semblablement (pour s'inciter tant plus d'en faire autant à ceux contre lesquels ils s'acheminent) ils ne cessent de flageoler par les chemins....

....

Chap. XVI: *Ce qu'on peut appeller religion entre les Sauvages Bresiliens des erreurs, ou certains abuseurs qu'ils ont entr'eux nommez Caraibes les detiennent: & de la grande ignorance de Dieu où ils sont plongez.*

....

p. 277

POUR donc entrer plus avant en matiere, il faut sçavoir qu'ils ont entre eux certains Prophetes qu'ils nomment *Caraibes*, lesquels allans & venans de village en village, comme les porteurs de Rogatons en la Papauté, leur font accroire que communiquans avec les esprits ils peuvent non seulement par ce moyen donner force à qui il leur plaist, pour veincre & surmonter les ennemis, quand on va à la guerre, mais aussi que ce sont eux qui font croistre les gosses racines & les fruicts, tels que i'ay dit ailleurs, que ceste terre du Bresil les produit. Davantage, ainsi que i'ay entendu des truchemens de Normandie, qui avoyent long temps demeuré en ce pays-la, nos *Tououpinambaoults* ayans ceste coustume que de trois en trois, ou de quatre en quatre ans, ils s'assemblent en grande solennité, pour m'y estre trouvé, sans y penser (comme vous entendrez) voici ce que i'en puis dire à la verité. Comme donc un autre François nommé Iaques Rousseau, & moy avec un truchement allions par pays, ayans couché une nuict en un village nommé *Cotiva*, le lendemain de grand matin, que nous pensions passer outre, nous vismes en premier lieu les sauvages des lieux proches, qui y arrivoyent de toutes parts: avec lesquels ceux de ce village sortans de leurs maisons se ioignirent, & furent incontinent en une grande place assemblez en nombre de cinq ou six cens. Parquoy nous arrestans pour savoir à quelle fin ceste assemblee se faisoit, ainsi que nous nous en enquerions, nous les vismes soudain separer en trois bandes: assavoir tous les hommes en une maison à part, les femmes en une autre, & les enfans de mesme. Et parce que ie vis dix ou douze de ces messieurs les *Caraibes*, qui s'estoyent rangez avec les hommes, me doutant bien qu'ils feroyent quelque chose d'extraordinaire, ie priay instamment mes compagnons que nous demeurissions là pour voir ce mystere, ce qui me fut accordé. Ainsi apres que les *Caraibes*, avant que departir d'avec les femmes & enfans, leur eurent estroitement defendu, de ne sortir des maisons où ils estoyent, ains que de là ils escoustassent attentivement quand ils les orroyent chanter: nous ayans aussi commandé de nous tenir clos dans le logis où estoyent les femmes, ainsi que nous desieunions, sans sçavoir encor ce qu'ils vouloyent faire, nous commençasmes d'ouir en la maison où estoyent les hommes (laquelle n'estoit pas à trente pas de celle où nous estions) un bruit fort bas, comme vous diriez le murmure de ceux qui barbotent leurs heures: ce qu'entendans les femmes, lesquelles estoyent en nombre d'environ deux cents, toutes se levans debout, en prestant l'oreille se serrerent en un monceau. Mais apres que les hommes peu à peu eurent eslevé leurs voix, & que fort distinctement nous les entendismes chanter tous ensemble, & repeter souvent ceste interiection d'accouragement, ((Music Notation Ic)) nous fusmes tous esbahis que les femmes de leur costé leur respondans & avec une voix tremblante, reiterans ceste mesme interiection, *He, he, he, he*, se prindrent à crier de telle façon, l'espace de plus d'un quart d'heure, que nous les regardans ne sçavions quelle contenance tenir. Et de faict, parce que non seulement elles hurloyent ainsi, mais aussi qu'avec cela sautans en l'air de grande violence faisoyent bransler leurs mammelles & escumoyent par la bouche, voire aucunes (comme ceux qui ont le haut-mal par-deça) tomboyent toutes esvanouyes, ie ne croy pas autrement que le Diable ne leur entrast dans le corps, & qu'elles ne devinssent soudain Demoniaques. Tellement qu'ayant leu ce que dit Bodin en sa Demonomanie, allegant Iamblique, de l'estase laquelle, dit-il, est ordinaire aux Sorciers, qui ont fait paction expresse avec le Diable, & sont quelquefois transportez en esprit, demeurant le corps insensible (combien que quelquefois aussi cela se face en corps & en ame) ioint, dit Bodin qu'il ne se fait point d'assemblee entre eux ou l'on ne danse: et mesmes par la confes-

Discours de l'auteur sur la grande solennité des Sauvages.

Chantrerie des Sauvages.
Hurlemens & contenances estranges des femmes Sauvages.

sion de quelques Sorcieres, qu'il nomme, elles disent en dansant, har, har, (c'est le he, he, de nos Sauvages) Diable, Diable, saute-ici, saute-la: les autres respondent, Sabbath, Sabbath, c'est à dire la feste & le iour du repos, en haussant les mains & ballets qu'elles tiennent en haut, pour donner certain tesmoignage d'allegresse, & que de bon coeur elles servent & adore le Diable, et aussi pour contrefaire l'adoration qui est deuë à Dieu, lequel souz la loy commandoit aux Israëlites d'eslever leurs mains à luy & qu'ils s'escovissent en sa presence. Considerant di-ie ces choses i'ay conclu, que le maistre des unes estoit le maistre des autres: assavoir que les femmes Bresiliennes & les Sorcieres par-deçà estoyent conduites d'un mesme esprit de Satan: sans que la distance des leiux, ny le long passage de la mer empeche ce pere de mensonge d'opperer ça & là en ceux qui luy sont livrez par le iuste iugement de Dieu. Ainsi oyans semblablement les enfans bransler & se tourmenter au logis où ils estoyent separez tout aupres de nous: combien qu'il y eust ia plus de demi an que ie frequentois les Sauvages, & que ie fusse desia autrement accoustumé parmi eux, tant y à pour n'en rien desguiser, qu'ayant eu lors quelque frayeur, ne sachant mesme quelle seroit l'issue du ieu, i'eusse bien voulu estre en nostre fort. Toutesfois apres que ces bruicts & hurlemens confus furent finis, les hommes faisans une petite pose (les femmes & les enfans se taisans lors tous cois) nous les entendismes derechef chantans & faisans resonner leurs voix d'un accord si merveilleux, que m'estant un peu rasseuré, oyant ces doux & plus gracieux sons, il ne faut pas demander si ie desirois de les voir de pres. Mais parce que quand ie voulois sortir pour en approcher, non seulement les femmes me retiroyent, mais aussi nostre truchement disoit que depuis six ou sept ans, qu'il y avoit qu'il estoit en ce pays-là, il ne s'estoit iamais osé trouver parmi les Sauvages en telle feste: de maniere adioustoit-il, que si i'y allois ie ne ferois pas sagement, craignant de me mettre en danger, ie demeuray un peu en suspens. Neanmoins parce que l'ayant sondé plus avant il me sembloit qu'il ne me donnoit pas grand raison de son dire: ioint que ie m'asseurois de l'amitié de certains bons veillards, qui demeuroyent en ce village, auquel i'avois esté quatre ou cinq fois auparavant, moitié de force & moitié de gré, ie me hazarday de sortir. M'approchant doncques du lieu où i'oyois ceste chantrerie, comme ainsi soit que les maisons des sauvages soyent fort longues, & de façon rondes (comme vous diriez les treilles des iardins par-deçà) couvertes d'herbes qu'elles sont iusques contre terre: à fin de de mieux voir à mon plaisir ie fis avec les mains un petit pertuis en la couverture. Ainsi faisant de là signe du doigt aux deux François qui me regardoyent, eux à mon exemple, s'estans aussi enhardis & approchez sans empeschement ni difficulté, nous entrasmes tous trois dans ceste maison. Voyans doncques que les sauvages (comme le truchement estimoit) ne s'effarouchoyent point de nous, ains au contraire, tenans leurs rangs & leur ordre d'une façon

Deu. 12.6.7.

Femmes Bresiliennes, & les Sorcieres par-deçà, possedees d'un mesme esprit de Satan.

Maisons des sauvages de quelle façon faites.

admirable, continuoyent leurs chansons, en nous retirans tout belle-
ment en un coin, nous les contemplasmes tout nostre saoul. Mais sui-
vant ce que i'ay promis ci-dessus, quand i'ay parlé de leurs danses en
leurs beuveries & *caouinages,* que ie dirois aussi l'autre façon qu'ils ont
de danser: à fin de les mieux representer, voici les morgues, gestes &
contenances qu'ils tenoyent. Tous pres à pres l'un de l'autre, sans se
tenir par la main ni sans se bouger d'une place, ains estans arrengez en
rond, courbez sur le devant, guindans un peu le corps, remuans seulement la iambe & le pied droit, chacun ayant aussi la main dextre sur ses
fesses, & le bras & la main gauche pendant, chantoyent & dansoyent de
ceste façon. Et au surplus, parce qu'à cause de la multitude il y avoit
trois rondeaux, y ayant au milieu d'un chacun trois ou quatre de ces
Caraibes, richement parez de robbes, bonnets & bracelets, faits de belles
plumes naturelles, naifves & de diverses couleurs: tenans au reste en
chacune de leurs mains un *Maraca,* c'est à dire sonnettes faites d'un
fruict plus gros que un oeuf d'Austruche, dont i'ay parlé ailleurs, à fin
disoyent-ils, que l'esprit parlast puis apres dans icelles pour les dedier à
cest usage, ils les faisoyent sonner à toute reste. Et ne vous les sçaurois
mieux comparer, en l'estat qu'ils estoyent lors, qu'aux sonneurs de
campanes de ces caphards, lesquels en abusant le pauvre monde par-deçà,
portent de lieu en lieu les chasses de sainct Antoine, de sainct Bernard
& autres tels instrumens d'idolatrie. Ce qu'outre la susdite description,
ie vous ay bien voulu encor représenter par la figure suyvante, du dan-
seur & de sonneur de *Maraca* ((Illustration A)).

OUTRE plus, ces *Caraibes* en s'avançans & sautans en devant,
puis reculans en arriere, ne se tenoyent pas tousiours en une place
comme faisoyent les autres: mesme i'observay qu'eux prenans souvent
une canne de bois, longue de quatre à cinq pieds, au bout de laquelle il
y avoit de l'herbe de *Petun* (dont i'ay fait mention autre part) seiche &
allumee: en se tournans, & soufflans de toutes parts la fumee d'icelle
sur les autres Sauvages, ils leur disoyent: A fin que vous surmontiez vos
ennemis, recevez tous l'esprit de force: & ainsi firent par plusieurs fois
ces maistres *Caraibes.* Or ces ceremonies ayans ainsi duré pres de deux
heures, ces cinq ou six cens hommes Sauvages ne cessans tousiours de
danser & chanter, il y eut une telle melodie qu'attendu qu'ils ne sçavent
que c'est de l'art de Musique, ceux qui ne les ont ouys ne croiroyent
iamais qu'ils s'accordassent si bien. Et de faict, au lieu que du commen-
cement de ce sabbat (estant comme i'ay dit en la maison des femmes)
i'avois eu quelque crainte, i'eu lors en recompense une telle ioye, que
non seulement oyant les accords si bien mesurez d'une telle multitude,
& sur tout pour la cadence & refrein de la balade, à chacun couplet tous
en traisnans leurs voix, disans en ceste sorte: ((Music Notation Id)), i'en
demeuray tout ravi: mais aussi toutes les fois qu'il m'en ressouvient, le
coeur m'en tressaillant, il me semble que ie les aye encor aux oreilles.

Quand ils voulurent finir, frappans du pied droit contre terre, plus fort qu'auparavant, apres que chacun eut craché devant soy, tous unanimement, d'une voix rauque, prononcerent deux ou trois fois d'un tel chant, ((Music Notation Ie)), & ainsi cesserent. Et parce que n'entendant pas encores lors parfaitement tout leur langage, ils avoyent dit plusieurs choses que ie n'avois peu comprendre, ayant prié le truchement qu'il les me declarast: il me dit en premier lieu qu'ils avoyent fort insisté à regretter leurs grands peres decedez, lesquels estoyent si vaillans: toutesfois qu'en fin ils s'estoyent consolez, en ce qu'apres leur mort ils s'asseuroyent de les aller trouver derriere les hautes montagnes, où ils danseroyent & se resiouiroyent avec eux. Semblablement qu'à toute outrance ils avoyent menacez les *Ouëtacas* (nation de Sauvages leurs ennemis, lesquels comme i'ay dit ailleurs sont si vaillans qu'ils ne les ont iamais peu dompter) d'estre bien tost prins & mangez par eux, ainsi que leur avoyent promis leurs *Caraibes*. Au surplus qu'ils avoyent entremeslé & fait mention en leurs chansons, que les eaux s'estans une fois tellement desbordees qu'elles couvrirent toute la terre, tous les hommes du monde, excepté leurs grands peres qui se sauverent sur les plus hauts arbres de leur pays, furent noyez: lequel dernier poinct, qui est ce qu'ils tiennent entre eux approchant de l'Escriture saincte, ie leur ay d'autres fois depuis ouy reiterer. Et de faict, estant vray-semblable que de pere en fils ils ayent entendu quelque chose du deluge universel, qui avint du temps de Noé, suyvant la coustume des hommes qui ont tousiours corrompu & tourné la verité en mensonge: ioint comme il a esté veu ci-dessus, qu'estans privez de toutes sortes d'escritures, il leur est malaisé de retenir les choses en leur pureté, ils ont adiousté ceste fable, comme les Poetes, que leurs grands peres se sauverent sur les arbres.

Opinion confuse du deluge universel entre les Ameriquains.

POUR retourner à nos *Caraibes*, ils furent non seulement ce iour-la bien receus de tous les autres Sauvages, qui les traitterent magnifiquement des meilleures viandes qu'ils peurent trouver, sans selon leur coustume, oublier de les faire boire & *Caou-iner* d'autant: mais aussi mes deux compagnons François & moy qui, comme i'ay dit, nous estions inopinément trouvez à ceste confrairie des Bacchanales, à cause de cela, fismes bonne chere avec nos *Moussacats*, c'est à dire, bons peres de famille qui donnent à manger aux passans. Et au surplus de tout ce que dessus, apres que ces iours solennels (esquels comme i'ay dit, toutes les singeries que vous avez entendues se font de trois en trois ou de quatre en quatre ans entre nos *Tououpinambaoults*) sont passez & mesmes quelquefois auparavant, les *Caraibes* allans particulierement de village en village, font accoustrer des plus belles plumasseries qui se puissent trouver, en chacune famille trois ou quatre, ou selon qu'ils s'advisent plus ou moins, de ces hochets ou grosses sonnettes qu'ils nomment *Maracas*: lesquelles ainsi parees fichans le plus grand bout du baston qui

Preparation des Maracas.

est à travers dans terre, & les arrengeans tout le long & au milieu des maisons, ils commandent puis apres qu'on leur baille à boire & à manger. De façon que ces affronteurs faisans accroire aux autres povres idiots, que ces fruicts & especes de courges, ainsi creusez, parez & dediez mangent & boivent la nuict: chasque chef d'hostel adioustant foy à cela, ne faut point de mettre auprès des siens, non seulement de la farine avec de la chair & du poisson, mais aussi de leur bruvage dit *Caou-in*. Voire les laissans ordinairement ainsi plantez en terre quinze iours ou trois semaines, tousiours servis de mesme, ils ont apres cest ensorcelement une opinion si estrange de ces *Maracas*, (lesquels ils ont presques tousiours en la main) que leur attribuant quelque saincteté, ils disent que souventesfois en les sonnans un esprit parle à eux. Tellement qu'en estans ainsi embabouynez, si nous autres passans parmi leurs maisons & longues loges, voiyons quelques bonnes viandes presentées à ces *Maracas*: si nous les prenions & mangions (comme nous avons souvent fait) nos Ameriquains estimans que cela nous causeroit quelque mal-heur, n'en estoyent pas moins offensez que sont les supersticieux & successeurs des prestres de Baal, de voir prendre les offrandes qu'on porte à leurs marmosets, desquelles cependant au deshonneur de Dieu, ils se nourrissent grassement & oysivement avec leurs putains & bastards. Qui plus est, si prenans de là occasion de leur remonstrer leurs erreurs, nous leurs disions que les *Caraibes*, leur faisant accroire que les *Maracas* mangeoyent & beuvoyent, ne les trompoyent pas seulement en cela, mais aussi que ce n'estoit pas eux, comme ils se vantoyent faussement, qui faisoyent croistre leurs fruicts & leurs grosses racines, ains le Dieu en qui nous croyons & que nous leur annoncions: cela derechef estoit autant en leur endroit, que de parler par-deçà contre le Pape, ou de dire à Paris que la chasse de saincte Genevieve ne fait pas pleuvoir. Aussi ces pippeurs de *Caraibes*, ne nous haissans pas moins que les faux prophetes de Iezabel (craignans perdre leurs gras morceaux) faisoyent le vray serviteur de Dieu Elie, lequel semblablement descouvroit leurs abus: commençans à se cacher de nous, craignoyent mesme de venir, ou de coucher és villages où ils sçavoyent que nous estions.

Lourde super-stition.

Erreur gros-sier.

1. Rois 18. 19

Verité chas-sant le men-songe.

TRANSLATION

History of a journey made into the land of Brazil, otherwise called America.... with illustrations, revised, corrected and much enlarged with significant discourses in this third edition. The whole collected on the spot by Jean de Léry, native of Lamargelle, district of Saint-Seyne, in the Duchy of Burgundy. For Antoine Chuppin, ((La Rochelle)), 1585

Chapter VIII: *Of the disposition, strength, stature, nudity, bodily bearing and ornaments of the Brazilian savages, both men and women, living in America, amongst whom I sojourned about a year.*

p. 109

Thus if it is a question of leaping, drinking and *Caouning*, which is almost their normal occupation, over and above song and the vocalising which they customarily employ in their dances, they have also some things for rousing their spirits. After they have gathered a certain fruit that is of the size of a water chestnut, and somewhat resembling it in shape, and which has a rather hard skin, when it is quite dry, the core having been removed, they insert instead of it some small stones, and stringing several together they make them into leg-pieces, which when attached to their legs make as much sound as would snail-shells disposed in the same way, indeed they are almost the same as little bells from our part of the world, of which also they are greatly covetous when some are brought to them.

Little bells made out of fruits.

More than this, there being in that country a kind of tree which bears a fruit as big as an ostrich egg, and of the same configuration, the savages, having pierced it through the centre (just as you see in France children piercing big nuts to make twirling tops), then having hollowed it out and put in it some little round stones, or else some grains of their large millet, which will be discussed elsewhere, then afterwards passing through it a stick of about a foot and a half long, they make of it an instrument which they call *Maraca*. This sounding louder than a pig bladder full of peas, our Brazilians usually have in their hand. When I treat of their religion, I will express the opinion that they set as much store by this *Maraca* itself as by its sound, after it has been decorated by them with beautiful feathers, and is dedicated to the function we shall see later....

Maraca noisy instrument made from a large fruit.

p. 114

Finally, adding to the things mentioned above the instrument called *Maraca* in his hand, and plumage of feathers which they call *Arroroye* about his loins, and the little bells made of fruits around his legs, you will see him then, just as I will depict him in another place, accoutred in the manner that he is, when he dances, drinks and gambols.

Accoutrement of the savages when drinking and dancing.

Chapter IX: *Of the great roots and big millet, from which the savages make flours which they eat instead of bread; and of their drink which they call* Caou-in.

p. 131

But our Brazilian women, bringing similarly to the boil, and also chewing then afterwards in their mouth this big millet, called *Avati* in their language, make of it again a drink of the same sort that we have heard they make of the roots mentioned above.... The savages call this drink *Caou-in*, which being cloudy and thick like dregs, has almost the taste of sour milk; and they have it red and white like we have wine.

Drink made of millet.

Caou-in; a sour drink.

p. 136

Similarly also, whether they drink much or little, apart from what I have said, that it never engenders melancholy in them. they have this custom of getting together every day to dance and enjoy themselves in their villages, and again the young marriageable men have something special, in that with each having one of those great plumages that they call *Aroroye* tied about their loins, and sometimes with their *Maraca* in their hand, and the dried fruits (of which I have spoken above) sounding like snail-shells, tied and disposed around their legs, they do practically nothing else during every night but coming and going, thus accoutred, leaping and dancing from house to house; so much so that seeing and hearing them so often doing this business recalled to me those who in certain places in our part of the world are called *valets de la feste*, who at the time of their patronal and other festivals that they hold for the saints and patrons of each parish, also go around in crazy clothes, with baubles in their fist and little bells on their legs, fooling and dancing the Morris-dance around the houses and squares.

Savages great dancers by day as well as by night.

But it should be noted at this point that in all the dances of our savages, whether they are following one another, as I will tell when speaking of their religion, or whether they are disposed in a circle, the women and girls are never mingled with the men. If they want to dance that is done by them separately.

Women and girls separated from men in the savages' dances.

Chapter XI: *Of the variety of the birds of America, quite different from ours; rundown of the large bats, bees, flies, gnats and other strange vermin of that country.*

p. 158

The other is called Canidé, having all its plumage under the belly and around the neck as yellow as fine gold; the upper part of the back, the wings and the tail, are of a blue so bright that it could not possibly be more so; one's impression is as though it were decked with a golden cloth below and mantled with violet-coloured figured damask above, and one is ravished by such beauty.

Canidé, bird of blue plumage.

The savages in their songs commonly make mention of this, saying and repeating often according to this music: ((Music-Notation)); that is to say, a yellow bird, a yellow bird, etc., for *iouue*, or *ioup* means yellow in their language....

Chapter XII: *Of some commoner fish among the savages of America, and of their way of fishing.*

p. 173

Camou-roupouy-oaussou, large fish.

Camouroupouy-ou assou is a very large fish (for also *Ouassou* in Brazilian language means big or fat, according to the accent one gives to it) which our Tupinambás often mention when dancing and singing, saying, and repeating often in this way of singing ((Music-Notation)), and it is very good to eat.

Chapter XIV: *Of the war, combats, daring and arms of the Brazilian savages*

p. 215

Inubia, large horns.

Fifes and flutes made of human bones.

In addition, either when leaving their region or when going away from each place where they stop and sojourn, with the object of notifying the others and keeping them informed, there are always some of them who with horns, which they call *Inubia*, of half the size and length of a pike-staff, but at the lower end about a foot wide like a shawm, sound off in the middle of the troops. Some even have fifes and flutes made from the arm- and thigh-bones of those who have earlier been killed and eaten by them, on which (apparently to incite themselves to do as much and more to those against whom they are setting out) they ceaselessly play while on their route....

Chapter XVI: *What may be called religion among the Brazilian savages; of the errors in which certain deceivers that they have among them, called* Caraibes, *keep them, and of the great ignorance of God in which they are sunk.*

p. 277

Caraibes, false prophets.

In order to go still further into this matter, one must know that they have amongst them certain prophets whom they call *Caraibes*, who coming and going from village to village, like merdicant friars around the Papacy[1], make them believe that in communicating with spirits

1. This translation is suggested in the following footnote on page 222 of Charly Clerc's edition: Sous cette expression, Léry entend sans doute les moines mendiants.

they can by that means not only give strength to any one to whom they are pleased to give it, to conquer and overcome enemies when he is going to war, but also that it is they who make the great roots and fruits grow, such as I have mentioned elsewhere that this land of Brazil produces. Moreover, just as I had heard from the interpreters from Normandy, who have lived in that country a long time, our Tupinambás having that custom that every three or every four years they assemble with great ceremony, and I having found myself there without expecting to (as you will understand), here is what I can truthfully tell about it. While then another Frenchman named Jacques Rousseau and I with an interpreter were going through the country, having slept for a night in a village called *Cotiva*, the next day in the early morning when we thought of getting on our way, we saw in the first place the savages from neighbouring places arriving there from all directions; those of this village leaving their homes joined up with them, and immediately formed an assembly in a large open space, to the number of five or six hundred. Halting thereupon to find out the purpose for which this assembly was being formed, and as we were enquiring about this, we saw them suddenly separate into three groups, namely all the men in one house separately, the women in another, and the children likewise. And because I saw ten or twelve of those gentlemen the *Caraibes*, who stationed themselves with the men, having no doubt that they would do something extraordinary, I urgently requested my companions that we should remain there to see this mystery, which was granted me. Thus after the *Caraibes*, before going away from the women and children, had strictly forbidden them to leave the houses where they were stationed, so that from there they could listen attentively when they heard them singing; having also ordered us to keep ourselves shut within the dwelling where the women were, just as we were having breakfast, without yet knowing what they would do, we began to hear, from the house where the men were (which was not more than thirty paces from the one where we were), a very soft sound, as you might say the murmuring of those who mumble their hours-devotions; when this was heard by the women, who were about two hundred in number, all rising into a standing position and listening, they pressed together into a close group. But after the men had gradually raised their voices and we had heard them distinctly singing all together, and repeating often this interjection of encouragement ((Music-Notation)), we were all amazed that the women for their part responded to them, and with trembling voice reiterating the same interjection, *He, he, he, he,* began to sound off, for the space of more than a quarter of an hour, in such a manner that we looking at them did not know how to comport ourselves. And in fact, not only because they howled in that way, but also because at the same time leaping into the air, with great violence that made their

Discourse by the author on the great ceremonial of the savages.

Manner of singing of the savages.

Howling and strange faces of the women savages.

breasts shake, and foaming at the mouth, some of them (like those who have epilepsy in our part of the world) fell down fainting away, so that I could not believe other than that the devil was entering into their body, and that they were becoming demoniacs. So much so that, having read what Bodin[1] says in his *Démonomanie,* citing Iamblicus[2], about the ecstasy which, he says, is normal to sorcerers who have made an express compact with the devil and are sometimes carried away in spirit, the body remaining insensible (although sometimes also that happens in the body and soul), added to the fact that Bodin says that there is never any assembly among them at which there is not dancing; and even by the confession of several sorceresses, whom he names, they say while dancing, *'har, har'* (this is the *he, he* of our savages) 'Devil, Devil, jump here, jump there', the other responding 'Sabbath, Sabbath', that is to say, the feast and the day of repose, while raising their hands and witches'-brooms which they hold aloft, in order to give definite witness of gladness, and that they willingly serve and adore the devil, and also in order to counterfeit the adoration that is due to God, who under the law commanded the Israelites to raise their hands to him, and that they should uncover themselves in his presence. Considering, I say, these things I have concluded that the master of the one group is the master of the other; seeing that the Brazilian women and the sorceresses in our part of the world were led by the same spirit of Satan, without the distance between the places or the long passage by sea preventing that father of lies from operating both here and there in those who are handed over to him by the just judgement of God. Thus hearing similarly the children stirring and getting agitated in the dwelling in which they were separately stationed quite close to us, though I had been among these savages already for more than half a year, and I was already otherwise quite at ease among them, nevertheless there is no use concealing the fact that experiencing in that situation some fear, and not knowing even what the issue of the affair might be, I would have wished myself in our fort. However, after these noises and confused howlings were over, the men making a little break (the women and children also being then quite silent) we heard them once again singing and making their voices sound with an agreement so delicious that, becoming somewhat reassured through hearing these sweet and more gracious sounds, there is no need to ask if I wanted to see them closely. But because when I wanted to go out and approach them, not only did the women hold me back, but also our interpreter said that during the six or seven years that had passed since

Deuteronomy 12; 6, 7.

Brazilian women, and sorceresses with us, possessed by the same spirit of Satan.

1. Jean Bodin, b. Angers, c. 1530; d. Laon, 1596; his *Démonomanie* was published in Paris in 1581.
2. Neoplatonist philosopher; b. Syria, c. 250 A.D.; d.c. 330

he came into that country he had never dared to be found among the savages in such a festival; so much so, he added, that I would not be prudent if I went there, as he feared I would put myself in danger, I remained for a while undecided. Nevertheless, because having question- ed him further it seemed to me that he did not give me sound reasons for what he said; added to the fact that I was sure of the friendship of certain good old men who lived in that village, with whom I had been four or five times before, half from fortitude and half from inclination, I took the chance of going out. Accordingly drawing near to the place from where I heard this singing, and the savages' houses being, as they are, very long and arched over (as you might say the vine-arbours of gardens with us) with greenery right down to the ground, in order to see better for my pleasure I made with my hands a little opening in the covering. Thus beckoning from there to the two Frenchmen who were looking at me, they being emboldened also by my example and ap- proaching without hindrance or difficulty, we all three entered into that house. Seeing then that the savages (as the interpreter anticipated) were not at all frightened of us, on the contrary, holding their ranks and their order in an admirable fashion they continued their songs, we, withdrawing softly into a corner, took our fill of contemplating them. But following what I have promised above, when I spoke of their dan- ces in their drinking-bouts and *caouinages,* that I would tell also the other way they have of dancing, in order better to describe them, here are the proud looks, gestures and facial expressions they have. Being quite close to each other, without holding hands and without moving from their place, and being thus disposed in a circle, bending forwards and raising their body a little, moving only the right leg and foot, also having each one his right hand on his buttocks, and his left arm and hand hanging down, they sang and danced in that manner. Further- more, there being on account of the multitude three circles, in the middle of each one three or four of those *Caraibes,* richly arrayed in robes, caps and bracelets made of beautiful natural feathers, bright and of various colours, holding besides in each of their hands a *Maraca,* that is to say rattles made of a fruit larger than an ostriche's egg, of which I have spoken elsewhere, in order they say, that the spirit may then speak afterwards within them so as to dedicate them to that service, they make them sound to the very utmost of their strength. And you would not know anything better to compare them with, in the state they were then, than the jingle-men around those humbugs who, imposing them- selves on poor people in our part of the world, carry from place to place the shrines of St. Anthony, or St. Bernard, and other such instru- ments of idolatry. Apart from the above description, I have tried to represent this in the following drawing of a dancer and a sounder of *Maraca* ((Illustration A)).

Facial ex- pressions of the savages dancing in a circle.

Caraibes dedicating Maracas.

Moreover these *Caraibes*, while advancing and leaping forwards and then recoiling backwards, do not always stay in one place as do the others; in fact I observed that taking often a wooden stick, from four to five feet long, at the end of which there was a herb *Petun* (which I have mentioned elsewhere), dried and lighted; turning around, and blowing in all directions the smoke from it upon the other savages, they said to them: 'In order that you may overcome your enemies, receive all of you the spirit of strength'; and thus did these master *Caraibes* several times. But those ceremonies having lasted thus almost two hours, these five or six hundred savage men not ceasing at any time to dance and sing, there was a tune of such a kind that, given that they do not know what the art of music is, those who have not heard them would never believe that they could sing so well together. And in fact, whereas at the beginning of this sabbath (being as I have said in the women's house) I had been in some fear, I had now as recompense such a joy that, not only hearing the consonant sounds so well rhythmicised by such a multitude, and above all in the cadence and refrain of the dance-song, at each verse everyone drawing out their voices, giving forth in this way ((Music-Notation)), I was altogether captivated; but also every time that I remember it with beating heart, it seems to me that I still have them in my ears. When they wanted to end, striking with their right foot on the ground more strongly than before, after each one had spit in front of him, all unanimously, in a raucous voice, pronounced two or three times to a tune of this sort ((Music-Notation)), and thus stopped. And because they had said several things that I, then not yet understanding perfectly all of their language, had not been able to understand, and having asked the interpreter to explain them to me, he told me in the first place that they had very insistently expressed sorrow for their deceased grandfathers who were so valiant; however, they were finally consoled by the fact that after their death they were certain of going to find them behind the high mountains, where they would dance and rejoice with them. Likewise they had to excess threatened the *Ouetacas* (a nation of savages who were their enemies, who as I have said elsewhere are so courageous that they have never been able to subdue them) with being soon captured and eaten by them, as their *Caraibes* had promised them. In addition they had interspersed and made mention in their songs that the waters having once upon a time so much overflowed that they overran all the earth, all the men in the world were drowned, except their grandfathers, who were saved on the highest trees of their country; this last point, which is the one of their beliefs that most closely resembles the holy scripture, I have at other times since then heard them reiterate. And in fact, it being probable that they have heard from father to son something about the universal flood which dates from the time of Noah, following the custom of men

Caraibes blowing on the other savages.

Confused idea about the universal flood among the Americans.

who have always corrupted the truth and turned it into a lie, joined as has been seen above to the fact that being deprived of all kinds of writings, it is difficult for them to retain things in their purity, they have added, as do poets, this fable, that their grandfathers were saved in the trees.

  To return to our *Caraibes*, not only were they well received that day by all the other savages, who treated them magnificently to the best meats they could find, without forgetting to give them a proportionate amount to drink and *Caou-iner*, as is their custom, but also my two French companions and I, who, as I have said, unexpectedly found ourselves at this confraternity of convivial drinkers, on that account made good cheer with our *Moussacats*, that is to say, good fathers of families who give nourishment to transients. And in addition to everything mentioned above, after these days of ceremonial (when as I have said all the monkey-tricks you have heard about go on every three or four years among our Tupinambás) are over, and even sometimes before that, the *Caraibes* go from village to village, especially to equip with the most beatiful combinations of plumage they can find, three or four from each family, or more or less acording to their judgement, those rattles or large shakers that they call *Maracas*; these being thus decked out, driving the longer end of the stick that is through them into the ground, and disposing them along all the length and in the centre of the houses, afterwards they then command that these be supplied with food and drink. In this way these imposters make the other poor simpletons believe that these fruits and mere gourds, thus hollowed out, ornamented and sanctified, eat and drink during the night; each head of a household adds to this belief by never failing to put before his own maracas not only meal with flesh and fish, but also some of their brew called *Caou-in*. Seeing these *Maracas* usually planted thus in the earth for a fortnight or three weeks, always looked after in the same way, they have after this sorcery so strange an opinion of them (which they have almost always in their hand) that, attributing to them some sanctity, they say that oftentimes when they shake them a spirit speaks to them. Being thus so much bamboozled, if we ourselves passed among their houses and long huts and saw some good meats presented to these *Maracas*, if we took and ate them (as we have often done) our Americans, considering that this would bring some evil upon us, are no less shocked than are the superstitious believers in and followers of the priests of Baal, to see removed the offerings brought to their idols, with which, however, to the dishonouring of God, they feed themselves plentifully and without effort, along with their whores and bastards. What is more, if taking thereupon the opportunity of remonstrating with them on their errors we were to tell them that the *Caraibes*, in making them believe that the *Maracas* ate and drank, were deceiving

Preparation of Maracas.

Clumsy superstition.

Gross error.

them not only in that, but also that it was not they, as they falsely boast, who made their fruits and their great roots grow, but the God in whom we believe and whom we announce to them, that would be the equivalent in their situation of speaking in our own against the Pope, or of saying in Paris that the reliquary of St. Genevieve does not bring rain. Thus these frauds the *Caraibes*, hating us no less than the false prophets of Jezebel (fearing to lose their fat pickings) did the true servant of God Elias, who similarly laid bare their abuses, beginning to hide from us, were afraid even to come to or sleep in the villages where they knew we were.

1. Kings 18; 19
Truth driving away the lie.

2 JUAN DE TORQUEMADA

Juan de Torquemada was born in Spain; the year has been variously given as 1550 (by A.C. Wilgus, *Histories and Historians of Hispanic America*, New York, 1965, p. 23), as 1563 (by Jose T. Medina, in a reference in Robert Stevenson's *Music in Aztec and Inca Territory*, Berkeley and Los Angeles, 1968, p. 194, n. 81), and as 1565? (by Stevenson in the same book). Torquemada was professed as a Franciscan in Mexico in 1579, became official Franciscan chronicler in 1609, and according to the title-page of the *Monarchia Indiana*, was Provincial of the Franciscan Order in Mexico in 1614.

Torquemada's account of the Indians in Mexico before and after Spanish rule was largely compiled from earlier accounts, chiefly those by the Franciscans Toribio de Benavente, called Motolinia (1490? -1565), who arrived with the original twelve missionaries at Tenochtitlán in June, 1524, and Geronimo de Mendieta (1525? -1604), who entered Mexico in 1554. The legend of the visit to the house of the Sun (pp. 26-27), for example, was derived from Mendieta (see the paraphrased translation quoted by Stevenson, *op. cit.*, p. 113) and the description of festal dances (pp. 32-34) followed that of Motolinia, partly *via* Mendieta (*op. cit.*, pp. 97-99). Robert Stevenson's book has further details about Torquemada's reliance on Mendieta (see especially his p. 119), and also some translated extracts from Torquemada's work (e.g., p. 171).

Juan de Torquemada, *Los veintiún libros rituales y Monarchia Indiana, con el origen y guerras de los indios occidentales*, Madrid, 3 vols., 1723 (first printed, Seville, 1615)

....

Vol.I, Book II, Chapter LXXXVIII: *De la manera, con que se servia el Rei Motecuhçuma, en su Comida, y la Gente, que le asistia à ella, y Audiencia, que daba, y Pasatiempos, de que gustaba, en aquella ocasion.*

....

p. 229

Asistian à la Comida (aunque desviados) seis Señores Ancianos, à los quales daba algunos Platos, del Manjar, que le sabia bien, y alli los comian con gran respeto, y veneracion. Serviase siempre con mucha Musica, de Flautas, Campañas[1], Caracoles, Huesos, Atabales, y otros Instrumentos, de poco deleite à los oidos de los Españoles, y no alcan-

---

1. Orig.: Campoñas

çaban otros mejores, ni tenian Musica de Canto (come la que usamos en voces concertadas) porque no sabian el Arte, hasta que de los Castellanos lo aprendieron (en especial fuè Maestro de èl, en esta Nueva Iglesia, el Apostolico Varon Fr. Pedro de Gante, Fraile Lego de la Esclarecida Orden de mi Glorioso Padre San Francisco) aunque en sus Bailes, y Fiestas cantaban en voces iguales, al son de su Teponaztli (como en otra parte decimos)....

Vol. II, Book VI, Chapter XLIII: *De como Tezcatlipuca apareciò à un su devoto, y lo embiò à la casa de el Sol.*

....

p. 78

Los Hombres devotos de estos Dioses muertos, à quien por memoria avian dejado sus mantas, dizen, que andaban tristes, y pensativos, cada uno con su manta embuelta acuestas, buscando, y mirando, si podrian vèr à sus Dioses, ò si les aparecerian. Dicen, que el devoto de Tezcatlipuca, que era el Idolo principal de Mexico, perseverando en esta su devocion, llegò a la Costa de la Mar, donde le apareciò en tres maneras, ò figuras, y le llamò, y dixò: Vèn aca, Pulano, pues eres tan mi amigo, quiero que vaias à la casa del Sol, y traigas de allà Cantores, è instrumentos, para que me hagas fiesta; y para esto llamaràs à la Ballena, y à la Sirena, y à la Tortuga, que se hagan Puente, por donde pases; pues hecha la dicha Puente, y dandole un Cantar, que fuese diciendo, y entendiendolo el Sol, avisò à su gente, y criados, que no le respondiesen al canto; porque à los que le respondiesen los avia de llevar consigo; y asi aconteciò, que algunos de ellos, pareciendoles melifluo el canto, le respondieron, à los quales trajò con el atabal, que llaman Huehuetl, y con el Tepunaztli. Y de aqui dicen, que començaron à hacer fiestas, y bailes à sus Dioses; y los cantares, que en aquellos arietos cantaban, tenian por oracion, llevandolos en conformidad de un mismo tono, y meneos, con mucho seso, y peso, sin discrepar en voz, ni en paso. Y este mismo concierto guardan en el tiempo de aora. Pero es mucho de advertir, que no les dejan cantar sus canciones antiguas; porque todas son llenas de memorias idolatricas, ni con insignias diabolicas, ò sospechosas, que representan lo mismo. Y es de notar, cerca de lo que arriba se dijò, que los Dioses se mataron à sî mismos, por el pecho, que de aqui dicen algunos, que les quedò la costumbre, que despues usaron, de matar los hombres, que sacrificaban, abriendoles el pecho con un pedernal, y sacandoles el coraçon, para ofrecerlo à sus Dioses, aunque (como en otra parte decimos) fuè en otra ocasion; porque como todo esto es fabula, asi tambien tiene poca verdad aver sido en este acto hecho.

T.1.lib.2.
cap.3.

Vol. II, Book IX, Chapter XXIII: *Donde se trata, de como aunque el oficio de los Sacerdotes, y de los otros Ministros Eclesiasticos antiguamente fue, tener cuidado de los Saccrificios, que en los Templos se hacian, era tambien su oficio ordinario, cantar loores, y alabanças al Dios que adoraban, y conocian.*

p. 210

Este mismo modo, que han guardado los Cantores, y Ministros de Dios, ha sido el de los Sacerdotes, y Ministros del Demonio, en sus Casas, y Templos, cantando alabanças, y loores, y haciendole gracias por los bienes, que entendian venirles de sus manos, y asi en tiempo de Paz, como de Guerra, guardaban esta costumbre. Y entendiendo este gran cuidado gentilico San Clemente, dice, que se deben confundir mucho los Christianos, considerando, que los Gentiles, cada dia, en despertando del sueño, vàn à los Templos de sus Idolos para hacerles honras; y antes que comiencen à exercitarse, en algun exercicio corporal, les hacen sus suplicaciones, y ponen todo cuidado en celebrar sus Fiestas. Y aunque de todos los Gentiles en general se entiende lo dicho, estos de esta Nueva-España tenian sus Cantares, y Alabanças Idolatricas, las quales cantaban de dia, y de noche, en los Templos, diferenciando las horas, porque unos servian para los dias, y otros para las noches, y otros para Dias, que nosotros llamamos feriados, y de entre semana, y otros para los Pasquales, y Festivos; à los quales cantos asistian los Sacerdotes, y Ministros, juntos en Coro, y Congregacion, y los cantaban tañendo, y bailando al derredor del Atambor, y Teponaztle (que es el instrumento, que en otra parte diximos) variando los sones, y bailes, para maior consonancia, harmonìa, y devocion. Y este era Sacrificio de alabança, que jamàs avia de faltar en el Templo; como queriendo el Demonio remedar à Dios, que en sus Iglesias es por este modo continuamente alabado.

D. Clem. li. 2. Const. A-post. ca. 33

Vol. II, Book IX, Chapter XXXIV: *Del tañer de las Campanas, y de los Veladores, que avia en los Templos, y Barrios, para llamar à las horas ordinarias de la administracion de los Oficios.*

p. 226

....Y aunque de los Tiempos antiguos, y pasados no sabemos, que en la Casa, y Templo de Dios huviese Campanas, para tañer, y llamar, con ellas, à las Gentes à la celebracion de las Fiestas, y otras ocasiones, que se ofrecian, como agora en esta Lei de Gracia se usa en las Iglesias; sabemos, empero, que avia Instrumentos Musicos de Viguelas, Citaras, Harpas, Organos, y Cimbalos, y de otros generos immensos, con que se celebraban; de los quales estos Gentiles modernos tambien usaron à sus tiempos, y horas.

De los Instrumentos, que sabemos aver mas usado, fueron unas Flautas, à manera de Cornetas, y de unos Caracoles, que sonaban como

Bocina. Con estos llamaban para las horas, que se cantaban en el Templo de dia, y de noche; como si dixesemos, à Maitines, à Prima, à Visperas, y las demàs horas, à que acudian los Sacerdotes, y Ministros à sus Sacrificios, y loores del Demonio. Hacian con esta solemnidad de instrumentos, y atabales, cada mañana fiesta al Sol, quando salia, con armonia, y estruendo singular, y saludabanle de palabra, como ofreciendole en aquella hora Sacrificio de alabança; y tràs esto sangre de Codornices, que para este fin mataban entonces, arrancandoles las cabeças con violencia, y fuerça, y mostrandolas al Sol ensangrentadas, y descabeçadas. Esta ceremonia de tanto ruido, y estruendo hacian todos los Sacerdotes juntos, teniendo cada qual una Codorniz en sus manos. La qual ceremonia acabada, se guisaban las Codornices, y se las comian estos dichos Satrapas, que à no ser el acto idolatrico, pudieran apetecer muchos esta ceremonia, pues en ella tenian seguro, y cierto el almuerço, y no malo. Hecha esta ceremonia, ofreciendole incienso luego, con la misma armonia, y musica de cuernos, y atabales. Los quales, como està dicho, se tañian à todas las horas, que de dia, ò de noche, se entraba à la Ofrenda del Incienso, y Sacrificio, y à los loores, y alabanças del Demonio. Haciendo en esto una manera de imitacion al tañer de las Campanas à las Horas Canonicas, con que en nuestras Iglesias Christianas se llama à los Ministros, y otras Gentes, para que se congreguen à los Oficios Divinos, y Festividades, con que se celebran.

Vol. II, Book X, Chapter XVI: *De la Fiesta, que se celebraba en este Mes Toxcatl al Dios Huitzilupuchtli, llamado de los Antiguos Marte.*
p. 263

Supr. lib. 6 cap. 21.

Marte, Dios de las Batallas, fue llamado de estos Indios, Huitzilupuchtli, cuia asimilacion queda probada en el Libro de la Verdadera, y Falsa Religion; y asi, no pretendo en este Capitulo mas que decir la Fiesta, que en este mesmo Mes se le hacia por estos Gentiles (con que casi todo èl era festivo) la qual era de esta manera......

Delante de estas Andas llevaban una manera de lienço, hecho de papel, que tenia veinte braças de largo, una de ancho, y un dedo de grueso. Este lienço, hecho de papel, llevaban muchos Mancebos, asidos con unas saetas, con mucho recato; porque no se quebrase, ni lastimase, todo pintado, en cuias pinturas debian de ir escritas todas las haçañas, que en su favor entendian aver hecho, y todos los Blasones, y epitectos, que le daban, en recompensa de las Victorias, que les concedia. Iban cantando delante de este falso Dios sus haçañas, y proezas, acto à solo Dios debido, à quien los de su Pueblo cantaron, diciendo, Dios de venganças, que obra libremente; y otros (en otra parte) cantemos à Dios, que gloriosamente se ha mostrado, hecho un Marte Divino, y un castigador de maldades, anegando al Rei Faraon, y matando toda su cavalleria......

Psalm. 95. Isaias 35.

....

Todas las Doncellas, que servian à este Dios, bailaban en este Fiesta: para cuio Baile se afeitaban las caras, poniendose color en las mexillas, y emplumandose los braços, hasta los codos, de una pluma colorada mui rica, y sobre sus cabeças Guirnaldas de Maiz tostado, que llaman Mumuchitl, à manera de açahar, ò Flores mui blancas. Bailaban à las bueltas de estas Donçellas los Satrapas, y Sacerdotes de este Dios: los quales llevaban emplumadas las cabeças con unas plumas blancas de Garça, ò de Gallina, y en la frente pendiente una rodaja de papel, à manera de Rosa, los rostros entintados, y parte de ellos juntamente con los labios enmelados, para que relumbrase, y hiciese visos sobre la tinta....Los que tañian el Teponaztli, ò Atambor, con que les hacian el son para bailar, no estaban presentes, como en los otros Bailes comunes, y ordinarios acostumbraban, sino en cierto Aposento, ò Sala metidos, de donde les tañian. De manera, que se oia el son, y no se veian las Personas, ni Instrumentos musicales. Toda la Gente de Palacio, y Hombres de Guerra, asi moços, como viejos, bailaban en otra parte, apartados de estos, todos travados de las manos, y culebreando, à manera de las danças, que los populares, asi Hombres, como Mugeres, hacen en Castilla la Vieja,....

Vol. II, Book X, Chapter XXIII. *De la Fiesta, que hacian estos Indios, en el undecimo Mes de su Kalendario, llamado Uchpaniztli, à la Diosa Teteuynan, Madre de todos los Dioses, y por otro nombre Tocitzin.*
p. 275

En el undecimo Mes del Kalendario Mexicano tenia su Dia, y Fiesta la Madre de los Dioses, llamada Teteuynan: y esta pienso, que es aquella Antigua Berecinta, tan celebrada de los Antiguos Gentiles, con este mismo nombre, como el Glorioso Augustino lo dice, aunque no con Sacrificios, y Ofrendas tan lascivas, y deshonestas, y con profanidad, y actos, mas de confusion, que de devocion, como esotros; segun parece, y es claro, y manifiesto, en las unas, y otras Fiestas. Llamaban à este Mes Uchpaniztli, y caia su primer Dia à los veinte y quatro ue Agosto, y fenecia à los doce de Septiembre. Pero cinco Dias antes, que entrara este Mes Uchpaniztli, cesaban todas las Fiestas del pasado, y quedaba el tiempo en sosiego, y calma, sin Fiesta, ni celebracion alguna. En entrando el primer Dia, bailaban en el Templo dicho, sin Teponaztli, ni Canto, sino en mui concertado, y mudo silencio, siguiendo sus compases al son de la fantasia, que era con la que los formaban; y aviendo bailado ocho dias à este tono, y silencio, componian à la Muger, que representaba la imagen de esta maldita Diosa, con sus adereços, y ornamentos; y acompañabanla grande numero de Mugeres (en especial de Medicas, y Parteras) y la primera vista que daban al Pueblo, era con un juego, à manera del de Cañas, que los nuestros acostumbran, en sus regocijos, quando usan de Alcancias, y no de Cañas. Hacian para este

D. August de Civitat. Dei, lib. 2. c. 4 & 5.

juego, unas pelotas, de una ierva, llamada Pachtli, otras de Espadañas, y Juncia, y otras con pencas de Tunas, y con estas cosas se tiraban las unas à las otras, y se ofendian, aunque no de manera, que se maltrata- sen, ni lastimasen, ni que les obligasen los golpes, à quejarse, ò à vengar- se de los recibidos de sus contrarias; y este Juego duraba quatro dias.....

....

Vol. II, Book XIII, Chapter XLVI: *De la Solemnidad. con que se hacian los Entierros, y Obsequias de los Reies de Mechoacan, que es Capitulo de notar.*
p. 524

Era Lei inviolable, que en esta ocasion havian de morir muchos, con el Rei; porque decian (falsa, y mentirosamente) que iban con èl, à servirle al otro Mundo....; un Plumagero, un Platero, que le hacia Joias, un Oficial de Arcos, y Flechas; dos, ò tres Monteros; algunos de aquel- los Medicos, que no le pudieron sanar, para emmendar la cura, que en esta Vida havian errado; un Truhan, y un Gracioso, que tenia cargo de contarle Novelas; un Tabernero, para el vino; iba un Tañedor, y un Bailador, y un Carpintero de hacer los Instrumentos Musicos, con que tañen; y otros muchos criados suios se ofrecian de su voluntad, à la muerte, para irle à servir, en aquella su jornada;....

A todos estos lababan, y bañaban, con gran cuidado, y luego los embadurnaban todo el cuerpo, con una tinta amarilla, de que ellos usaban, y les ponain Guirnaldas, en sus cabeças, y puestos, en renglera, unos tras otros, hacian una larga Procesion delante de las andas, del Cuerpo del Difunto, el qual sacaban al punto de la media noche de Palacio, y le acompañaban ciertos Musicos, tañendo con unos huesos de Caimanes, en unas rodelas de Tortugas. Iban las Andas en hombros de sus Hijos, y de los Señores mas Principales de el Reino, y los Señores de los Pueblos de Eneani, Zacapu, Heriti, Vanacaye, que eran quatro Pue- blos, conjuntos al de Pazquaro, que era la Corte, que eran de sus mas cercanos Deudos; iban cantando ciertos Cantares, en que decian loores, y alabanças del Señor, cuio Cuerpo llevaban à quemar, y otras cosas, ordenadas, segun el acto en que iban ocupados. Todos estos, que acom- pañaban este Cuerpo, llevaban sus insignias de Valientes Hombres; y mui acompañado de lumbres, iban tañendo Trompetas, è iban muchos criados barriendo las calles, y caminos, y decianle: Señor, por aqui has de ir, mira no pierdas el camino, y de esta manera lo llevaban hasta el Patio de los Teocales, ò Templos grandes, donde ia estaba puesta una grande hacina de leña seca, concertadamente, una sobre otra. En este lugar daban quatro bueltas con èl, à la redonda, con grande pausa, y solemnidad de Musica. Luego lo ponian sobre aquel monton, y rimero de leña, con todo su aparato, y atavio, como lo traian, y tornaban sus Parientes à decir su Cantar, como antes, quando salieron de su casa; y acabado, ponian Fuego à la leña, que como era de Pino, y mui seca, ardia luego; y mientras estaba ardiendo este desventurado Cuerpo, iban achocando con Porras, y Macanas a los Ministros, que iban à servirle à la otra Vida, segun estos ciegos Hombres creian; pero diciendo Verdad, ibanle acompañando à las penas del Infierno; y para que no sintiesen la muerte, los emborrachaban primero; que quando no tuvieran otro peca- do, para ir al Infierno, este bastaba, pues es vicio contrario à la Virtud de la Templança, la qual nos està tan encomendada; y en detestacion de este bestial vicio, dice el Glorioso Padre San Agustin: El borracho entre- gandose del vino, el vino se entrega en èl; es abominado de Dios, despre- ciado de los Angeles, hacen burla de èl los Hombres; es despojado de las Virtudes, confundido de el Demonio, y menospreciado de los Hom- bres......

D. August. lib. de Poe nitent.

Vol. II, Book XIV, Chapter IV: *Que se dice la Honra, que se hacia al Rei, ò Señor, que en Guerra prendia enemigo, la primera vez; y se dicen otras cosas tocantes à la Guerra.*
p. 541
....Por esto querian estos Indios, que los que lo eran suios tuviesen valor, y osadia, y que por su Persona hiciesen hechos de grande Fama, y mientras esto no hacian, aunque estuviesen elegidos, y confirmados, y en la posesion de su Señorio, parecia que no estaban contentos, ni usaban libremente de la execucion, y dignidad de Señor, como los otros, que ià se havian mostrado ser valientes Hombres en las Guerras: porque tenian de costumbre, que ni los Señores, ni los Hijos de Señores no se ponian Joias de Oro, ni de Plata, ni Piedras preciosas, ni mantas ricas de labores, ni pintadas, ni plumajes en la cabeça, hasta que huvie- sen hecho alguna valentia, matando, ò prendiendo, por su mano ò alguno, ò algunos en la Guerra; y mucho menos la otra Gente de mas bajo estado, sino era que llegaba à merecerlo, por haçañas notables, que huviese hecho, en la Republica, ò contra sus enemigos: por lo qual quando la primera vez el Rei, ò Señor, prendia alguno en la Guerra, luego despachaba sus mensageros, para que de su casa le trajesen las mejores Joias, y vestidos, que tenia, y que corriese la voz de que el Rei, ò Señor, havia prendido, por su sola Persona, en la Guerra, un Prisione- ro, ò mas, y bueltos los mensageros, con las ropas, luego componian, y vestian al que el Señor havia preso, y hacian, unas como andas, el las quales le traìan, con mucha fiesta, y Solemnidad, y llamabanlo Hijo del Señor que lo havia prendido, y hacianle la honra, que al mismo Señor (aunque no de veràs porque era para darle mas dura muerte) y el preso delante, y todo el despojo enemigo, delante venian los de la Guerra mui regocijados, y los del Pueblo salian à recibirlos, con Trompetas, y Boci- nas, Bailes, y Cantos, y à las veces los Maestros de los Cantos compo- nian algun Cantar propio, del nuevo vencimiento, y al preso, que venia

en las andas, saludaban todos, primero que al Señor, ni otro ninguno, y decianle: Seais mui bien venido, pues sois llegado à vuestra casa, no os aflijais, que en vuestra casa estais, luego saludaban al Señor, y à sus Cavalleros. Y sabida esta primera Victoria del Rei, ò Señor, por los otros Pueblos, y Provincias, los Señores comarcanos, Parientes, y Amigos venianle à ver, y à regocijarse con èl, traiendole Presentes de Joias de Oro, de Piedras finas, y mantas ricas, y èl recibialos, con mucha alegria, y haciales gran Fiesta de Bailes, y Cantos, y de mucha comida, y tambien les repartia, y daba muchas mantas; y los Parientes mas cercanos, quedabanse con èl, hasta que llegaba el Dia de la Fiesta, que havian de sacrificar, al que havia prendido, porque luego que llegaban al Pueblo, señalaban el Dia.

Vol. II, Book XIV, Chapter XI: *De la manera, que estos Naturales tenian de Bailes, y Danças, y de la gran destreça, y conformidad, que todos guardaban, en el Baile, y en el Canto.*
p. 550
Una de las cosas principales, que en toda esta Tierra havia, eran los Cantos, y Bailes, asi para solemniçar las Fiestas de sus Demonios, que por Dioses honraban, con los quales pensaban, que les hacian gran servicio, como para regocijo, y solaz proprio; y por esta causa, y por ser cosa de que hacian mucha cuenta, en cada Pueblo, y cada Señor, en su Casa tenia Capilla, con sus Cantores, componedores de Danças, y Cantares, y estos buscaban, que fuesen de buen ingenio, para saber componer los Cantares en su modo de Metros, ò Coplas, que ellos tenian. Y quando estos eran buenos, con trabajos, tenianlos en mucho; porque los Señores en sus Casas, hacian cantar muchos Dias en voz baja. Ordinariamente cantaban, y bailaban, en las principales Fiestas, que eran de veinte en veinte dias, y en otras menos principales. Los Bailes mas principales, eran en las Plaças, otras veces en casa del maior Señor, en su patio, porque todos los Señores tenian grandes patios: bailaban tambien en casa de otros Señores, y Principales. Quando havian havido alguna victoria en Guerra, ò levantaban nuevo Señor, ò se casaban, con alguna Señora principal, ò por otra novedad alguna, los Maestros componian nuevo Cantar, demás de los generales, que tenian de las Fiestas de los Demonios, y de las haçañas antiguas, y de los Señores pasados. Proveian los Cantores algunos Dias, antes de la Fiesta, lo que havian de cantar. En los grandes Pueblos eran muchos los Cantores; y si havia cantos, ò danças nuevas, aiuntabanse otros, con ellos, porque no huviese defecto el Dia de la Fiesta. El Dia que havian de bailar, ponian luego por la mañana una grande estera en medio de la Plaça, adonde se havian de poner los Atabales, y todos se ataviaban, y aiuntaban en casa de el Señor, y de alli salian cantando, y bailando: unas veces començaban los Bailes por la mañana, y otras à la hòra que aora es de Misa Maior; y à la

noche tornaban cantando al Palacio, y alli daban fin al canto, y Baile, ià noche, ò à gran rato andado de la noche, y à las veces à la media noche. Los Atabales eran dos; el uno alto, y redondo, mas grueso que un Hombre, de cinco palmos en alto, de mui buena madera, hueco de dentro, y bien labrado, por de fuera pintado; en la boca ponainle su cuero de Venado, curtido, y bien estirado; desde el bordo, hasta el medio, hace su diapente, y tañenle por sus puntos, y tonos, que suben, y bajan, concertando, y entonado el atabal con los cantares. El otro Atabal, es de arte, que sin pintura, no se podria dàr bien à entender: este sirve de contra bajo, y ambos suenan bien, y se oien lejos. Llegados los Bailadores al sitio, ponense en orden à tañer los Atabales, y dos Cantores, los mejores, como Sochantres, comiençan desde alli los cantos; el Atabal grande encorado, se tañe con las manos, y à este llaman Huehuetl; el otro se tañe, como los Atabales de España, con palos, aunque es de otra hechura, y llamanle Teponaztli. El Señor con los otros Principales, y viejos, andan delante los Atabales bailando; y hinchen tres, ò quatro braças al derredor de los Atabales, y con estos otra multitud que và ensanchando, y hinchendo el corro. Los que andan en este medio, en los grandes Pueblos, solian ser mas de mil; y à las veces mas de dos mil; y demàs de estos, à la redonda anda una procesion de dos ordenes, de Mancebos, grandes Bailadores. Los delanteros, son dos Hombres sueltos, de los mejores Bailadores, que vàn guiando el Baile. En estas dos ruedas, en ciertas bueltas, y contenencias, que hacen, à las veces miran, y tienen por compañero al de enfrente; y en otros Bailes, al que và junto, ò tràs è'. No eran tan pocos los que iban en estas dos ordenes, que no llegasen à ser cerca de mil, y otras veces mas, segun los Pueblos, y las Fiestas. En su antiguedad, antes da las Guerras, quando celebraban sus Fiestas, con libertad, en los grandes Pueblos se aiuntaban tres, y quatro mil, y mas à bailar: mas aora como se ha disminuido, y apocado tanta multitud, son pocos los que se juntan à bailar. Queriendo començar à bailar tres, ò quatro Indios levantan unos silvos mui vivos; luego tocan los Atabales, en tono bajo, y poco à poco vàn sonando mas; y oiendo la Gente bailadora, que los Atabales comiençan, por el tono de ellos, entiende el cantar, y el baile, y luego lo comiençan. Los primeros Cantos vàn en tono bajo, como bemolados, y despacio; y el primero es conferme à la Fiesta, y siempre le comiençan aquellos dos Maestros, y luego todo el Coro lo prosigue, juntamente con el Baile. Toda esta multitud trae los pies tan concertados, como unos mui diestros Dançadores de España; y lo que mas es, que todo el cuerpo, asi la cabeça, como los braços, y manos, trae tan còncertado medido, y ordenado, que no discrepa, ni sale uno, de otro medio compàs, mas lo que uno hace con el pie derecho, y tambien con el izquierdo, lo mismo hacen todos, y en un mismo tiempo, y compàs; y quando uno baja el braço izquierdo, y levanta el derecho, lo mismo, y al mismo tiempo, hacen

todos. De manera, que los Atabales, el Canto, y Bailadores, todos llevan
su compàs concertado, y todos son conformes, que no discrepa uno de
otro una jota; de lo qual los buenos Dançadores de España, que los vèn,
se espantan, y tienen en mucho las Danças, y Bailes de estos Naturales,
y el gran acuerdo, y sentimiento, que en ellos tienen. Los que andan
mas apartados, en aquella rueda de fuera, podemos decir, que llevan el
compasillo, que es de un compàs hacer dos, y andan mas vivos, y meten
mas obra en el Baile; y estos de la rueda, todos son conformes, unos à
otros. Los que andan en medio de el corro, hacen su compàs entero; y
los movimientos, asi de los pies, como del cuerpo, vàn con mas grave-
dad, y cierto levantan, y bajan los braços con mucha gracia. Cada Verso,
ò Copla repiten tres, ò quatro veces, y vàn procediendo, y diciendo su
Cantar, bien entonado, que ni en el Canto, ni en los Atabales, ni en el
Baile sale uno de otro. Acabado un Cantar, dado caso que los primeros
parecen mas largos, por ir mas despacio, aunque todos no duran mas de
una hora, apenas el Atabal muda el tono, quando todos dejan el Cantar;
y hechos ciertos compases de intervalo (en el Canto, mas no en el Baile)
luego los Maestros comiençan otro Cantar un poco mas alto, y el compàs mas vivo, y asi vàn subiendo los Cantos, y mudando los tonos, y
sonadas, como quien de una baja, muda, y pasa à una alta, y de una
Dança, en un contracompàs. Andan bailando algunos Muchachos, y
Niños, Hijos de principales, de siete, y de ocho Años, y algunos de
quatro, y cinco, que cantan, y bailan, con los Padres; y como los Muchachos cantan en prima voz, ò tiple, agracian mucho el canto. A tiempos tañen sus Trompetas, y unas Flautillas no mui entonados; otros dan
silvos, con unos hueseçuelos, que suenan mucho; otros andan dis-
fraçados, en trage, y en voz, contrahaciendo à otras Naciones, y mudando el lenguaje. Estos que digo, son Truhanes, y andan sobresalientes,
haciendo mil visajes, y diciendo mil gracias, y donaires, con que hacen
reir à quantos los vèn, y oien; unos andan como viejas, otros como
bobos. A tiempos les traen bebida, y de ellos salen à descansar, y à
comer, y aquellos bueltos, salen otros, y asi descansan todos sin cesar el
Baile. A tiempos les traen alli Piñas de Rosas, y de otras Flores, ò
Ramilletes, para traer en los manos, y Guirnaldas, que les ponen en las
Cabeças, demàs de sus atavìos que tienen para bailar, de Mantas ricas, y
plumajes; y otros traen en los manos, en lugar de Ramilletes sus Plu-
majas pequeños hermosos. En estos Bailes sacan muchas divisas, y seña-
les, en que se conocen los que han sido valientes en la Guerra. Desde
hora de visperas, hasta la noche, los Cantos, y Bailes, se vàn mas avivan-
do, y alçando los tonos, y la sonada es mas graciosa, que parece que
llevan un aire de los Himnos, que tienen el Canto alegre. Los Atabales
tambien vàn subiendo mas; y como la Gente que baila es mucha, oiese
gran trecho, en especial adonde el Aire lleva la voz, y mas de noche,
quando todo està sosegado: que para bailar en este Tiempo proveian de
muchas, y grandes Lumbres, y cierto ello todo era cosa de vèr.

Vol. III, Book XVII, Chapter III: *De como los Indios fueron enseñados en la Musica; y cosas, que pertenecen al servicio de la Iglesia, y lo que en esto han aprovechado.*

p. 213

NO menos habilidad mostraron para las Letras los Indios, que para los Oficios Mecanicos, porque luego, con mucha brevedad, aprendieron à Leer, asi nuestro Romance Castellano, como Latin, y Tirado, ò Letra de mano; y el Escrivir por consiguiente, con mucha facilidad. Començaron à Escrivir en su Lengua, y entenderse, y tratarse, por Cartas, como nosotros: lo qual, antes tenian por maravilla, que el Papel hablase, y dixese à cada uno lo que el ausente le queria dar à entender. Contrahacian, al principio, mui al proprio las materias que les daban: y si les mudaban Maestro, luego ellos mudaban la forma de la Letra, en la del nuevo Maestro. En el segundo Año, que les començaron à enseñar, dieron à un Muchacho de Tetzcuco, por muestra, una Bula, y sacòla tan al natural, que la Letra que hiço parecia el mismo Molde; puso el primer renglon de la Letra grande, como estaba en la Bula, y abaxo sacò la Firma del Comisario, y un Jesus, con una Imagen de Nuestra Señora, todo tan al proprio, que parecia no aver diferencia del Molde, à la que èl sacò: y por cosa notable, y primera la llevò un Español à Castilla, para mostrarla, y dàr que vèr con ella. Despues se fueron haciendo mui grandes Escrivanos de todas Letras, chicas, y grandes, quebradas, y goticas: y los Religiosos les aiudaban à salir Escrivanos, porque los ocupaban à la continua en escrivir Libros, y Tratados, que componian, ò trasuntaban de Latin, ò Romance, en sus Lenguas de ellos. El Año de 1570, que fue à España el Padre Frai Geronimo de Mendieta, dice, que llevò un Libro del *Contemptus Mundi,* buelto en Lengua Mexicana, escrito de letra de un Indio, tan bien formada, igual, y graciosa, que de ningun Molde pudiera dàr mas contento à la vista: y mostrandolo al Licenciado Don Juan de Ovando, que à la saçon era Presidente de Consejo de Indias, agradòle tanto, que se quedò con èl, diciendo, que lo queria dàr al Rei Don Felipe Segundo, de este Nombre, nuestro Señor. Demàs de el Escrivir, começaron luego los Indios à pautar, y apuntar, asi Canto-Llano, como Canto de Organo, y de ambos Cantos hicieron mui buenos Libros, y Psalterios, de letra gruesa, para los Coros de los Frailes, y para sus Coros, con sus Letras grandes, mui iluminadas: y no iban à buscar quien se los enquadernase, porque ellos juntamente lo aprendieron todo: y lo que mas de notar es, que sacaban Imagenes de Planchas, de mui perfectas Figuras, que quantos las veian se espantaban; porque de la primera vez les hacian, ni mas, ni menos, que la Plancha.

El tercero Año los pusieron en el Canto, y algunos se reian, y burlaban de los que los enseñaban, y otros los estorvaban, diciendo, que no saldrian con ello, asi porque parecian desentonados, como porque parecian tener flacas voces: y à la verdad, no las tienen comunmente, ni las pueden tener tan recias, ni tan suaves, como los Españoles, andando, como andan, descalços, y mal arropados, y comiendo poco, y flacas viandas; pero como ai muchos en que escoger, siempre ai buenas Capillas, y algunos Contrabaxos, Altos, Tenores, y Tiples, que pueden competir con los escogidos de las Iglesias Catedrales. El primero que les enseñò el Canto, juntamente con Frai Pedro de Gante, fue un Venerable Sacerdote Viejo, llamado Frai Juan Caro, que bien barato, y cumplido se mostraba con ellos, pues sin saber palabra de su Lengua, ni ellos de la Española, se estaba todo el Dia enseñandoles, y hablandoles, y platicandoles las Reglas del Canto en Romance, tan de proposito, y tan sin pesadumbre, como si ellos fueran meros Españoles: y los Muchachos estaban la boca abierta mirandole, y oiendole mui atentos, à vèr lo que queria decir. Y aunque algunos de nosotros tomaban ocasion de reirse de esta su santa bondad, y flema, de otra manera la consideraba, aquel Señor, que se agrada de los coraçones sencillos, y llanos; y asi la favoreciò, obrando como Soberano, y Poderoso Artifice, entre aquel Maestro, y sus Discipulos; que poco, ni mucho no se entendian; de suerte, que sin medio de otro Interprete, los Muchachos en poco tiempo lo entendieron de tal manera, que no solo lo entendieron, y salieron con el Canto Llano, mas tambien con el Canto de Organo: y despues acà unos à otros se lo vàn enseñando, y ai entre ellos muchos, y mui diestros Cantores, y Maestros de Capilla; tanto, que en cada Capilla de Cantores ai, por lo menos, cinco, y seis, y mas, que se vàn cada Año remudando en el Oficio de Maestros, y Capitanes, que guian, y rigen à los otros. La primera cosa, que aprendieron, y Cantaron los Indios, fue la Misa de Nuestra Señora, que comiença: *Salve Sancta Parens.* No ai Pueblo de cien Vecinos, que no tenga Cantores, que Oficien las Misas, y Visperas en Canto de Organo, y con sus Ministriles, è Instrumentos de Musica; ni ai Aldehuela apenas, por pequeña que sea, que dexe de tener siquiera tres, ò quatro Indios, que Canten cada Dia en su Iglesia las Horas de Nuestra Señora, especial en la Provincia de Mechoacàn, y Xalisco.

Los primeros Instrumentos de Musica, que hicieron, y usaron, fueron Flautas: luego, Chirimias: despues, Orlos: y tràs ellos, Vihuelas de Arco: y tràs ellas, Cornetas, y Baxones; finalmente, no ai genero de Musica, que se use en la Iglesia de Dios, que los Indios no lo tengan, y usen, en todos los Pueblos Principales, y aun en los no Principales: y ellos mismos lo labran todo, que yà no ai que traerlo de España. Una cosa puedo afirmar con verdad, que en todos los Reinos de la Christiandad (fuera de las Indias) no ai tanta copia de Flautas, Chirimias, Sacabuches, Trompetas, Orlos, Atabales, como en solo este Reino de la Nueva España. Organos tambien los hacian, casi todas las Iglesias, donde ai Religiosos. Y aunque los Indios (por no tener caudal para tanto) no toman el cargo para hacerlos, sino Maestros Españoles, los Indios son los que labran todo lo que es menester para ellos, y ellos los tañen en nuestros

Conventos. Los demàs Instrumentos, que sirven para solàz, y regocijo de las Personas Seglares, los Indios los hacen todos, y los tañen: Rabeles, Guitarras, Discantes, Vihuelas, Harpas, y Monacordios; y con esto se concluie, que no ai cosa que no hagan: y lo que mas es, que pocos Años despues, que aprendieron el Canto, començaron ellos à componer, de su ingenio, Villancicos en Canto de Organo, à quatro Voces, y algunas Misas, y otras Obras, que mostradas à diestros Cantores Españoles, decian ser de escogidos juicios, y no poder ser de Indios.

Sobre enseñarles la Gramatica Latina, y la Latinidad, huvo muchos pareceres, asi entre los Frailes, como entre otras Personas: y antes, que se la enseñassen, tuvieron muchas contradiciones, con raçones aparentes, que los de la contraria opinion daban, mas al fin prevalecio la raçon verdadera; de que era justo, que à lo menos algunos Naturales entendiesen, en alguna manera, lo que contiene la Sagrada Escritura, y los Libros de los Sagrados Doctores, asi para que ellos mismos se fixasen, y fortaleciesen mas de veras en las cosas de Nuestra Santa Fè, como para que pudiesen satisfacer à los otros Indios, de quan diferentemente vamos fundados los Christianos, en lo que creemos, y seguimos, de lo que ellos, y los demàs Gentiles avian creìdo, y seguido, sin fundamento, ni camino, ni rastro de ninguna verdad. A los principios pasòse trabajo grande, y hallaron no poca dificultad los Religiosos, que eran sus Maestros; porque puesto caso, que sabian mui bien su Lengua, como en ella no se avian tratado semejantes materias, no hallaban terminos con que explicarles las Reglas Gramaticales: y asi, era mui poco lo que aprovechaban, y casi desmaiaban, y desconfiaban los Discipulos, y aun los Maestros. Mas como en todas las demas cosas, en que los Siervos de Dios, en el principio hallaban dificultad, tuvieron propicio, el auxilio Divino, asi quando plugo al Espiritu Santo (que es el verdadero Maestro de todas las Artes, y Ciencias) de abrirles los Entendimientos, vieron la puerta, que el Señor les abria, y hallaron terminos, de nuevo compuestos, por donde con facilidad se pudieron declarar, y dàr à entender las Reglas de la Gramatica; y asi, en pocos Años, salieron tan buenos Latinos, que hacian, y componian Versos mui medidos, y largas, y congruas Oraciones, en presencia de los Virreies, y de los Prelados Eclesiasticos, como se dice en otra parte.

TRANSLATION

(I.ii.88) *Of the manner in which King Moctezuma's feasts were served, of those who were present there, of the audience he gave and the pastimes he used on those occasions.*

Present at the feast, although set apart, were six elders whom he knew well, to whom he gave certain dishes, and they ate them there with great respect and veneration. He was always provided with a great deal of music on flutes, bells, shell trumpets, bone scrapers, drums and other instruments, of little pleasure to Spanish ears, and they achieved nothing better, nor did they have vocal music like that we use in vocal ensembles, for they did not know this art until the Castilians taught them (friar Pedro de Gante, lay-brother of the illustrious Order of my glorious father St. Francis, was in particular a master of that art in that new Church), although in their dances and feasts they sang in unison to the sound of their teponaztli, as we have said elsewhere.

(II.vi.43) *How Tezcatlipoca appeared to one of his devotees, and took him to the house of the Sun.*

The devotees of these dead gods, who as a momento had left them their cloaks, are said to have gone about sad and thoughtful, each one wrapped in his cloak, searching and looking to see if they could see their gods, or if they would appear to them. They say that the devotee of Tezcatlipoca, who is the principal idol of Mexico, persevering in this his devotion, reached the sea-coast, where he appeared to him in three manners or figures, and called him and said: 'Come hither, Pulano; since thou art so much my friend, I command thee to go to the house of the Sun and bring thence singers and instruments, to make me a festival; and therefore thou shalt call the Whale and the Mermaid and the Turtle to make a bridge by which thou mayest pass over.' Now when that bridge was made, and he was given a song saying what he was, and the Sun had heard him, he ((the Sun)) told his people and servants not to answer that song, for he ((the devotee)) was to take away with him those who answered him. Now it so befell that some of them, to whom the song seemed mellifluous, answered him, and these he brought back with the drum which they call huehuetl and the teponaztli. They say that from thenceforth they began to hold feasts and dances to their gods; and the songs which they then sang they took for prayer, keeping them fixedly in the same tone and gesture, with much sense and weight, without changing the voice or step. And this same concert they keep until this day. But mark well that they should not be allowed to sing their old songs, for they are all full of memories of idolatry, nor ((use)) devilish and suspect symbols which represent the same. And note here that it was said that the gods killed themselves by stabbing their breasts, from which, some say, arose the custom they afterwards used of killing the men they sacrificed, opening their breasts with a flint knife and drawing out their hearts to offer to their gods, although, as I have said elsewhere, it was for another reason; for as all this is fable, so there is little likelihood that it should have been thus.

(II.ix.23) *Where it is shown that, although the office of the priests and the other ministers was anciently to watch over the sacrifices done in the temples, it was also their ordinary office to sing praises to the god they adored and knew.*

This same fashion, which the singers and ministers of God have kept, was that of the priests and ministers of the Devil in his house and temples, singing hymns and praises, and thanking him for the good things which they supposed came to them from his hands, and thus in time both of peace and war they held to this custom. And understanding this great heathen devotion, St. Clement says that the Christians should be much dismayed to consider that the Gentiles every day when they waken go to the temples of their idols to do them honour, and before they begin to take any bodily exercise they make their supplications to them, and take every care to celebrate their festivals. And although this saying is to be understood of all the heathen in general, those of this New Spain kept their idolatrous songs and praises, differentiating between the hours, so that some served for days and others for nights, others for the days which we call ferias within the week, and others for festive periods and days. In these songs the priests and ministers joined in chorus and the congregation assisted, and they sang them dancing around players of the drum and teponaztli (which is that instrument we have spoken of elsewhere), varying the music and dances for greater fitness, conformity and devotion. And this was the rite of praise which was never allowed to fail in the temple, as though the Devil sought to ape God, who in his churches is thus continually praised.

(II.ix.34) *Of the bell-ringing, and of the watchmen that were in the temples and quarters to call to the ordinary hours of administration of the offices.*

And although we do not know whether in ancient and vanished times there were bells in God's house and temple, to be struck to call the people to celebrate the feasts and other occasions that arose, as is now the gracious rule in the churches, nonetheless we know that musical instruments of the nature of vihuelas, guitars, harps, organs and harpsichords and of many other kinds were used to celebrate them, of which these modern pagans likewise made use in their ritual times and hours.

Of the instruments which we know they most used, there were certain flutes like cornetts and certain shells which they sounded like trumpets. With these they called to the services which were sung in the temple by day and by night, as if we were to say 'to Matins, to Prime, to Vespers', and to the other hours at which the priests and ministers hastened to their sacrifices and praises of the Devil. Every morning with this solemnity of instruments and drums they celebrated the rising Sun with music and extraordinary din, and saluted him with words, offering him at this hour sacrificial praise, and besides that the blood of quails, which they killed for this purpose at that time, tearing off their heads with violence and force, and showing them to the Sun bleeding and headless. This ceremony with all its noise and din was performed by all the priests together, each one holding a quail in his hands. This ceremony ended, they cooked the quails, and the said satraps ate them, which rite, if it were not idolatry, might attract many people, and by it they considered their meal sure and certain, and nothing ill. This ceremony accomplished, they immediately offered up incense to the same sounds and the music of horns and drums, which as said before they played at all the hours of the day or night when they began their incense-offering and sacrifice and lauds and praises of the Devil, thus making a kind of imitation of the bell-tolling at the canonic hours by which in our Christian churches we call the ministers and other folk to the divine offices and festivals that are celebrated.

(II.x.16) *Of the festival which was celebrated in this month Tóxcatl to the god Huitzilopochtli, whom the ancients called Mars.*

Mars, the god of battles, was called by these Indians Huitzilopochtli, whose assimilation is easily proved in the Book of True and False Religion (vi.21 above); and so in this chapter I pretend no more than to tell of the festival made to him in this month by these pagans (for whom nearly all this month was a festival), which was after this manner......

Before this litter they had raised a kind of canvas made of paper, twenty fathoms long, one broad, and one fingerbreadth thick. This paper canvas was borne by many young men, ((and)) was fastened to arrows very carefully, lest it be broken or hurt, and all painted, in which pictures had to be shown all the exploits which they thought he had done in their favour, and all the honours and epithets they gave him in recompense for the victories he had given them. They went before this false god singing his deeds and honours, an act due to God alone, to whom his people sang, saying : ((&c.))

All the maidens who served this god danced in this festival; for which dance they made up their faces and painted their cheeks, and adorned their arms up to the elbows with a very rich-coloured feather, and on their heads garlands of toasted maize, which they call Mumuchitl, like orange-blossom or white flowers. The satraps and priests of this god danced alternately with these maidens; they bore on their heads heron or hen feathers, and hanging down from their foreheads a small paper disk like a rose, their faces painted, and some too with their lips spread with honey, that it might shine and be seen above the paint......... They who played the Teponaztli, or drum, which provided the sound for the dance, were not present, as was the custom in the other common and ordinary dances, but were placed in a certain chamber or room nearby, in which they played, so that one might hear the sound and not see the players or the instruments. All the people of the palace, and warriors, both young and old, danced in another place apart from them, all with hands joined, and in a writhing line, like the dances which the peasants, both men and women, have in Old Castile..........

(II.x.23) *Of the festival which these Indians made in the eleventh month of their calendar, called Ochpaniztli, to the goddess Teteuynan, mother of all the gods, otherwise named Tocitzin.*

In the eleventh month of the Mexican calendar the mother of gods, called Teteuynan, had her day and festival; and I think she is that same Berecynthia of old, much celebrated of the ancient Gentiles by that same title, as the glorious St. Augustine says *(De civitate Dei,* II, chapters 4 and 5), though not with such lascivious and vile sacrifices and offerings, and with profanity and displays of confusion more than devotion, as those other did, as it appears and is made clear and manifest in the one and the other festival. They called this month Ochpaniztli, and its first day fell on the 24th of August, and it ended on the 12th of September. But for five days before the beginning of this month Ochpaniztli all the previous festivities ceased, and they spent the time in peace and quiet, without any festival or ceremony whatever. When the first day of the month began, they danced in the said temple, without teponaztli or song, but yet well concerted together and quite silent, setting their rhythm to the fancy of her who led them; and when they had danced for eight days in this manner and this silence, they adorned that woman. who represented the image of this accursed goddess with her finery and ornaments, and a great many women (especially the female doctors and midwives) accompanied her, and the first sight that people had of them was with a sport like the stick-game with which our people amuse themselves, but they used missiles and not sticks. For this game they made balls from a herb called Pachtli, others of long leaves and rushes, and others of the leaves of the prickly pear; and with these things they would aim at and hit each other, but not so as to hurt or wound each other, nor to be obliged to complain or avenge themselves for the blows they had received; and this game lasted for four days.....

(II.xiii.46) *Of the solemnity with which were held the burials and obsequies of the King of Michoacán, which is a chapter to be noted.*

It was an inviolable law that many people had to die on this occasion, with the King; for they said (falsely and mendaciously) that there went with him, to serve him in the next world: ((many people, including))... a feather-worker; a silversmith to make him jewels; an archer-officer; two or three huntsmen; some of the doctors who had not been able to cure him, to learn to cure better, as they had done ill in this life; a jester and a clown to tell him stories; a taverner for the wine; there went an instrumentalist and a dancer, and a carpenter to make the musical instruments they played; and many others of his servants offered to die willingly, that they might come to serve him on this his journey....

They washed and bathed all these people with great care, and immediately thereafter daubed their bodies all over with a yellowish paint they used, and set garlands on their heads, and having placed them in a line one beside the other, made a long procession before the dead man's bier, which they brought out of the palace at the point of midnight, accompanied by certain musicians playing with cayman-bones on tortoise-shells. The bier was borne on the shoulders of his sons and of the greatest nobles of the kingdom, and the lords of the cities of Eneani, Zacapu, Heriti, Vanacaye, which were four cities near to Pátz-cuaro (which was the Court) and were his nearest relatives; they went chanting certain songs, which gave praise and honour to the King whose body they were taking to be burnt, and other things ordained in the rite in which they were engaged. All those who accompanied this corpse carried the insignia of men of rank, and accompanied by many torches they went forward playing trumpets (while many servants barred the streets and roads), and said to him: 'O Lord, by this way must thou go; beware lest thou mistake the road'. In this manner they bore him to the Court of the Teocallis, or great temples, where there had already been set a great pile of dry sticks heaped up on top of each other. They encircled this place with him four times with great sedateness and musi-cal solemnity. After this they placed him on that pile of wood, with all his trappings and finery they had carried with him, and his relatives took up their song as before when they left his house; and this com-pleted, they set fire to the pile, which being pine-wood and very dry burned quickly; and while this wretched body was burning they struck with clubs and cudgels those ministers who were to serve him in the other life — as those blind men believed — but to speak the truth they were accompanying him to the pains of hell; and in order that they should not feel their death they had first been made drunk, which, if no other sin could have sent them to hell, was enough, for it is a vice contrary to the virtue of temperence so much commended to us; and in detestation of this beastly vice, the glorious father St. Augustine says: ((&c.))

(II.xiv.4) *Which tells the honour they paid to the King or nobleman who had taken an enemy in battle the first time, and other things touching battle.*

....Therefore these Indians desired that their people should have valour and audacity, and that they should do in person deeds of great fame; and so long as they did not do this, notwithstanding they had been elected and confirmed and in the possession of their rank, it seems that they were not satisfied, nor could they use the station and dignity of a nobleman freely, as did the others who had already shown themselves valiant men in the wars; for it was a custom that neither the noblemen nor the sons of noblemen should wear golden or silver jewels, or precious stones, or richly fashioned or painted cloaks, or feathers on their heads before they had done some valiant action, killing or taking prisoner one or more people in war; and much less so the others of lower rank, unless they should have come to earn it by notable exploits done for the state or against its enemies. For this reason, when the King or a nobleman had for the first time taken a prisoner in war, at once he sent his messengers to bring him from his house the best jewels and clothes he had, and to spread the news that the King or nobleman had himself personally taken in the war one or more prisoners; and when the messengers had returned with the clothes, they at once adorned and dressed him who had been taken prisoner, and made a kind of litter on which they brought him with great festival and solemnity, and called him the son of the nobleman who had captured him, and did him the same honour as that nobleman (though not in truth, for it was to give him a worse death). And the prisoner leading, and with all the enemy spoil, the warriors proceeded very merrily, and the townsfolk came out to receive them with high and low trumpets, dances and songs; and sometimes the singing masters would compose some special song of the new victory; and everyone saluted the prisoner in his litter before they did the nobleman or anyone else, and said to him: 'Be very welcome, for you are come to your own house; be not afflicted, for you are at home'; and afterwards they saluted the nobleman and his warriors. And when the other cities and provinces learned of this the King's or nobleman's first victory, the neighbouring nobles, his parents and his friends came to see him and make merry with him, bringing him presents of golden jewels, precious stones and rich cloaks; and he received them with much joy, and made for them a great festivity of dance and song and a big banquet, and also distributed gifts among them, and gave them many cloaks; and his nearest relatives he kept with him until the chief day of the festivity, when the prisoner was to be sacrificed, for as soon as they had reached the city that day was settled upon.

(II.xiv.11) *Of the manner which these natives had of dancing, and of the great dexterity and conformity they all kept in dancing and singing.*

One of the principal things in this whole country were the songs and dances, both to solemnize the feasts of their demons which they took for gods, with which they thought to do them great service, as also for their own enjoyment and relaxation; and for this reason, and because it was a thing on which they set much importance, in every town and in every nobleman's house there was a group of musicians with its singers and makers of dances and songs, and they sought out those who had a good talent and knowledge of making songs in such metres or stanzas that they had. And if they were good and hardworking, they were highly esteemed, for on many days the noblemen had private singing in their houses. The regular singing and dancing was at the principal festivals, which were every twenty days, and at others less important. The most important dances were in the public squares, at other times in the greatest nobleman's house, in his courtyard, for all the noblemen had great courtyards, and they also danced in the houses of other noblemen and famous men. When they had won a great victory in battle, or installed a new lord, or some great lady was married, or for some other new occurrence, the song-masters would make a new song, other than the usual ones which they had handed down from the devils' festivals, their ancient exploits and the great men of old. The singers practised for some days before the festival what they had to sing. In the large cities there were many singers, and if there were new songs or dances, they gathered others together with themselves, so that there should be no defect on the chief day of the festival. On the day on which the dance was to be, early in the morning, a great mat was set in the midst of the square, on which the drums were to be placed, and everyone adorned themselves and met together in the nobleman's house, and came out from there singing and dancing; sometimes the dances began in the morning, and sometimes at the hour when we now have High Mass; and at night they returned, singing, to the palace, and there ended their singing and dancing after dark, or well into the night, and sometimes in the middle of the night. There were two kinds of drums: one high and round, fatter than a man, five palms high, made of very good wood, hollow inside, and well fashioned, painted outside; on the top they set a deerskin, cured and well stretched; between the side and the middle there is the difference of a fifth, and they strike ((the head)) in various places and ((thus produce)) various pitches which they raise and lower, matching exactly the drum's rhythm and pitch with the songs. The other drum is of such a nature that without a picture it could not easily be described; this one serves as a lower part, and they both sound well and are heard from afar. When the dancers have reached the set place, they position themselves to play the drums, and the two best singers, like choirmasters, lead the song. The great leather-covered drum is played with the hands, and this one they call Huehuetl; the other is played with sticks like the Spanish kettledrums, though it is made of another shape, and they call it Teponaztli. The chief noblemen, with the other men of rank and the elders dance immediately around the drums, and they stretch ((to a depth of)) three or four fathoms from the drums; and along with them is another multitude extending and stretching somewhat further. The people placed in this middle position would in the great cities usually be more than a thousand, and sometimes more than two thousand; and outside them a procession composed of young men, great dancers, goes round in two files. The leaders are two picked men chosen from the best dancers, who head the dance. In these two circles, in certain figures and formations, they sometimes face and take for partner the man in front, and in other dances the man beside or beyond. There would be enough people in these two circles to amount to about a thousand, and at other times more, varying with the city and the festival. In the olden days before the wars, when they celebrated their festivals freely, in the great cities three or four thousand and more would join together in the dance; but nowadays, when such a multitude has diminished and waned, they who dance together are but few. When they wish to start dancing, three or four Indians strike up some very lively whistles; at once the drums start playing softly, and little by little they grow louder; and when the dancers hear the drums begin, they know from their sound the song and dance, and they begin it at once. The opening songs are gentle, as if in a minor key, and slow; and the first one identifies the festival, and always these two leaders start it, and at once the whole chorus takes it up together with the dance. All this multitude moves its feet as unanimously as the most dexterous dancers of Spain; and what is more, they move their whole bodies, head, arms and hands, in such united order and agreement that not one man varies from the others half a measure, but what one man does with his right foot, and also with his left, they all do the same thing simultaneously and to the same beat; and when one man lowers his left arm and raises his right, they all do the same at the same time, Thus the drums, the song and the dancers all move to one identical beat, and all agree together, so that not one man varies a jot from another; for which reason, when the best dancers of Spain see them they are astonished, and esteem highly these natives' dances and the great conformity and feeling they show in them. Those who are furthest, in an outer circle, might be said to move at double speed, that is, two units in the time of one, and they move faster and put more energy into the dance; and those in this circle all agree together. Those in the middle of the ring dance at normal speed, and they move both feet and body more gravely, and indeed they raise and lower their arms with much grace. Each line or stanza is repeated three or four times, and they proceed and sing their song so uniformly that in neither song, drums nor dance does one person vary from another. When one song is finished, supposing that the first one should seem too long because of its slow speed, although none lasts more than an hour, hardly has the

drum changed its ((dance-identifying)) sound-formula than all stop singing; and after a few bars' rest (in the song, but not in the dance) at once
the leaders begin another song rather louder and quicker, and thus they
intensify the songs and change the tunes and timbres as one changes
from a low, quiet and grave song to a quick one, and from one dance to
another with a contrasting beat. Among the dancers are boys and children, sons of leading men, seven and eight years old, and some of four
and five, who sing and dance with their fathers; and as the boys sing in
a high or treble voice, they a add much charm to the singing. Sometimes people play trumpets and little flutes, not too well; others make
very shrill whistle-sounds with little bones; others disguise their dress
and voice, imitating other peoples and changing their own language.
These I speak of are jesters, and they somersault about, making a thousand faces and saying a thousand jokes and quips, so that those who see
and´hear them laugh; some go as old women, others as simpletons.
Drink is brought at times, and then some leave to rest and eat, and
when they return others leave, and so everyone rests without the dance
stopping. Sometimes they bring wreaths of roses or other flowers, or
little branches in their hands, and garlands on their heads, over and
above the trappings of rich cloaks and feathers they wear to dance; and
others instead of little branches bear in their hands beautiful small
feathers. These dances are divided into many sections, with signals to
distinguish those who have been valiant in battle. From vesper-time
until nightfall the songs and dances grow livelier, the tunes more penetrating, their execution more engaging, so that they seem to have the air
of a Christian hymn with a gay tune. The drums also become more
insistent, and as many people are dancing, all is audible at a great
distance, especially when the open air carries the voices, and all the
more at night, when everything is at rest; and in order to dance at this
hour many great torches were provided, and certainly all this was a
sight to be seen.

(III.xvii.3) *How the Indians were taught music, and those things which
pertain to the service of the Church, which benefited greatly thereby.*
  The Indians showed themselves no less skilful in letters than in
manual crafts, since they at once with great despatch learnt to read not
only our Castilian Spanish but also Latin, and cursive handwriting, and
subsequently to write with great facility. They began to write in their
own language, and to understand and write letters to each other, as we
do, whereas previously they regarded it as a marvel that paper could
talk, and could tell each one what he who was absent wished to tell
him. At first they copied very exactly the material given to them, and if
their teacher were changed they promptly changed their form of writing into that of the new teacher. In the second year from the beginning

of training they gave a youth from Tetzcuco a Bull for a model, and he copied it so faithfully that it appeared like the very print. He put down the first line in large type, as it was in the Bull, and below copied the signature of the Commissioner, and a picture of Jesus with a statue of Our Lady, all so exactly that there seemed no difference from the printed original he was copying; and because it was so remarkable, it was taken to Castile by a Spaniard in order to show it and have it seen. Later they became very good scribes for all types of script, small and large, separated[1] and Gothic, and the religious helped them to become scribes, keeping them constantly busy writing books and treatises which they composed or translated from Latin or Spanish into their own languages. In the year 1570 the friar Geronimo de Mendieta, he says, went to Spain and took a copy of the *Contemptus Mundi* translated into the Mexican language and written by the hand of an Indian — a hand so well formed, regular and handsome that no print could have given greater pleasure to the eye. When this was shown to the lawyer Don Juan de Ovando, who at the time was President of the Council of the Indies, it was so much to his liking that he kept it, saying that he wished to present it to King Philip the Second, our Ruler. Besides writing, the Indians soon began to make staves for and to notate both plainsong and polyphonic music, and they made very fine books of both kinds of music, and also Psalters in large script for the friars' choirs and for their own choirs, with the capitals highly illuminated. They did not need to look for anyone to do the binding for them since they learnt all about that too. What is more remarkable is that they copied book-illustrations with very perfect depictions, which astonished any who saw them, because at the first try they made them with nothing taken from or added to the original.

In their third year ot training they proceeded to singing, and some people laughed and ridiculed those who were teaching them; others hindered them, saying that they could not make any progress in this, either because they seemed to make false notes or because they seemed to have weak voices. It is true that neither did they have — nor could they((hope to have)) — voices as strong or as sweet as those of the Spaniards, going barefoot and poorly clothed as they did, and eating little food and that of poor quality. Nevertheless, since there are many persons to choose from there are always good choirs, and some basses, altos, tenors and trebles who could compete with those of the best of the cathedral choirs. The first to teach them singing, along with Fray Pedro de Gante, was a venerable old priest named Fray Juan Caro, who moved quite freely and courteously among them; without knowing a word of their language, nor they of Spanish, he spent whole days teach-

---

1. Quebrado (literally "broken") is a technical term in typography.

ing them and talking to them, and telling them the rules of singing in Spanish with as much purpose and with as little trouble as if they had actually been Spaniards. The youths were open-mouthed with wonder, and listened most attentively trying to follow what was being said. Although some of us took occasion to laugh at his saintly simplicity and serenity, it was viewed differently by the Lord, Who takes pleasure in simple and plain hearts, and therefore favoured the task, intervening ((in His)) capacity as the supreme and all-powerful Maker ((to assist the contact)) between this master and his disciples. Though they understood each other neither much nor indeed little, the result was that without the intervention of another interpreter, very soon the youths understood to such a degree that not only did they comprehend and achieve success with plainsong, but also with polyphonic music. From that time on they have taught each other, and among them there are many who became very skilled singers and choirmasters, so much so, that in any choir of singers are at least five or six or more who take it in turn each year to hold the offices of choirmaster and leading singer, to guide and lead the others. The first thing the Indians learnt and sang was the Mass of the Virgin Mary which begins *Salve sancta parens.* There is no settlement of one hundred households which does not have singers who perform Masses and Vespers in polyphony, together with their players of reed-instruments and other instrumentalists; there is scarcely a hamlet, however small, which does not have at least three or four Indians who sing every day in their church the Hours of the Virgin Mary, especially in the provinces of Michoacán and Jalisco.

The first musical instruments that they made and played were flutes; then shawms, next small reed-instruments, and after these bowed string-instruments, and after these cornetts and bass reed-instruments. There is indeed no kind of music used in God's church that the Indians do not have and use in all the principal towns and even in the less important ones; they make all these instruments themselves, so that there is no longer any need to import any from Spain. There is one thing that I can say with assurance, namely that nowhere in all the realms of Christendom outside of the Indies is there such a profusion of flutes, shawms, sackbuts, trumpets, small reed-instruments and drums as in the kingdom of New Spain alone. They even made organs for almost all churches where there are resident friars. And although the Indians — because they lack the means — are not in charge of making organs, but ((work under)) Spanish masters ((at the craft)), it is the Indians who ((actually)) make all the parts required, and then play them in our conventual churches. Such other instruments as are played to give pleasure to the laity, the Indians make and play them all — small fiddles, guitars in two sizes, vihuelas, harps and keyboard string-instruments. The conclusion is that there is nothing that they cannot learn to do. What is more, only a few years after they learnt singing, they themselves began independently to compose polyphonic villancicos in four parts, and some Masses and other works; the which, when shown to accomplished Spanish singers were taken to be the work of cultivated experts, which could not possibly be by Indians.

On the question of teaching them Latin grammar and the Latin tongue there were many opinions, among the friars as among other people, and before it might be taught there were many objections, with seeming reasons being given by those with the contrary opinion; but in the end true reason prevailed. Namely, that it was right that at least some natives should understand in some fashion what is contained in the sacred Scriptures and in the books of the Doctors of the church, not only in order that they themselves might understand and thereby be strengthened more truly in the things of our Holy Faith, but also that they might convince the other Indians upon how firm a foundation our Christian faith is based ((as compared to)) the way in which they and all the other heathens have believed and followed, which rests on no foundation, nor true way, nor any truth whatever. To begin with, this involved excessively hard work, and the religious who were their teachers experienced no little difficulty, although they ((i.e., the Spanish religious)) knew their language very well, since each matter had never been dealt with in it they could not find terms with which to explain to them the rules of grammar. Therefore their progress was scanty, so that they almost gave up, through loss of confidence amongst the pupils, and indeed even among the teachers too. However, as in all other things in which the servants of God had difficulty at the beginning, they found Divine favour and help, so when it pleased the Holy Spirit (who is the veritable Teacher of all the arts and sciences) to unlock their understandings, they saw the door which the Lord opened to them, and they found terms, newly coined, through which they could with facility expound and explain the rules of grammar. Consequently, in a few years some ((of them)) became such good Latinists that they were able to write well balanced verses, and make long and coherent speeches in the presence of the Viceroys and of the church prelates, as has been related elsewhere.

3 NICHOLAUS GODIGNUS

Nicolao Godinho was born in 1561 and died in Rome in 1619. His book, as its title implies, was compiled from reports sent from Ethiopia by two pioneer Jesuit missionaries there, João Nunes Barreto and André de Oviedo. Barreto became a Jesuit in 1544 and went to Africa soon after. He was named patriarch of Ethiopia by João III in 1555. Oviedo was born in 1518, succeeded Barreto as patriarch in 1562, and died in Ethiopia in 1580.

Nicholaus Godignus, S. J., *De Abassinorum rebus deque Aethiopiae Patriarchis, I.N. Barreto et A. Oviedo*, Lyons, 1615

Book I, Chapter XXII: *De Abassinorum festis, & aliis ad sacra pertinentibus*

....

p. 136

Nihil ex scripto recitant, sed memoriter omnia. Cum Matutinum dicitur, praeter consuetas, quae ante aram, lampades sunt, in quibus arvina pingui, loco olei, fovetur ignis, lumen aliud neque in templo, neque in odeo est. Non alternis, sed omnes simul singulos decantant Psalmorum versus. Matutini lectio ad principalem templi ianuam inconditis profertur clamoribus. Nemo sedens recitat: concessum senibus, ut ligneis innitantur adminiculis, cum sunt defessi. Sacra omnia partim Chaldaeo, partim Aethiopico continentur idiomate. Quaecumque proferunt, sic exprimunt, ut oris et corporis motum ad illa accomodent. Itaque pronuntiant flentes, quae significant fletum; ridentes, quae risum; saltantes, quae saltum; contenta voce, quae clamorem; submissa, quae silentium; quidquid denique proferunt, ita corporis motu indicant, ut non minus dicentis gestu, quam voce percipiatur. Ea musica instrumenta, quae vocamus organa, generis vocabulo ad speciem contracto, quorumque frequens nostris in templis usus, usque ad Gregorii XIII tempus, ne de nomine quidem noverant. Is Pontifex in Aethiopiam artifices misit, qui ea inibi fabricarent. Duo apud eos erant cymbalorum genera, quaedam certo e lapide, e ferro alia confecta; utraque & figura, & sono, & arte nostris dissimilia. Nunc aere utuntur campano, ut apud nos fit, eoque pulsato populum convocant ad templum. Supplicationibus ac pompis valde sunt dedici. Singulas post horas, quas recitant, supplicantes fanum circumeunt, eo saepius, quo festus dies maiori colitur celebritate. Contingit, ut in una eademque pompa tritenos & amplius circa templum conficiant gyros. Hisce autem in pompis quatuor, vel quinque argenteae, baculorum instar, feruntur cruces, totidem thuribula; haec manu dextra, illae sinistra; interque Psalmorum & hymnorum cantus multa miscentur crepitacula. Caeterum tanta pietatis & interni affectus significatione divina officia peraguntur, ut tenere lacrymas nequeant, qui intersunt.

TRANSLATION

Nicolao Godinho, *Concerning the affairs of the Abyssinians and concerning the Patriarchs of Ethiopia, J.N.Barreto and A.Oviedo*, Lyons, 1615
(I.xxii) *Of the Abyssinians' festivals, and other things pertaining to their rites*

They perform nothing from writing, but everything from memory. When they say Matins, apart from the usual torches before the altar, in which grease burns instead of oil, there is no other light in the church, nor in the choir. They chant the psalm-verses, not alternately, but each one all together. The Matins lesson is said at the principal door of the church, amid confused shouting. No one recites seated; the older men are allowed to lean on wooden props when they are tired. The whole service is partly in the Chaldean and partly in the Ethiopic language. Whatever they say, they accompany with suitable movements of face and body. Thus they speak weeping the words of tears; laughing those of laughter; leaping those of leaping; loudly those of clamour; softly those of silence; in short, whatever they utter, they show with such bodily gesture as to be understood no less through the speaker's signs than through his voice. That musical instrument we call the organ, to restrict the general word to that species we often use in church, they did not know even by name until the time of Gregory XIII.[1] This Pope sent craftsmen into Ethiopia to build them there. They had two kinds of cymbals, one made of a certain stone, the other of iron; both were different from ours in shape, sound and fashion. Nowadays they use a bell in the air, as we do, to call the people to church. There are many occasions set apart for thanksgiving and festivals. After each of their services the worshippers proceed about the building, the more often as the festival celebrated is important. It can happen that in one celebration the church is encircled thirty and more times. In these celebrations they carry four or five silver crosses like sceptres in their right hands, and as many thuribles in their left; and many rattles join with the sung psalms and hymns. For the rest, they carry out the divine offices with so much piety and inward feeling that those who are present can hardly restrain their tears.

1. Pope 1572-1585.

4 CHARLES DE ROCHEFORT

John Davies of Kidwelly in Carmarthenshire was an industrious translator from the French.[1] The author of the original of his *The History of the Caribby-Islands*, whose name Davies did not mention, is usually given as Charles de Rochefort, though the work is sometimes attributed to L. de Poincy, with de Rochefort as reviser. It is clear from the following passage in its preface (which Davies shortened considerably) that it is a compilation at second hand:

C'est-pourquoy nous avons aporté un soin diligent & scrupuleus à ne rien ajouter de notre, dans ce qui est essenciel, que l'ordre & les liasons qui ne se trouvoient pas en des pièces détachées. Et nous n'avons fait à parler proprement, que préter la main à ces nobles Voyageurs, pour décrire & arranger leurs narrations, sans en alterer le sens: & pour enchasser & mettre en oeuvre fidèlement, les precieus materiaus qu'ils nous avoient confiez. Aussi seront ils en toute rencontre les garens autentiques de nos Relations; n'y ayant rien en tout cet Ouvrage qu' ils n'ayent veu, qu'ils n'ayent examiné, qu'ils n'ayent même corrigé, s'il en a été besoin, & où, en un mot, ils ne donnent une pléne aprobation: Veu qu'en éfet, ce livre n'est presque qu'une copie de leurs riches Originaus.[2]

((This is why we have exercised a diligent and scrupulous care in adding nothing of our own, in any essential thing, but the order and the continuity which are not found in separate pieces. And to speak truly we have only lent a hand to these noble travellers, in order to describe and arrange their narratives, without changing their meaning, and in order to exhibit and put faithfully to use the precious materials that they have confided to us. Thus they will be at every juncture the authentic guarantors of our accounts, there being nothing in all this work that they have not seen, that they have not examined, that they have not even corrected when there was need, and to which they would not give full approval, seeing that in fact the book is almost nothing but a copy of their rich originals.))

The *Histoire naturelle* went into a second edition, in which

1. See Joseph E. Tucker, "John Davies of Kidwelly, 1627(?)-1693, translator from the French. With an annotated bibliography of his translations", *Papers of the Bibliographical Society of America*, 44 (1950).
2. Charles de Rochefort, *Histoire naturelle et morale des Iles Antilles*, Rotterdam, 1658, Preface, page b verso.

some changes were made. Here, for example, are two versions of a passage whose translation by Davies is printed here:

Histoire naturelle (1658, p. 362):

Ils aiment passionément la musique, & tous les instrumens qui rendent quelque Harmonie, & à peine y en a-til aucun qui ne sache jouër de la flute et d'une espece de hautbois, qui étant de differente grosseur font un asses bon accord & rendent un son fort melodieus.

Ibid. (1665, p. 405):

Ils aiment passionement la musique & tous les instrumens qui rendent quelque harmonie, tellement qu'a péne trouve t-on aucun parmy eus, qui ne sache jouër du flageollet, ou d'une sorte de flûtes de different grosseur, qui font un accord fort agreable.

Comparison with Davies's translation shows that he worked from the first edition. Davies's book was re-issued in the same year, unchanged but for a new title-page in which it was called *The History of Barbados* ((etc.)). The *Histoire naturelle* appeared in 1681 in a *Derniere edition, Reveuë & augmentée par l'Autheur* with an account of the British colonies of North America, *"tiré fidelement des memoires des habitans des mêmes Colonies, en faveur de eus, qui auroyent le dessein de s'y transporter pour s'y établir"*. A Dutch translation had been published in 1662, in Rotterdam, where also all the French editions appeared.

John Davies of Kidwelly, trans. ((from the French of Charles de Rochefort)). *The History of the Caribby-Islands, viz. Barbados, St. Christophers, St. Vincents, Martinico, Dominico, Barbouthos, Monserrat, Mevis, Antego, &c. in all XXVIII*, London, 1666

Chapter VI: *Of the more honourable Employments of the European Inhabitants of the Caribbies; their Slaves; and their Government.*
p. 200

....

As concerning the Slaves, and such as are to be perpetual Servants, who are commonly employ'd in these Islands, they are originally Africans, and they are brought over thither from the Country about Cap-vert, the Kingdom of Angola, and other Sea-ports which are on the Coasts of that part of the world; where they are bought and sold after the same manner as Cattle in other places.

....

p. 202

They are great Lovers of Musick, and much pleas'd with such Instruments as make a certain delightful noise, and a kind of harmony, which they accompany with their voices. They had heretofore in the Island of S. *Christophers* a certain Rendezvouz in the midst of the Woods, where they met on Sundays and Holidays after Divine Service, to give some relaxation to their wearied bodies: There they sometimes spent the remainder of that day, and the night following, in dancing and pleasant discourses, without any prejudice to the ordinary labours impos'd on them by their Masters: nay, it was commonly observ'd, that after they had so diverted themselves, they went through their work with greater courage and chearfulness, without expressing any weariness, and did all things better than if they had rested all night long in their huts. But it being found, that the better to enjoy themselves in these publick Meetings, they many times stole the Poultry and Fruits of their Neighbours, and sometimes those of their Masters, the *French* General thought fit to forbid these nocturnal assemblies: So that now if they are desirous to divert themselves, they are enjoyn'd to do it within their own Neighbourhoods, with the permission of their Masters, who are willing enough to allow them convenient liberty.

....

Chapter VIII: *By way of Digression giving an account of the Apalachites, the Nature of their Country, their Manners, and their ancient and modern Religion.*

....

p. 235

They are passionate lovers of Musick, and all instruments that make any kind of harmony, insomuch that there's very few among them but can play on the Flute, and a kind of Hawboy, which being of several bigness, make a passably good harmony, and render a sound that is very melodious: They are mightily given to dancing, capering, and making a thousand postures, whereby they are of opinion they disburthen themselves of all their bad humours, and that they acquire a great activity and suppleness of body, and a wonderful swiftness in running. They heretofore celebrated solemn dances at the end of every harvest, and after they had made their Offerings to the Sun upon the Mountain of *Olaimi*; but now they have no set and appointed time for these divertisements.

Their voice is naturally good, mild, flexible, and pleasant; whence it comes that many among them make it their endeavour to imitate the singing and chirping of Birds; wherein they are for the most part so fortunate, that like so many *Orpheus's* they entice out of the woods to follow them, those Birds which think they hear only those of their own species: They do also by singing alleviate the hard labour they are addicted unto, and yet what they do, seems to be done rather

out of divertisement, and to avoid idleness, than out of any consideration of advantage that they make thereof.

Their Language is very smooth, and very plentiful in comparisons: That spoken by the Captains and all persons of quality, is more
elegant and fuller of flourishes than that of the common sort of people:
Their expressions are very precise, and their periods short enough:
While they are yet children, they learn several songs, made by the
Jaouas in honour and commendation of the Sun; they are also acquaint-
ed with several other little pieces of Poetry, wherein they have com-
prehended the most memorable exploits of their Kings, out of a design
to perpetuate the memory thereof among them, and the more easily
transmit it to their posterity.

All the Provinces which acknowledge the King of *Apalacha* for
their Sovereign, understand the language commonly spoken in his
Court; yet does not this hinder but that each of them hath a particular
dialect of its own, whence it comes that the language of some, is in
some things different from that of others of the Inhabitants: The Provinces of *Amana* and *Matica*, in which there are to this day many
Caribbian Families, have retained to this present many words of the
ancient idiome of these people, which confirms what we have laid down
for a certain assertion, to wit, that being known by the same name, and
having many expressions common to them with the Inhabitants of the
Caribby-Islands, those Families have also the same origine with them, as
we have represented in the precedent chapter. [1]

They heretofore adored the Sun, and had their Priests, whom
they called *Jaouas*, who were very superstitious in rendring to him the
service which they had invented in honour of him: their perswasion
was, that the raies of the Sun gave life to all things; that they dried up
the earth; and that once the Sun having continued four and twenty
hours under an eclipse, the earth had been overflown; and that the great
Lake which they call *Theomi*, was rais'd as high as the tops of the
highest Mountains that encompass it; but that the Sun having recovered
the eclipse, had, by his presence, forc'd the waters to return into their
abysses; that only .the Mountain dedicated to his honour, and wherein
his Temple was, was preserv'd from that deluge; and that their Predeces-
sors, and all the beasts which are at present in the woods and upon the
earth, having retir'd to the said Mountain, were preserv'd for the re-
population and recruit of the whole earth: So that they conceive themselves to be the most ancient people of the world; And they affirm, that
from that time they have acknowledg'd the Sun for their God.

....

1. Where it was maintained that the Apalachites came originally from Apalacha,
i.e., the region of the Appalachian Mountains, here called Florida (p. 241).

The service they rendred the Sun consisted in saluting him at his rising, and singing hymns in honour of him: They observed the same Ceremonies also in the evening, entreating him to return, and to bring the day along with him: And besides this daily service which every one performed at the door of his house, they had also another publick and solemn service, which consisted in sacrifices and offerings, and was perform'd by the *Jaouas*, four times in the year, to wit, at the two seed-times, and after the two harvests, upon the Mountain of *Olaimi*, with great pomp, and a general concourse of all the Inhabitants of the six Provinces.

....

Chapter XVII: *Of the Employments and Divertisements of the Carib-*
bians.

....

p. 307

To divert themselves they also make several Musical Instruments, if they may be so called, on which they make a kind of harmony: Among others they have certain Tabours or Drums made of hollow Trees, over which they put a skin only at one end ((*de Roche-*
fort added: à la façon des Tambours de Basque)): To this may be added a kind of Organ which they make of Gourds, upon which they place a cord made of the string of a reed which they call *Pite*; and this cord being touch'd makes a sound which they think delightful. The concerts of divers other Savages are no better than theirs, and no less immusical to their ears who understand Musick. In the morning, as soon as they are up, they commonly play on the Flute or Pipe; of which Instrument they have several sorts, as well polish'd and as handsom as ours, and some of those made of the bones of their Enemies: And many among them can play with as much grace as can well be imagin'd for Savages ((de Rochefort added: bien qu'en cela ils n'approchent pas des François)). While they are playing on the Flute, the Wives are busie in making ready their breakfast.

Sometimes also they pass away the time in singing certain Airs, the burthens whereof are pleasant enough; and in that Exercise they sometimes spend half a day together, sitting on their low stools, and looking on their fish while it is broiling. They also put pease or small pebble-stones, as the *Virginians* do, into gourds, through the midst whereof they put a stick which serves for a handle, and then shaking them they make a noise: This is the invention the women have to quiet their children. Most of the *Caribbian* Songs consist of bitter railleries against their Enemies; some they have also on Birds, and Fishes, and Women, commonly intermixt with some bawdery; and many of them have neither rhime nor reason.

Many times also the *Caribbians* of the Islands joyn Dancing to their Musick, but that Dancing is regulated according to their Musick. There are some Barbarians excessively addicted to that Exercise, as for instance the *Brasilians*, who, as *de Lery* affirms, spend day and night in dancing: And we have said elsewhere, that there are many Savages who make their imaginary felicity of the other life to consist in dancing. But the *Caribbians* use Dancing particularly at their solemn Entertainments in their *Carbet*, or publick house. These Entertainments are ordered after this manner: Some days before the meeting the Captain gives notice to every house, that all may appear at the *Carbet* at the day appointed: In the mean time the Women make a kind of strong drink of bak'd *Cassava*, and better prepar'd then that which they ordinarily drink; and as they adde to the dose of the Ingredients, so is the drink the stronger, and more apt to intoxicate: The men go a fishing, or catching of Lizards; for as to other meat they seldom prepare any for their own Tables, unless they have Strangers to entertain: On the day appointed both men and women paint their bodies with divers colours and figures, and adorn themselves with their Crowns of Feathers, their richest Chains, Pendants, Bracelets, and other Ornaments: Those among them who would appear most gallant rub their bodies with a certain Gum, and blow the Down of diverse Birds upon it. In fine, they all put on their best faces, and endeavour to make the greatest shew they can at this solemnity, priding it in their Plumes, and all their other gallantry: The women bring thither the Drink and Messes they have prepared, and are extreamly careful that nothing be wanting, which may contribute to the solemn entertainment: Our *Caribbians* spend all that day and the best part of the night in eating and drinking, dancing, discoursing and laughing: And in this Debauch they drink much more than ordinary, that is, they make a shift to get drunk; and the women will not be much behind them, especially when they can get any Wine, or *Aqua-vitae* to promote the work: So that what we have said of their ordinary sobriety holds not at these Meetings; no more than it does at their going to their Wars, and at their return thence: and yet take them at the worst, their excesses come much short of those of the *Brasilians*, who in their Debauches drink three or four days without ceasing, and in their drunkenness engage themselves in all kind of Vices.

Their drunkenness and their debauches are frequent, as hapning upon these several occasions: 1. When there is any Councel held concerning their Wars: 2. When they return from their Expeditions, whether they have prov'd successful or not: 3. Upon the birth of their first Male Children: 4. When they cut their Childrens hair: 5. When they are at age to go to the Wars: 6. When they cut down trees, in order to the making of a Garden and building of a House: 7. When they launch a new Vessel: And lastly when they are recovered of some disease: They call these assemblies *Ouicou,* and since they nave conversed with the *French, Vin,* that is, *Wine.*

But on the contrary they have also their Fasts, wherein they betray the ridiculousness of their humour: For, 1. they fast when they enter into adolescency: 2. When they are made Captains: 3. At the death of their Fathers or Mothers: 4. At the death of the Husband or Wife: 5. When they have killed one of their Enemies the *Arouagues;* this last occasion of fasting they glory very much in.

5 ADAM OLEARIUS

The first edition of John Davies's translation of Olearius (1603-1671) and Mandelslo was printed in 1662. The German original was first published in Schleswig in 1647, and there was a second, enlarged edition in 1656. A French translation first appeared in Paris in 1656, a Dutch translation in Amsterdam in 1658[1]. Davies made his translation from the French, not from the German. In his dedicatory statement, to *"the Right Worshipfull*, the Governour and Fellowship of English Merchants, for discovery of *New Trades*, in Muscovy, Russia, &c.", he made these comments:

> It is not unknown to you, what opposition this Negotiation met withall from the several Parties therein concern'd: and consequently, you can best judge, what advantages may be made thereof, in order to the Interest of this Nation....Adam Olearius, a Person, by his near relation to the Embassy, (Whereof he was Secretary) his Knowledge of the Mathematicks, but particularly his Acquaintance with the Languages of the Countries, through which they Travell'd, ((was)) perfectly accomplish'd for a Work of this Nature. What he writ of these Travels in his own Language, the *German*, was so kindly receiv'd, that it soon after Travell'd into several others, which gave some encouragement to the rendring of them into English.

In his *Preface to the Reader* Davies noted that Mandelslo was educated at the Duke of Holstein's Court. "Hearing of an Embassy intended for Muscovy and Persia, he would needs be one in it". Mandelslo went on to India, leaving Ormuz in 1638. Davies's translation of Mandelslo's account of this journey, which seems but loosely related to the original, is not quoted here. E.G. Cox remarks that "the English version and the French translation of 1719 contain material not found in the original German". Cox mentions an edition published in Bombay in 1931[2]. There is an edition of the 1656 print by Eberhard Meissner, printed in Berlin (GDR) in 1959. A translation into Russian (A. Olearij, *Opisanie putešestvija v Moskoviju,* St. Petersburg, 1906) is referred to in K. Vertkov, 'Beiträge zur Geschichte der russischen Guslitypen', *Studia instrumentorum musicae popularis* (Musikhistoriska museets skrifter, 3, ed. Ernst Emsheimer), I, ed. Erich Stockmann, Stockholm, 1969, p. 140.

---

1. These details from Samuel H. Baron, *The travels of Olearius in seventeenth century Russia,* Stanford, 1967, Preface, p.viii. Amsterdam University Library has a Dutch translation printed in Amsterdam in 1682, made from the French, not listed by Baron.
2. *A. Reference Guide to the Literature of Travel,* 3 vols., Seattle, 1935, 1938, 1949, i, 171.

Samuel Baron made his translation of the Russian journey (he was not concerned with the parts dealing with Persia and the journey there) from the second German edition of 1656, with some omissions. He commented (Preface, p. ix) on the English translation:

> ...the translator evidently was more concerned with felicity than with accuracy. Many passages were excised, and many others transposed, with no indication to the reader that this had been done. Although the translator did preserve the sense of most of the passages he included, he made a great many errors and on occasion even improvised.

The passages from Davies's translation reprinted here have been compared with the 1696 Hamburg edition of the German, whose text is quoted whenever this seemed desirable. References to Baron are also given for passages concerning Russia. Olearius's illustrations, one of which is reproduced here as illustration B, were drawn from life, most by Olearius himself, a few by Dr. Hartmann Gramann, the embassy's physician (Baron, p. xii).

John Davies of Kidwelly, trans., *The Voyages and Travells of the Ambassadors sent by Frederick Duke of Holstein, to the Great Duke of Muscovy, and the King of Persia, Begun in the Year MDCXXXIII and finish'd in MDCXXXIX....whereto are added the travels of John Albert de Mandelslo, (a Gentleman belonging to the Embassy) from Persia, into the East-Indies.... Written originally by Adam Olearius, Secretary to the Embassy... The Second Edition Corrected,* London, 1669

The First Voyage into Muscovy (1634)
p. 7

The Musick of Muscovy

The 23. ((July)) at ((midday)) dinner ((near Ladoga)), was the first time we heard any of the Country Musick, which consisted of a Lute and Violin ((1696: mit einer Lauten und Geigen; cp. Baron, 49)), with some voices, singing aires to the honour of their *Czaar, Michael Federovits,* and perceiving they were permitted, they fell a-Dancing after a strange manner. The men and women danc'd much after the same manner, every one alone, making strange faces, with as strange gesticulations; the motions of the hands, shoulders, and hips, being more violent than those of the feet, which they do but gently stir, not moving as it were from the same place. The women have commonly handkerchers in their hands, fring'd with silk of divers colours, which they cast about their heads.

....

p. 9

The 14. ((August))......the Messengers sent by the *Pristaf* return'd from *Moscou,* and oblig'd us to prepare for our Entrance, which
we made the same day in the order following:

1. The *Strelits,* or *Muscovian* Musketiers, who had convoy'd us,
march'd in first.
2. After them, *Jacob Scheve,* our Harbinger, *Michael Cordes,*
Captain of the ship, and *John Algueyer,* Clark of the Kitchen,
all three abreast.
3. Three led Horses, to be presented to the Great Duke; one
black, and two, dappled-grey.
4. A Trumpetter.
5. Marshall, or Steward.
6. Three of our Gentlemen a-breast. ((etc))

. . . .

The Second Voyage into Muscovy and Persia (1635)

p. 31

Their Ceremonies of marriage are very odd. When a Country
fellow marries a Lass out of another Village, he goes a hors-back to fetch
her, sets her behind him, and makes her embrace him with the right
hand. He hath in his hand a stick cleft at the top, where he puts a piece
of brass money, which he gives to him who opens the wicket, through
which he is to pass. Before, rides a man that playes upon the Bag-pipe
((1696: ein Sackpfeiffer)), as also two of his friends, who, having naked
swords in their hands, give two Stroaks therewith, cross the Door of the
House, where the marriage is to be consummated, and then they thrust
the point of one of the swords into a beam, over the Bridegroom's
head, which is done to prevent Charms, which, they say, are ordinary in
that Country. 'Tis to the same end that the Bride scatters little pieces of
Cloath, or red Serge by the way, especially where cross-ways meet, near
Crosses, and upon the Graves of little Children dead without baptism,
whom they bury in the High-ways. She hath a Veil over her face while
she is at the Table, which is not long; as soon almost as the Guests are
set down, the married couple rise, and go to bed. About two hours after
they get up, and are brought to sit down at the Table. Having drunk
and danc'd till such time as they are able to stand no longer, they fall
down on the floor, and sleep together like so many swine.

*The Cere-
monies of
marriages
in* Livonia

....

Their first publick Audience ((at the court of Czar Michael Federovits))
(1636)

p. 39

As soon as we were return'd to our Lodgings ((after the audience)) came one of the Great Duke's Carvers, named *Knez Simon Petrouits Luon*, with forty dishes of meat from his Majesty, all Fish, fry'd things, and pulse, it being in their Lent: and twelve pots of several sorts of drinks.

· · · ·

We sate down, but most of the dishes being dress'd with Onions and Garlick, we eat very Little, and sent the rest to our friends in the City. But what we spar'd in meat, we made good in drink, whereto we were partly encourag'd by the *Persian* Ambassadors, who being lodg'd near us, gave us the divertisement of their Bagpipes, and Hautbois ((1696: mit Heerpaucken, Schalmeyen und Trompetten lustig hören; cp. Baron,98)), and partly by the excellent Wines, which the Great Duke had sent us.

p. 68

When their Great Lords, *Knez*, and *Bohares* dispose of their Children in marriage, there is appointed on the Bride-groom's side a Woman, whom they call *Suacha*, and another on the Brides, who joyntly take order for the Nuptials. That on the Brides part, goes upon the Wedding-day to the Bridegroom's Lodgings, and there makes ready the Nuptial bed......

····

The Ceremonies in the Church.

In the Church, where the Benediction is to be given, they cover some part of the floor with Crimson Taffeta, upon which the young Couple stand, having over them another piece of the same stuff. Before they are married, the Priest makes them go to the offering, which consists in Fish, Fry'd Meats, and Pastry. That done, the married receive the Benediction, which is given by holding Images over their heads, and the Priest taking the man by the right hand, and the woman by the left at the same time, asks them three times, whether it is with their consent that they are married, and whether they will love one another, as they ought to do. Having both answer'd, yes, all the Company joyn hands, and the Priest sings the 128. Psalm, he one verse, and the Company the next, dancing at the mean time, much after the same manner as they do in these parts, who sing and dance at the same time.....The Marriage-Ceremonies being thus over, the Bride is put into her Sledge, which is encompas'd with six Torches, or Wax-candles, and the Bridegroom gets on horse-back to return to his own house, where the Wedding is kept.

....Having eaten, the young Couple go to bed, and all withdraw, save only one of the old servants of the house, who walks before the Chamber-door, while the kindred and friends are busied about all manner of charms, which they think may be advantageous to the New-married Couple.

This servant coming ever and anon to the door, asks whether the business be done. As soon as the Bridegroom answers that it is, the Trumpets and Timbrels ((1696: Trompetten und Heerpaucken: cp. Baron, 168)) which only expect the word, are plaid upon, and make an excellent noise, till such time as the stoves are made ready, when the New-married-couple bath themselves, but apart. They are wash'd with water, Hydromel and Wine, and the Bride sends to the Bridegroom a shirt, embroider'd with Gold and Pearls at the collar and extremities, and a rich Crabit. The next two dayes are spent in entertainments, dancing, and other divertisements, the Women making their advantage of the opportunity, while their husbands are drunk, to the loss of their honours. ((1696: Die folgenden zweene Tage werden mit grossem über-flüssigen essen, trinken, tantzen und allerhand Lust, die sie nur er-dencken können, zugebracht; worbey sie allerhand Music gebrauchen, und unter andern ein Instrument, so sie Psaltir nennen, is fast wie ein Hackebret, habens auff dem Schoss liegen, und greiffens mit Fingern als eine Harffe, wie in vorhergehender Figur beym Küntzgenspiel augedeutet worden. Da dann manches Weib... (etc.). That is: The following two days are spent in great and over-abundant eating, drinking, dancing and whatever kind of pleasure they can think of; they use various kinds of music, amongst others an instrument which they call a psaltery which is almost the same as a hackbrett, being held laid on the lap and plucked with the fingers as is a harp, as has been indicated in the foregoing illustration ((see Plate B. Cp. Baron. p. 168.))

The Travels of the Ambassadors from Muscovy into Tartary and Persia MDCXXXVI

p. 155

As we march'd along, we had before us our loud Musick, which consisted in Hawboyes, Timbrels, Cornets, and Tabours, but particular-ly in a kind of Instrument, called *Kerrenai*. These are made somewhat like our Hawboyes, save that they are of Brass, being above eight foot in length, and at the extremity, above two foot Diameter. There were four of these Instruments, and those who play'd on them made a halt ever and anon, and stood in a Circle as our Trumpetters, holding up the end of their *Kerrenai* to the sky, and making a noise, which hath not only nothing of harmony in it, but is more like a dreadful howling than any thing of Musick. There were also common Hawboyes, which they call *Surnatzi*, and earthen Timbrels, made like our Butter-pots. ((1696: Da sahe und hörte man fremde Feld-Spiele und Music. Ihrer vier ritten vor uns her, hielten zum of tern gegen einander stille, bliesen Instrumente, so von Kupffer als Schalmeyen *formiret*, bey vier Ellen lang, deren Aussgang im diametro bey einer Ellen, werden *Kerrenai* genant. Diese hielten sie im Blasen gen Himmel, und machten mehr ein grausahm Gebrülle, als einen anmuthigen Thon. Neben diesen waren auch *Surnatzi* oder gemeine Schalmeyer. Item viel Heerpaucker, so die Paucken als länglichte Töpffe vor sich über die Pferde hangen hatten. Item etliche mit langen Krumhörnern, Handpaucken, und dergleichen.)) Having march'd on a little way in this Company, the *Chan* ordered all to make a second halt, that the Ambassadors might drink, causing in the mean time, a certain Buffoon, or Jeaster, one of those whom they call *Tazusch*, to make wry-faces, and shew a thousand postures. He also used Castagnets, and sung very pleasant songs. ((1696: mit einer Klapper und Gesange allerhand seltzame Possen)).

Within a quarter of a League of the City ((of Isfahan)) there was a body or battalion of above two thousand foot, most *Armenians*. This battalion consisted of five Regiments, distinguish'd one from the other by so many Colours, which were fasten'd to the top of a great and long Pole, so that it was as much as a man could do to carry one of them. They had their particular musick, consisting of Pipes and other Instruments, one whereof was very remarkable, and consisted of two brass Basins, which they struck one against the other. ((1696: worbey auch eine sonderliche Music mit grossen Cymbeln, welche als Messinge Schüsseln gestalt, zusammen geschlagen wurden: Pfeifen und andere seltzame Instrumente, die man nicht alle beobachten kunte, mit welchen sie sich freudig hören liessen...)) All these people bid us also very welcome, and express'd their joy at our arrival, some by clapping their hands, others by turning their Caps about their heads, or flinging them up into the air. There the Governour commanded a third halt to be made, that the Ambassadors might drink once more. Coming near the City-Gate, we were entertain'd with another band of musick, consisting of Timbrells, Hawboyes, Trumpets, and other Instruments, which joyning with those of our Company made such a noyse as would have drown'd Thunder it self. ((1696: Als wir zur Stadtmaur naheten, stunden auff derselben auch viel Heerpaucker, Schalmeyer und Trompeter, welch neben andern Sängern ein solch Jubelgeschrey macheten, dass man kaum sein eigen Wort hören kunte.))

....

p. 156

We had Musick, while we were at Meal. The Musick consisted of Lutes and Viols, very poorly plaid on: as also of Tabours and Voices, which made a wretched kind of Harmony. ((1696: Unter währender Mahlzeit wurde musiciret mit Lauten, Geigen, Handpaucken und singender Stimme, welches eine frembde und wilde Harmonie gab.)) The two Pages who had fill'd the Wine at the Collation, danc'd to the sound of all these Instruments: so that they seem'd as if they would give us a taste of the delights of the Terrestial Paradise, after the hardship we had suffer'd since our coming from *Moscou*. The Governour's Palace lyeth upon the ascent of a little Hill, whence might be discover'd all the houses about the City; and he had commanded all the Inhabitants to set a row of Lamps in their windows, which represented to our eyes above twenty thousand Stars, enough to dispel the greatest darkness of the night, and added much to the divertisement, which they endeavoured to give all our senses, while the Musick of the Hawboys and Timbrels made all the Rampiers of the City to resound again. ((1696: auff den Stadtmauren die Heerpaucken und Schalmeyen lustig gehöret wurden.))

....

p. 158

January 9 ((1637)). The *Armenian* Bishop gave the Ambassadors a Visit. He came to their Lodgings with the Cross and Banner, having many Priests marching before him, who were all in their Pontifical Robes, with Wax-Candles in their hands. As they came into the Court they fell a singing and playing on their Timbrels, Hawboies, and little Bells, ((1696: Im Eintritt des Hofes fiengen sie an zu singen und klingen mit Cymbeln, Schellen und Handpaucken,)) and brought us a present of two Pitchers of Wine, and a dish of Apples, in the midst whereof they had planted a Wax-Candle lighted. They were above three hours in discourse with the Ambassadors, concerning the business of their Religion, and when they took leave of them, they re-iterated the intreaty they had made to them before, of employing their intercession to the Governour, for the building of their Church.

....

p. 161

The same day, which is, according to the accompt of the *Persians*, the 21. day of *Ramesan*, they celebrated their *Auschur*, or solemn Feast, in memory of *Haly*, their great Saint and Patron. The Ceremonies and Devotions were performed in a House built for that purpose, without the City. The Governour, his *Calenter*, and the other chief Officers, were in a Gallery of the said House, and opposite to the Gallery, there was an open Chair, about eight foot high, which was

A Feast in memory of Haly.

A Persian Priest pleasantly dress'd.

plac'd under a piece of Linnen Cloath which had been pitch'd there, for the convenience of the *Chatib*, that is, their Prelate, who sat in the said Chair, clad in a blew Garment, which is the Mourning-Colour of that Country. He spent above two hours in reading in a Book, which they call *Machtelnama*, containing the Life and Actions of *Haly*, singing with a loud and dolefull, yet clear and intelligible Voice, and that without any intermission, unless it were when he came to some remarkable Passage, or some Moral Sentence, whereof he only said the first Word, leaving the rest to be sung out by the other Priests, whereof there stood a great number about the Chair. One of those Priests cry'd out at the end of every passage, *Luanet Chudai ber kuschendi Aaly bad*, that is, *Gods Curse be on him who kill'd Haly*: whereto the whole Assembly answer'd, *bisch bad kem bad*, that is, *rather more than less...* When the *Chathib* hath given over Reading the *Chan* sends him a Garment of Silk,

A Procession.

which he immediately puts on, and then there were conducted, in Procession, three Camels carrying Coffins, cover'd with black Cloath, to represent those of *Haly*, and his two Sons, *Hassan* and *Hossein...* and at last many men carrying on their Heads little Boxes cover'd with Feathers, and Flowers of several colours, in which the *Alchoran* lay open.

These last Danc'd and Leap'd, in cadence to a certain dolefull Musick of Hawboyes, Timbrels, Flageolets and Tabors. ((1696: Diese hüpfften und sprungen nach einer traurigen Music von grossen Cymbeln, Sintz, Pfeiffen, Hand- und Heerpaucken.)) On the other side, many young Boyes Danc'd and Sung together, clapping one another upon the shoulders, and crying *Heder, Heder*, which is the name of *Haly, Hassan, Hossein*; and with these Ceremonies they took their way towards the City. Upon this day the Death of *Haly* is celebrated all over *Persia*: but *Mahomet*, their great Prophet, hath no particular Festival.

....

p. 162

MARCH

The first of *March*, which according to their Almanack, called by them *Taguim*, is the fourteenth of *Scheual*, the *Persians* celebrated another Feast, which they call *Chummehater*, in memory of that day, on which *Haly* took possession of the Estate of his Cousin and Father-in-law *Mahomet*. The *Chan* treated us again this day very Magnificently, near the River under a Tent, where, during the time of the Entertainment, he gave us the Divertisements of several sorts of Dances, and among others that of a Youth of about twenty years of age, who Danc'd to the Musick of two little Cimbals, ((1696: mit 2 kleinen Cymbeln,)) which he himself play'd on excellently well; as also that of a *Moor*, or black *Arabian*, who leap'd and danc'd between the Porcelane

Dishes, wherein the Meat had been brought up, with such exactness, that he broke not one.

p. 203

We had also, while we were at Dinner, the Divertisement of their Musick, and the Activity of those Courtezans. The Musick consist- ed of Lutes, Violins, Flageolets, Hawboies, and Timbrels, which he who play'd upon the Timbrel, accompany'd with a wretched inharmonious Voice, which disorder'd the little Consort there was in their pretended Consort. ((1696: Sie hatten gleichwoll unter der Mahlzeit sonst ihre Lust an der Music und etlichen Schauspielen. Die Instrumente in der Königlichen Music wahren Hand-Paucken, Pfeiffen, heimliche Schall-meyen, Lauten und Geigen, darein sang der Hand-Paucker in unsern Ohren gar einen jänierlichen Thon.))

Musick.

p. 204

Aug. the 28. the Augustine Friers came to intreat the Ambassa- dors to honour them with their Presence the next day, at the Celebra- tion of the Festival of their Patron St.*Augustine*. They desired the same favour of the *Muscovian Poslanick, Alexei Savinouits,* as also of an *Armenian* Bishop, and the *English* Merchants, who, though of a diffe- rent Religion, and that in *Europe* they would have made some difficul- ty to be present at the Ceremonies of the *Roman-Catholick* Church, live like Brethren and true Christians, among their common Enemies.

Celebrate the Festival of St. Au- gustine.

There were in the Monastery in all, but six *Spanish Monks,* and yet they had built a very vast Structure, with a very fair Church belong- ing to it, which had two Steeples, but somewhat low, a stately Cloister, several Cells, and a large Garden.

The Ambassadors went thither on Horseback, in regard that, though the Monastery were within the City, yet was it above a League from our quarters; and the Religious men, who receiv'd them at the entrance of the Monastery, conducted them straight to the Church, which was adorn'd with abundance of Pictures, and Gilt in several places. They presently began Mass, during which we had pretty good Musick, for one of their Monks had some skill upon the Organ, and our Musicians had brought thither their Lutes and Violins.((1696: Bey ge- haltener Messe wurde auff einem, gegen dem Altar über gelegenem er- habenen Chor mit einem Positive neben unsern dazu erbetenen Musi- canten musiciret.))....

....

Two Arme-
nian *Lords*
visit the
Ambassadors.

About this time *Seferas-beg*, Governour of *Armenia*, accompany'd by his two Brothers, came to see the Ambassadors, with a design
to make acquaintance, and contract Friendship with them. They were
all three persons of an excellent good disposition, free in their Conversation and Civil, which gain'd so much upon the nature of the Ambassador *Brugman*, who lov'd people of that Kidney, and was himself of a
free Humour, that he presented the two Elder, each of them, with a
handsome Fowling-piece, and the younger with a Case of Pistols. They
took these Presents so kindly, that, to express their gratitude, they
resolv'd to make an Entertainment for the Ambassadors, for which they
appointed the 18 of *September*, and entreated them to bring all their
Retinue along with them. They sent us Horses to bring us, and some of
the *Armenian* Merchants to accompany us.

Musick.

We were invited to sit down, and to eat of the Fruit and Conserves, which were brought in, during which we had the Divertisement
of Musick and Dancing. And as a further honour to us, the Patriarch
was sent for, who came in immediately, having about him a Cassock of
water'd Chamlet of a Violet Colour, and attended by two Priests clad in
black, with Caps on their Heads. He was no ill Company: but the
second of the two Brethren, whose name was *Elias-beg*, made the best sport
of any in the company. For, to heighten the Divertisement of the
Ambassadors, he would needs play on the *Tamera*, which is an Instrument used by the *Persians* instead of the Lute: and then he call'd for

*Porcelane
Musick.*

seven Porcelane Cups, full of water, and striking them with two little
sticks, he accorded them with the Lute....

p. 206

*The second
private
Audience.*

The 19 ((September, 1637)). The Ambassadors had their second
private audience, which the King gave them in another apartment, at
the end of a Garden, and which lasted not above half an hour; in regard
the Council took time to consider of the Memorials they receiv'd in
writing from them. It is ordinary to stay and Dine at the Court after the
Conferences; therefore I shall forbear repeating the Circumstances, unless something in particular oblige me thereto: as it happen'd this day,
in that the King having heard that the Ambassadors had Musicians in
their Retinue, he sent them word, that he would gladly hear their
Musick. It consisted of a base Viol, a Tenor, and a Violin, which play'd
about half an hour, till the King sent us word, that that Musick was not
ill, but that he thought that of the Country as good as it. ((1696:
Wurde derwegen eine *Viol di Gamba*, Bandor und Discant Viole ge-

hohlet, und bey einer Stunden musiciret, welches dem König zwar woll-
gefallen hatte, aber doch gleichwoll mit ihrer Music, der sie gewohnet,
nicht tauschen wollen.))

*The Am-
bassadors
treated by
the English.*

The 25 of *September,* the *English* made an entertainment for the
Ambassadors and all their Retinue, which, in Magnificence, surpass'd all
the rest. Their House or Lodge was in the *Basar,* near the *Maiden.* The
Structure was of great extent, divided into several appartments, and had
a very fair Garden. We were at first brought into a Gallery, where we
found Fruits and Conserves laid upon the floor, which was cover'd with
Tapistry, according to the custom of the Country; and having done
there, we pass'd into a great Hall, where we found the Table furnish'd
and serv'd after the *English* fashion.

They forgot not to drink the healths of most of the Kings and
Princes of *Europe,* and we had the Divertisement of Musick upon the
Virginals. ((1696: Unterdessen wurde ein wollklingend Clav-Cymbel
von einem ihrer Diener geschlagen.)) After Dinner, we were brought
into an open Hall, which look'd into a Garden, where we found a
Collation of Conserves, with the best Wine the Countrey could afford.
And whereas we had often seen the Dancing-women of the Country,
they sent for some *Indian* Women of the same profession. There were
brought six young Women, whereof some had their Husbands with
them, who also either Danc'd or Play'd upon Violins ((1696: so auch
Täntzer und Spielleute)); some came in alone. They were all somewhat
of an Olive-colour, but had excellent good features, a delicate smooth
Skin, and very handsome Bodies. They had about their Necks much
Gold and Pearls, and in their Ears Pendants of Gold or Silver, glistering
with Jewels and Spangles.

*Indian
Dancing-
Women.*

*Handsome
and well
shap'd*

Some of them had Bracelets of Pearl, others of Silver, but they
had all Rings on their Fingers, and among the rest, they had upon the
Thumb, upon which, in the place where the Stone should be, there was
a piece of Steel, about the bigness of a Crown-piece of Silver, and so
well polish'd, that it serv'd them for a Looking-glass. They were
Cloath'd after a particular manner, having on a kind of Stuff, which was
so thin, that there was not any part of the Body but might be seen by
the Company, save only what was hidden by the Drawers which they
wore under their Petticoats. Some wore Caps on their Heads, others had
them dress'd in Tiffany, and some had silk Scarfs, wrought with Gold
and Silver, which crossing their shoulders reach'd down to the ground.
Some were bare-foot, others were shod after a very strange manner.
They had above the instap of the foot a string ty'd, with little Bells
fastened thereto, whereby they discover'd the exactness of their Cadence, and sometimes corrected the Musick it self; as they did also by
the *Tzarpanes,* or *Castagnetts,* which they had in their hands; in the
managing whereof they were very expert. Their Musick consisted of

Their habit.

Timbrels, according to the *Indian* way of Playing on them, Tabors, and Pipes.

The *Indian* Timbrels are two foot long, but broader in the middle than at the extremities, much after the fashion of our Barrels. They hang them about their Necks, and play on them with their fingers. ((1696: Ihr Spielwerck waren Indianische Paucken, Persche Sintz oder Handpaucken und Flöthen. Die Indianischen Paucken sind einer Ellen lang und schmal, fast wie eine Tonne formieret, die Boden ungleicher Grösse, welche, wenn sie geschlagen werden, am Thon eine Quart unterschieden. Sie werden aber auff beyden Seiten mit blossen Händen geschlagen, deswegen man sie an einem Riemen umb dan Halsz hänget.)) The postures of these *Indian* Women in their dancing are admirable. Their hands and feet are alwayes in action, as is also their whole Body: and many times, they address themselves to some particular person of the Company, either by an inclination of the Body, or to get the little Present they expect, which they very handsomely beg, either by stretching out their hands, yet so that it seems to be done without any affectation, but as a necessary consequence of the Dance. They are much more pleasant in their Conversation than the Women of the Countrey. All these Dancing-women are common prostitutes, and very free to shew all their postures for money, nay to do beyond what might be expected from them. It was far-night ere we got away, which oblig'd the *English* to bring us home to our Lodgings.

p. 207

About this time, I went to the Suburbs of *Tzulfa,* with the intention to visit some *Armenian* Merchants, with whom I had had occasion to make acquaintance at the entertainments which had been made us. Coming near the Church, I saw going thither one that was to be Married, whom I had the curiosity to follow, purposely to see the Ceremonies of the Marriage. In the front of the Procession march'd the ordinary Musick, consisting of Timbrels, and Tabors ((1696: Es wurden Heerpaucken und messinge Cymbeln vorher gespielt)), and after them went a Youth of about twelve or fifteen years of age, who had a wax Candle in his hand...While the Communion was administred, they sung, and play'd on certain great Cymbals, which the *Armenians* call *Hambar-zon.* ((1696: Bey Empfangung des Abendmahls wurde gesungen, und mit ihren bereiteten Cymbeln, welche sie auff Armenisch *Hambarzon* nennen, geklungen.)) They never communicate without that kind of Musick, which they believe to be so much the more necessary, in that they say our Saviour, when he was to feed four thousand men with seven Loaves, went first up into the Mountain, where he offered his Prayers in Sacrifice to God, and that while he pray'd, two Angels came down from Heaven, and play'd upon that kind of Cymbals. After the Communion, they cast Rose-water upon the new-Married couple, and all the company, and ty'd a Scarf about the Bride's right hand, by which the Bridegroom draws her after him to the Church door, where all the Company get on Horse-back, to goe to the place where there is a Feast prepared for them. For the first three nights after the Marriage, the Married couple touch not one another.

Coming out of this Church, I pass'd by another, where hearing a great noise, I went into it. The noise was made by striking with a great stick upon a deal board that was hung up, which the *Armenians* are forc'd to make use of instead of Bells, the *Persians*, it seems, not permitting them to make use of any..((1696: Nach diesem gieng ich in eine andere Kirche, woselbst sie auff dem Thurm an statt der Glocken, welche sie vor den Persern nicht haben dürffen, ein dürres Bret auffgehencket, und mit einem Knöppel daran schlagen, wenn ihr GottesDienst zu verrichten ist.))...

The Baptism of the Armenians.

p. 215

The same day, the *Mehemander* came to give us notice, that the King intended within eight days to goe for *Kaschan*, and that if we could be ready against that time, we might make our advantage of the convenience, as far as that City. Which oblig'd us to put all things in readiness for our journey: and the 12. we made an entertainment, in order to our departure, whereto were invited the same persons who had been at the first, save that the acquaintances, which the Ambassador *Brugman* had made in the Suburbs of *Tzulfa*, occasion'd his invitation ·of several *Armenians* to this, who had not been at the former.

In the afternoon, there was running at the Ring, at which Divertisement was present also the *Portuguez* Agent, who manag'd the Viceroy's affairs at the Court, and a rich *Jew*, who drove a great trade between the *Indies* and *Constantinople*. The Walls, Windows, and tops of the neighbouring houses were full of *Persians* and *Armenians*, who came thither to see that Divertisement.

The noise of the Trumpets and Tymbrels continu'd all the time, as did also that of our Artillery, which the Ambassador *Brugman* ordered to be discharg'd at all the healths that were drunk, and that so often, that Father *Joseph*, our Interpreter, who knew that they might hear every shot at the King's Palace, fearing his Majesty should take it ill, was forc'd to represent to him the Tyrannical humour of that Prince, and the danger, whereto he expos'd not only his own person, after the Ambassadors were departed, but also all that belong'd to the Embassy. He told him, that is was no extraordinary thing to see that Prince exercise his cruelties upon all sorts of persons, without any regard of their Quality or Character, and intreated him to command that there should be no more shooting. But all these Remonstrances prevail'd nothing with the Ambassador, who ordered the Trumpets to sound, and the Guns to be fir'd as much as at any time before. We understood since, that the King was so incens'd against the said Ambassador, as well for this action, as another, whereof I shall presently give an account, that he was upon the point of ordering him to be cut in pieces, and it may be all of us with him, if the prudence and moderation of the Chancellor had not prevail'd with him to forbear, by representing to him, that the Prince his Master, who, no doubt approv'd not the insolences of that Ambassador, would be sure to punish them, as soon as he were advertised thereof.

6 JOHN SCHEFFER

John Scheffer was born in Strasbourg in 1621. He migrated to
Sweden as a mature and versatile scholar, and was welcomed by Queen
Christina, who obtained for him in 1648 the professorship of Rhetoric
and Law at the University of Uppsala. The Latin original of *The History
of Lapland* was published in Frankfurt in 1673, with the title *Lapponia,
id est, regionis Lapponum et gentis nova et verissima descriptio.* The
work was published in translations into German (1675), French (1678)
and Dutch (1682). A Swedish translation by Hendrik Sundin, with
additional material and notes, was published in Uppsala in 1956 as *Acta
Lapponica* VIII. The bibliographical footnotes to these extracts are
drawn from the notes to Sundin's translation.

The writer of the Preface to the English translation introduced
the book with the following words (this is the Preface in full):

The Reader may please to take notice, that the diligent and
learned Author of this History, (to the writing of which he was
commanded, and therein assisted by the Chancellor of *Sweden*)
hath in the whole work taken care to justify what he relates,
from the faith of authentic records, the testimony of Historians,
and the Discourses of *Laplanders* themselves, with whom he had
ready opportunities of converse. And this he hath don so precisely, that having in the contexture of his work, given a full
account of what he thought observable in the writings, or
narratives to which he refers; he afterwards constantly puts
down at length the very words of his Authors, a great part of
which are in the Swedish Tongue. Now in this Edition we have
spared our selves the labor of such repetition; which we hope
will not be regretted by the Reader, who we suppose would not
have bin much edified by them. As to the subject here discours'd of, twill not be needfull to give a character of it. Military Action, and those public murders in which other Histories
triumph, have no share here. Hunger, cold and solitude are enemies that engage all the fortitude of this People: and where so
much passive valor is necessary, we may dispense with the want
of Active. Amidst the barbarity and darkness which reign in
Lapland, there appear strictures of light, which will entertain
the eie of the most knowing observer; as the Stars are no less
remarkable then is the Sun it self. However the Reader will not
fail to meet here with what may gratify his curiosity. Warmer
Climates having all the comforts and necessaries of life plentifully bestowed upon them, are but a more distant home; where
we have little else talk'd of, then what we daily see among our

selves: but here it is indeed, where, rather then in *America*, we have a new World discovered: and those extravagant falsehoods, which have commonly past in the narratives of these Northern Countries, are not so inexcusable for their being lies, as that they were told without temtation; the real truth being equally entertaining, and incredible.

The illustrations in the English translation were redrawn, in reverse position compared with the Frankfurt print. They are here reproduced in the original form. The illustrations marked A-B, C-D, E and F (corresponding respectively to plates C1 to C6 here) have indications of the dimensions of the drums depicted. Three of these also have the explanation *Pes Romanus Lucae Peti*. This was not shown in the English version; its reference is to Lucas Paetus, *De mensuris et ponderibus Romanis et Graecis*, Venice, 1573. In the second plate in that work measurements are given for the following:

> *Schema legitimi Pedis;* one unit of this measures 2.3 cm. *Mensura Palmi quo hodie Ro: Architecti utuntur*; one unit measures 1.8 cm.
>
> *Mensura coloñiani et statiliani Pedis*; one unit measures 7.2 cm. *Schema maioris Cuiusdam Pedis postremorum temporum crediti*; one unit measures 1.8 cm.

It was presumably the first of these to which Scheffer referred the measurement he indicated as *Pes Romanus Lucae Peti*.

John Scheffer, Professor of Law and Rhetoric at Upsal in Sweden ((trans. Acton Cremer)), *The History of Lapland, wherein are shewed the Original, Manners, Habits, Marriages, Conjurations, &c. of that People*, Oxford, 1674

Chapter X: *Of the heathenish Gods of the* Laplanders

....

p. 42

I come now to their Sacrifices and other Ceremonies used to their Gods. First it is observable that they are performed only by men, all women being excluded; they esteeming it as great a crime for a woman to offer Sacrifice as to frequent the consecrated places. They never offer Sacrifice till they have enquired of their God whether he will accept it or no. This they do with a certain instrument which they call *Kannus*, not unlike the old fashioned Drums, from whence they are usually called Laplandish Drums, and shall be exactly described hereafter. This Drum being beaten, and some Songs sung, they bring the designed Sacrifice to *Thor*, who if he signifies by a ring in the Drum

that the Sacrifice is pleasing to him, they fall presently to work: otherwise they carry it to the Sun, and so to *Storjunkar*, till one of them will
accept of it. The manner of it is thus. They pull off some of the hair at
the bottom of the beasts neck, and bind it to a ring which is fastned to
the Drum, then one of them beats the Drum, and all the rest sing these
words, *What sayst thou ô Great and Sacred God, dost thou accept this
Sacrifice, which we design to offer unto thee?* And while they chant
these words, they repete the name of the mountain where they are:
then if the ring rests on that part of the Drum where the God is
pictured, they take it for granted that the God is pleased, and so proceed to the Ceremony; or else they carry the Sacrifice to *Thor*, and use
the like form of words, *Father God will you have my Sacrifice. Peucer*[1]
either thro false intelligence, or misapprehension, relates this business
somthing differently, they have (saies he) a brasen Drum whereon they
paint several sorts of Beasts, Birds, and Fishes, such as they can easily
procure: bolt upright upon this Drum they fix an iron pearch, upon
which stands a brasen Frog, which at the beating of the Drum falls
down upon some of the pictures, and that creature whose picture the
Frog touches, they sacrifice....

Chapter XI: *Of the magicall Ceremonies of the* Laplanders

....

p. 46

As to the bequeathing their familiars to their Children, they
suppose it the only means to raise their family; so that they excell one
another in this art, according to the largeness of the legacies they receive. From hence it is manifest, that each house hath peculiar spirits,
and of different and quite contrary natures from those of others. And
not only each distinct family, but single persons in them also have their·
particular spirits, sometimes one, two, or more, according as they
intend to stand on the defensive part, or are maliciously inclined and
design to be upon the offensive: so that there are a set number of
obsequious spirits, beyond which none hath. But however some of
these will not engage themselves without great solicitation, and earnest
entreaties, when others more readily profer themselves to litle children, when they find them fit for their turn, so that diverse of the
Inhabitants are almost naturally Magicians. For when the devil takes a
liking to any person in his infancy, as a fit instrument for his designs, he
presently seases on him by a disease, in which he haunts them with

---

1. The reference is to Casparus Peucerus, *Commentarius de praecipuis divinationum generibus*,
Wittemberg, 1560.

several apparitions, from whence according to the capacity of his years and understanding he learns what belongs to the art. Those which are taken thus a second time see more visions, and gain greater knowledg. If they are seased a third time, which is seldom without great torment, or utmost danger of their life, the devil appears to them in all his shapes, by which they arrive to the very perfection of this art; and become so knowing, that without the Drum they can see things at greatest distances, and are so possessed by the devil, that they see them even against their will. For example, not long since a certain *Lap*, who is yet alive, upon my complaint against him for his Drum, brought it to me; and confest with tears, that tho he should part with it, and not make him another, he should have the same visions he had formerly: and he instanc't in my self, giving me a true and particuliar relation of whatever had happened to me in my journy to *Lapland*. And he farther complained, that he knew not how to make use of his eies, since things altogether distant were presented to them.

As for the art, it is, according to the diversity of the instruments they make use of in it, divided into two parts: one comprehends all that to which their Drum belongs, the other those things to which knots, darts, spells, conjurations, and the like refer. First concerning the drum, as being peculiar to the *Laplanders*; and called by them *Kannus*, or *Quobdas*; it is made out of a hollow piece of wood, and must either be of pine, fir, or birch tree, which grows in such a particular place, and turns directly according to the Suns course; which is, when the grain of the wood, running from the bottom to the top of the tree, winds it self from the right hand to the left. From this perhaps they believe this tree very acceptable to the Sun, which under the image of *Thor* they worship with all imaginable devotion. The piece of wood they make it of, must be of the root cleft asunder, and made hollow on one side, upon which they stretch a skin: the other side, being convex, is the lower part, in which they make two holes, where they put their fingers to hold it. The shape of the upper side is oval, in diameter almost half an ell, very often not so much; it is like a kettle drum, but not altogether so round, nor so hollow; neither is the skin fastned with little iron screwes, but wooden pegs. I have seen some sowed with the sinews of Rain-dears. *Olaus*[1] termed the drum very improperly an anvil, tho I believe he only meant by this a drum, as will appear hereafter. This perhaps made the Engraver mistake, who made a Smith's anvil for it, placing a Serpent and a frog upon it, with a Smith's hammer by. The *Laplanders* use only a drum, which perhaps because they beat it with a hammer, was by *Olaus* called an anvil. They paint upon the skin several

---

1. Olaus Magnus, *Historia de gentibus septentrionalibus,* Rome, 1555.

pictures in red, stained with the bark of an Alder tree. They draw near the middle of the drum several lines quite cross, upon these they place those Gods, to whom they pay the greatest worship, as *Thor* the chief God, with his attendance, and *Storjunkar* with his: these are drawn on the top of the line; after this they draw another line parallel to the former, only half cross the drum, on this stands the image of Christ with some of his Apostles. Whatever is drawn above these two lines represents birds, Stars, and the Moon; below these they place the Sun, as middlemost of the Planets, in the very middle of the drum, upon which they put a bunch of brazen rings when they beat it. Below the Sun they paint the terrestrial things, and living creatures; as Bears, Wolves, Rain-dears, Otters, Foxes, Serpents: as also Marshes, Lakes, Rivers, &c. This is the description of the drum according to *Sam. Rheen*[1], of which this is the picture ((see Illustration C1)).

I have observed that severall of their drums have not the same pictures upon them, I have three very different; one, which is here set down, marked by the letter B. They are described differently by *Tornaeus*[2], in which the figures are distinguished so as to refer to several places, of which there are chiefly three. In the first stands *Norland*, and other Countries of *Sweden*, which are placed on the South side of the drum, and are separated by a line from the rest; in this also is contained the next great City, where they trafic most; as in the drums made at *Torne*, or *Kiemi*, there is drawn the City *Torne*, with the Temple, Priest, and Governour of the *Laplanders*, and many others with whom they have any concerns: as also the highway that lies betwixt them and *Torne*, by which they discover when their Priest, or Governour will come; besides other affairs managed in those parts. On the North part, *Norway* is described with all that is contained in it. In the middle of these two stands *Lapland*, this takes up the greatest part of the drum: in it are the several sorts of beasts that are in the Countrey, here they picture herds of Rain-dears, Bears, Foxes, Wolves, and all manner of wild beasts, to signifie when, and in what place they may find them. If a tame Rain-dear be lost, how they may get him againe. Whether the Rain-deers young ones will live. Whether their net fishing will be successfull. If sick men will recover, or not. Whether women great with child shall have a safe delivery. Or such, or such a man will die of such a distemper, or by what other; and other things of the like nature which they are desirous to know. I cannot give an account of the reason for

---

1. Samuel Rheen, *En kortt Relation om Lapparnes Lefwarne och Sedher*, ed. K.B. Wiklund, *Sverige landsmål*, XVII, i, 1897.
2. Johannes Tornaeus, *Berättelse om Lapmarckerna och Deras Tilstånd*, ed. K.B. Wiklund, *Sverige landsmål*, XVII, iii, 1900.

this difference in the drums, unless it is that some of them are made for more malicious designs, others again for each man's private purpose. Upon this account I believe, according to the nature of the business they intend, they add, and blot out, and sometimes wholly change the figures. But that you may the better understand the diversity of the drums, here are two represented to you, both which I had out of the Study of the Chancellour of the Kingdom ((see Illustration C2)). The two greater Figures represent, one the upper, the other the lower side of the Drum, and so do also the two lesser.

Besides these two drums, I had also a third given me by the same Lord of as great a size as any that can be usually met with ((see Illustration C3)).

To these I add a fourth, given me by the Illustrious Baron Lieutenant *Henry Flemming*, mark't with the letter F ((see Illustration C4)).

Now there are two things required to fit the drum for use, and Index and a Hammer, that shews among the pictures the thing they enquire after, with this they beat the drum. The Index is the bunch of brazen rings mentioned before. They first place one great ring upon the drum, then they hang severall small ones upon that; the shape of the Index's is very different, for of these I have one made of copper, of the bigness of a *Dollar*, with a square hole in the middle, several small chains hanging about it instead of rings. Another hath an Alchymy ring, on which a small round plate of copper is hung by little chains. I have seen another also of bone, in the shape of the Greek Δ, with rings about it; and others of a quite different make. I have described mine under the drums A, and B, by the mark G: but the common sort of rings are of copper, and those upon the Chancellors drums are altogether such. Some Writers call these rings serpents, or brazen frogs, and toads; not that they resemble them, but because by them they signifie these creature, whose pictures they often use in their conjuring, as supposing them very grateful and acceptable to the Devil. The *Laplanders* call the Index *Arpa*, or *Quobdas*; and make it indifferently of any sort of metal. The hammer they use in raising their familiars, is not the Smith's; which was the errour of him that drew it in *Olaus Magn.* but is an instrument belonging only to the *Laplanders*, and called by a peculiar name by them: it is made of a Rain-deers horn, branching like a fork, this is the head of the hammer, the other part serves for the handle. The instrument is placed under the two drums A. B. with the letter H, with the hammer they beat the drum, not so much to make a noise, as by the drumming to move the ring lying on the skin, so as to pass over the pictures, and shew what they sought after. This is the description of the drum, with all its necessaries as it is used by the *Laplanders* that are subject to the *Swedes*; the *Finlappers* also that are under the Crown of

Danemarke, make use of drums something different in fashion from the former; yet however the difference is so small, that I believe their drums are not of a different kind from ours, but made only for some particular uses. I shall give an account of one of those, described in *Wormius's* Study[1], who saies that the *Laplanders* drum, which "they use in their magic, and by beating which they discover those things they desired, is made of an oval piece of wood hollowed, in length a foot, in breadth ten inches; in this they make six holes, and put a handle to it, that they may hold in the left hand, whilst they beat it with the other; upon it they stretch over a skin, painted with diverse rude figures, drawn with blood, or red; upon this lies a piece of brass, in the shape of a Rhomboides, somewhat convexe, about two inches in diameter, in the middle of this, and at each corner hangs a small chain. The instrument, with which they beat the drum, is of bone, six inches long, about the thickness of a little finger, and made much like the Latine T."

This instrument the *Laplanders* use for diverse designs, and are of opinion that whatever thay do it is don by the help of this. For this reason they have it in great esteem and reverence, taking such care in securing it, that they wrap it with the Index, and hammer, up in a Lambskin, and for its greater safety, lay it in some private place. But I think it an errour, to suppose them to lay it in a Lambskin: for it is written in some places *Loomskin*, which signifies the skin of a bird that lives altogether in the water. They think it so sacred, and holy, that they suffer no maid that is marriageable to touch it; and if they remove it from place to place, they carry it the last of all, and this must be don too only by men; or else they go with it thro some untrod way, that no body may either meet or follow them. The reason they give for their great care in this particular, is, because they believe if any one, especially a maid that is marriageable, should follow the same way, they would in three daies time at least fall into some desperate disease, and commonly without any hopes of recovery. This they seem to verifie by many examples, that we may give the more credit to it; and we have the less reason to doubt the truth of this, since the devil severely commands his worship to be observed, and suffers not those rites and customs he hath imposed to be violated, so long as God is pleased to grant him this liberty. Now because it may happen sometimes that a woman may out of necessity be constrained to go that way, by which the drum hath bin carried, the devil is so favorable as to permit it without any danger, upon condition she first offers a brazen ring to the drum.

In the next place, because they believe they can effect very strange things by the drum, we will shew what they are, and the manner

---

1. Olaus Wormius, *Museum Wormianum,* Leiden, 1655.

used to perform them. These are three, belonging either to their hunting, their sacred affairs, or lastly the enquiring into things far distant. I
find four chiefly mentioned by another Writer, the first is, the knowing
the state of affairs in forreign Countries. The second, what success their
designs in hand will meet. With the third, how to cure diseases. The
fourth, what Sacrifices their Gods will be pleased to accept, and what
beast each God desires or dislikes most. As to the way in making
enquiries, it is not the same among all these artists. But the great thing
they generally observe, is, to stretch the skin very stiff, which is don by
holding it to the fire. The next is, that they beat not altogether in the
same place, but round about the Index; then that they beat softly at
first, presently quicker, and continue this till they have effected their
intent. The drummer first lifts up the drum by degrees, then beats
softly about the Index, till it begins to stirr, and when it is removed
some distance from its first place to either side, he strikes harder, till
the Index points at something, from whence he may collect what he
sought for. They take care also that as well he that beats the drum, as
those that are present at the ceremony, should be upon their knees. As
to the occasions of their beating thus, the later of those is already
discoursed of. Now we proceed to the rest, the first of which is concerning their enquiries into things acted in remote parts. Those who
desire to know the condition of their friends, or affairs abroad, whether
distant five hundred, or a thousand miles, go to some *Laplander*, or
Finlander skilfull in this art, and present him with a linen garment, or
piece of silver, as his reward, for satisfying them in their demands. An
example of this nature is to be seen upon record, at *Bergen*, a famous
Market Town in *Norway*, where the effects of the German Merchants
are registred; in this place there was one *John Delling*, Factor then to a
German, to whom a certain *Finlapper* of *Norway* came with *James
Samaousuend*: of him *John Delling* enquired about his Master then in
Germany; the *Finlapper* readily consenting to tell him, like a drunken
man presently made a great bawling, then reeling and dancing about
several times in a circle, fell at last upon the ground, lying there sometimes as if he were dead, then starting up on a suddain, related to him
all things concerning his Master, which were afterwards found to agree
to what he reported. There are many more instances of this kind: the
most considerable, is one concerning a *Laplander*, now living, who gave
Tornaeus an account of the Journey he first made to *Lapland*, tho he
had never seen him before that time; which, altho it was true, *Tornaus*
dissembled to him, least he might glory too much in his devilish prac-
tises, and rely upon them, as the only means whereby he might attain
to truth. The autority of this man is so considerable, that it may gain
credit enough to the Story. As to the method taken in making dis-
coveries, it is very different. *Olaus Magn.* described it thus, the drummer

goes into some private room, accompanied by one single person, besides his wife, and by beating the drum moves the Index about, muttering at the same time several charms, then presenlty he falls into an extasie, and lies for a short time as if dead; in the mean while his companion takes great care, that no gnat, flie, or other living creature touch him; for his Soul is carried by some ill *Genius* into a forreign Countrey, from whence it is brought back with a knife, ring, or some other token, of his knowledg, of what is done in those parts; after this rising up, he relates all the circumstances belonging to the business that was enquired after; and that they may seem certainly so, he shews what he hath brought from thence. *Petr. Claud.*[1] makes no mention either of the drum, charms, company, or those things he brings with him; but saies he casts himself upon the ground, grows black in the face, lying as if dead for an hour or two; according as the distance of the place is, of which he makes enquiry; when he awakes he gives a full account of all affairs there. It is clear from what was said before, that they made use of a drum; and 'tis observed that for this sort of conjuring the lower part of the drum, whereby they hold it, was commonly shaped like a cross. One of this make was given me by the Lord *Henry Flemming*, Colonel of a foot Regiment in *Finland*, the Figure of it is in the page foregoing ((see Illustration C5)).They hang about it several claws, and bones of the creatures they take. That several persons also, as well men as women, are permitted to be present at this ceremony, is asserted by *Sam. Rheen* in his history, where he saies that the drummer sings a song, called by them *Joiike*, and the men and women that are present sing likewise, some in higher some in lower notes, this they call *Duura*. Next as to the casting themselves on the ground, there are various relations, some think them not really, but only in appearance dead; others are apt to believe that the soul departs from the body, and after its travell abroad. returns again. But without doubt this is false, for it is impossible, for either man, or devil, to restore the soul to the body it hath once left. So that I believe the devil only stifles the faculties of the soul for a time, and hinders their operations. Now after the drummer falls down, he laies his drum as near as possibly on his head, in this posture. ((see Illustration C6)).

Those in the mean time that are present, leave not off singing all the time he lies sweating in this agony; which they do not only to put him in mind, when he awakes, of the business he was to know; but also that he might recover out of this trance, which he would never do, (as they imagine) if they either ceased singing, or any one stirred him with their hand or foot. This perhaps is the reason why they suffer no flie, or

---

1. Peder Claussøn (Friis), *Norriges Oc Omliggende Øers sandfaerdige Bescriffuelse*, Copenhagen, 1632.

any living creature to touch him; and it is upon this account only that they watch him so diligently, and not out of any fear they have least the devil should take away his body; which opinion of *Peucers* is altogether false. It is uncertain how long they lye in this manner, but it is commonly according as the place where they make their discovery, is nearer or farther off; but the time never exceeds 24 houres, let the place be at never so great a distance. After he awakes he shews them some tokens to confirm their belief in what he tells them. This is the first and chiefest use they make of the drum.

The next is, how to know the event of their own concerns, and what success their hunting will have, or any other business which they undertake, for they seldom venture on any thing, without first consulting that. In order to the knowing this, they place the bunch of rings on the picture of the Sun in the drum; then they beat, singing at the same time; if the rings go round towards the right hand, according to the Suns course they promise to themselves good health, fortune, and great encrease both of men and beasts; if contrary, towards the left, they expect sickness and all the evils attending on ill success. We may easily ground this opinion of theirs upon the other mentioned above, where they believe the Sun the only Author of all productions. Wherefore when the Index moves according to his motion, it portends prosperity by following his course, from whom they expect all the good they receive. This is the way they take in all their more weighty affairs, as in a journey, hunting, removing their habitations, or any such like thing, of which something before, and more hereafter. Before they hunt they make particular observation which way the Index turns, whether East, West, North, or South; and collect from thence where their game lies. Other things for which the drum is serviceable, are, first, the discovering the nature of diseases, whether they arise from any disorder in the body, or are caused by magic; this being known, then to find the remedy for them, which is commonly by sacrifice to one or other of their angry Gods, but chiefly to *Storjunkar*, who bears greatest autority among them, and if not appeased, leaves them small hopes of recovery. Wherefore the sick person vows a sacrifice, either of a Rain-deer, Bull, Goat, or Ram, or something of this kind to one of the *Storiunkars*, that stands upon the mountains. The sacrifice is not left to the disposal of the sick man, but must be made according to the directions of the drummer; for he is supposed to be the only man able to advise them in this case, he first discovers which of the Gods is displeased, and what sort of sacrifice is most acceptable to him, for they refuse several, and the same also at several times. But before the drummer appeases their Gods, they give him a copper and a silver ring, putting them on his right arm, then he begins a song, and beats the drum, and all that are present joyn with him in a *Chorus*; after this according to the place, to which the Index points, he directs them. These are the things commonly done by the drum. The last thing for which they think it necessary, is, the accomplishing their wicked designs, as impairing mens health, or depriving them of their lives; which is frequently enough practised among them, tho not altogether so publicly as heretofore. Some of them account this only unlawful, and exclude themselves out of the number of those, which use it, thinking the other uses of the drum to consist chiefly in doing good. But however this mischievous Art continues still too much among them. Several inhabitants of *Kiema* in *Lapland* were apprehended in the year 1671, with drums, for this purpose so large, that they could not be removed from thence, but were burnt in the place. Among those *Laplanders* there was one four score years of age, that confessed he was bred up in this art from his childhood, who in 1670 upon some quarrell about a pair of mittens, caused a Boar of *Kiema* to be drowned in a Cataract, for which he was condemned to die, and in order to that was to be carried in chains to the next town in *Bothnia*, but in the journy he contrived so by his art, that on a suddain, tho he seemed well, and lusty, he died on the sledge, which he had often foretold he would sooner do, then fall into the Executioners hands. As to the ceremonies used in this particular, either in their words, gesture, or any other thing, I can give no account, finding none in those writings, from whence I collected the rest. The reason for this, I suppose, is, because they themselves keep this secret, as the great mystery in their art; or that no one would enquire into them, least they should be thought guilty of this damnable sin.

7 LUCAS DEBES

Lucas Jacobson Debes was born on the Danish island of Falster in 1623. He was Christian minister at Thorshavn in Strömö, the main island of the Faeroes, and died in 1676. His book on the Faeroes was printed at Copenhagen in 1673; there is a modern edition published at Thorshavn in 1903.

Lucas Jacobson Debes, *Faeroae & Faeroa Reserata: that is, a Description of the Islands and Inhabitants of Foeroe, being seventeen Islands subject to the King of Denmark, lying under 62 degrees 10 min. of North Latitude. Wherein several Secrets of Nature are brought to Light, and some Antiquities hitherto kept in Darkness, discovered. Englished by J((ohn)) S((terpin))*, London, 1676

Chapter V: *Of the Qualities of the Inhabitants.*

p. 273

They are not inclined to any unprofitable pastimes, but delight themselves most in singing of Psalms on holy days, except in their Weddings, and at Christmas, that they recreate themselves with a plain Dance, holding one another by the hand, and singing some old Champions Ballad: but they use not them to exercise themselves at any scandalous play.

Chapter VI: *Of the Policie.*

p. 281

The Provincial Judge ((at the annual Spring Sessions)) giveth the sentence, having under him 36 men established by Law, six for every division, and the sworn Recorder, that Registreth what is done and judged, as long as the Court is kept; all the Clergy being there also, the Service of God is celebrated every day in the forenoon, with Preaching and Singing in the Church; and in the afternoon, when the Bell rings, the Court is kept.....The same day in the evening, both Ecclesiastical and Civil, gather themselves in the Sessions-house, to Feast and be merry together, where according to an antient custome they drink the healths of his Majesty, of the Queen, and of the Prince, the Counsels, their Governours, and other principal healths, with the following Ceremony and Speech. First one of the eldest Priests begins a verse of a Psalm, which they sing out together, after which the same Priest alone sings it in Latine, according to the antient manner, and the guests answer, singing in Latine as followeth.

The Priest sings.
1. *Omnis Speritus,*
2. *Benedicamus Domino,*
3. *Benedicite,*

The people answers,
1. *Laudet Dominum,*
2. *Deo gratias,*
3. *Domino.*

Chapter VII: *Of Religion.*

p. 337

....This I must blame in our people of *Feroe,* that almost all of them know the most part of the old Gyants Ballads; not only those that are Printed in the Danish Book of Ballads, but also many more of the Champions of *Norway,* that may be forgotten elsewhere, here in fresh Memory, being usually Sung in their Dances.

....

p. 339

.....For all their household sitting for the most part at home in Winter, they exercise themselves continually in singing of Psalms; so that they know more of them without Book, then can here be credibly related; Wherefore, when the Congregation doth meet with the Priest in their Church to serve God, they have no need of a Reader to direct their singing; but the Priest beginneth, and all the hearers sing of themselves after him, how difficult soever the Psalm may be; for they not only sing without book, but almost all the men have their Psalm books with them, and antient hearers, being so well informed, teach also their children.....

8 SIMON DE LA LOUBÈRE

Before being entrusted with plenipotentiary status in Louis XIV's mission to the King of Siam in 1687, Simon de la Loubère, who was born in Toulouse in 1642, had been secretary to the French Ambassador to Switzerland from 1672 to 1676. The chief object of the Siam enterprise was to secure commercial advantages for the French as against the Dutch and the English. The mission had diplomats, Jesuits and 636 soldiers in six warships. It arrived in September, 1687, and la Loubère left on January 3, 1688, returning by way of Batavia. Besides his book on Siam he wrote on literary and mathematical subjects, and died in 1729.

His *Du royaume de Siam* was first published in two volumes in both Paris and Amsterdam in 1691. In 1969 there was published a facsimile reprint of the English translation, with an introduction by David K. Wyatt (from which the information in the previous paragraph was derived). Wyatt gave the following estimate of La Loubère's book:

> This book is the best of its kind partly because of the author's careful attention to detail and his well-organized format, but primarily because of his great reasonableness and intelligence....The information with which he provides us, whether of physical geography, manners and customs, political and social structure, or religion and administration, remains extremely useful to our understanding of Thai culture and society. Nearly three centuries have passed since he wrote, yet much of what he saw in 1688 is still to be seen in Thai villages, monasteries, and homes. La Loubère's remarkable book serves to provide us with that essential sense of continuity of past and present which so vibrantly characterizes Thailand yesterday and today.[1]

The two illustrations of musical instruments and the notation of a Siamese song (Illustrations D1 to D3) have been taken from the Amsterdam print of the original French. The illustrations were redrawn in a smaller size for the English translation, and the song notation there differs in a few small details from that in the Amsterdam print.

A New Historical Relation of the Kingdom of Siam. By Monsieur de la Loubere. Envoy Extraordinary from the French King, to the King of Siam, in the years 1687 and 1688....Done out of French, by A.P. Gen. R. S. S., London, 1693

1. Simon de la Loubère, *The Kingdom of Siam*, with an Introduction by David K. Wyatt, Kuala Lumpur, 1969, p. viii.

Part II, Chapter XII, p. 68: *Concerning Musick, and the Exercises of the Body*.

Musick is not better understood at *Siam*, than Geometry and Astronomy. They make Airs by Fancy, and know not how to prick them by Notes. They have neither Cadence, nor quaver no more than the *Castilians*: but they sometimes sing like us without words, which the *Castilians* think very strange; and in the stead of words, they only say *noi, noi*, as we do say *lan-la-lari*. I have not remark'd one single Air, whose measure was triple, whereas those are without comparison the most familiar to the *Spaniards*. The King of *Siam*, without shewing himself, heard several Airs of our *Opera* on the Violin, and it was told us that he did not think them of a movement grave enough: Nevertheless the *Siameses* have nothing very grave in their Songs; and whatever they play on their Instruments, even in their Kings march, is very brisk.

> The *Siameses* have no Art in Singing.

They understand not more than the *Chineses* the diversity of Parts in composition; they understand not the Variety of the Parts; they do all sing Unisons. Their Instruments are not well chose, and it must be thought that those, wherein there appears any knowledge of Musick, have them brought from other parts.

> They have not several parts in their Consorts.

They have very ugly little *Rebecks* or Violins with three strings, which they call *Tro*, and some very shrill Hoboys which they call *Pi*, and the *Spaniards Chirimias*. They play not ill, and accompany them with the noise of certain copper Basons, on each of which a man strikes a blow with a short stick, at certain times* in each measure. These Basons are hung up by a string, each has a Pole laid a-cross upon two upright Forks: the one is called *Schoungschang*, and it is thinner, broader, and of a graver sound than the other, which they call *Cong*.

> Their Instruments: the Rebeck, Hoboy, Basons.
>
> *The Ear guides them, no person beating the Time.

To this they add two sorts of Drum, the *Tlounpounpan*, and the *Tapon*. The wood of the *Tlounpounpan* is about the size of our Timbrels, but it is cover'd with skin on both sides like a true Drum, and on each side of the wood hangs a leaden ball to a string. Besides this the wood of the *Tlounpounpan* is run through with a stick which serves as a handle, by which it is held. They rowl it between their hands like a Chocolate-stick, only that the Chocolate stick is held inverted, and the *Tlounpounpan* strait: and by this motion which I have described, the Leaden Balls which hang down from each side of the *Tlounpounpan*, do strike on each side upon the two Skins.

> The *Tlounpounpan*.

The *Tapon* resembles a Barrel; they carry it before them, hung to the Neck by a Rope; and they beat it on the two Skins with each fist. They have another Instrument composed of Bells[1], which they

> The *Tapon*

---

1. The word *timbre* in this paragraph was left as dots in the translation; however, the *Errata* list at the end of Volume II gives 'Bells'.

call *Patcong*. The Bells are all placed successively every one on a short stick, and planted perpendicular on a demi-circumference of Wood, like to the felleys of a little Wheel of a Coach. He that plays on this Instrument is seated at the center cross-legg'd; and he strikes the Bells with two sticks, one of which he holds in his right hand, and the other in his left. To me it seems that this Instrument had only a fifth redoubled in extent ((Original: n'avoit qu'une quinte redoublée d'étenduë)). but certainly there was not any halfnotes, nor any thing to stop the sound of one Bell, when another was struck.

The Consort which follows the King in his Marches.

The March which they sounded at the entrance of the Kings Ambassadors, was a confused noise with all these Instruments together: The like is sounded in attending on the King of·*Siam*; and this noise, as fantastical and odd as it is, has nothing unpleasant, especially on the River.

Instruments accompanying the Voice.

They sometimes accompany the Voice with two short sticks, which they call *Crab*, and which they strike one against the other; and he that sings thus, is stiled *Tchang cap*. They hire him at Weddings with several of those Instruments I have mentioned. The people do also accompany the Voice in the Evening into the Courts of the Houses, with a kind of Drum called *Tong*. They hold it with the Left hand, and strike it continually with the Right hand. 'Tis an earthen Bottle without a bottom, and which instead thereof is covered with a Skin tyed to the Neck with Ropes.

Trumpets and Drums.

The *Siameses* do extreamly love our Trumpets, theirs are small and harsh, they call them *Tre*; and besides this they have true Drums, which they call *Clong*. But tho' their Drums be lesser than ours, they carry them not hanging upon their Shoulder: They set them upon one of the Skins, and they beat them on the other, themselves sitting cross-leg'd before their Drums. They do also make use of this sort of Drum to accompany the Voice, but they seldom sing with these Drums but to dance.

They have false ones to make a show.

On the day of the first Audience of the King's Ambassadors, there were in the innermost Court of the Palace an hundred Men lying prostrate, some holding for show those ugly little Trumpets which they sounded not, and which I suspect to be of wood, and the others having before them every one a little Drum without beating it.

9 LIONEL WAFER

The date and place of Lionel Wafer's birth and death are un-known; the *Dictionary of National Biography* suggests 1660? -1705? for his dates. When discussing in the *New Voyage* the Cuna Indians' words for numbers, Wafer wrote:

> In my Youth I was well acquainted with the *High-Land*, or primitive *Irish* language; both as it is spoken in the North of *Ireland*, particularly at the *Navan* upon the *Boyne*, and about the town of Virgini((a)) upon *Lough Rammer* in the Barony of *Castle Raghen*, in the County of *Cavan*; and also in the *High-Lands* of *Scotland*, where I have been up and down in several *Places*.

As a result of a gunpowder injury on May 5, 1681, during a crossing of the Isthmus of Darien, Wafer and four companions were with the Cuna Indians there for about four months. They then marched towards the Atlantic, and after a week's journey came to the mouth of the Conceptión River, near which they boarded friendly ships which had come to look for them.

Wafer's *New Voyage* was published in a second edition, with added material, in 1704. It was translated into Dutch and published with a Dutch translation of Dampier's *Voyages* in 1700, and in German with a German translation of Dampier in 1707. Different French trans-lations appeared in 1706 and 1714. It was reprinted for the Hakluyt Society in 1934, edited, with introduction, notes and appendices, by L.E. Elliott Joyce. This has been drawn upon for much of the infor-mation given here, and page references in Elliott Joyce are given for the extracts printed.

In his Preface to the second edition of his book, Wafer defended his account of the Indian way of "conjuring" in these terms:

> ...I think it very convenient to take this Opportunity of vindi-cating my self to the World, concerning some Circumstances in the Relation I have given of the Indian way of Conjuring (called by them Pawawing) and of the White Indians; at which several of the most eminent Men of the Nation seem'd very much startled. But I hope that the Testimony of all the Scotch Gentlemen and others, who have been there since me, will be look'd upon by all good Men, as a sufficient authority to con-firm the Truth of what I have asserted concerning those Mat-ters; since none of them, neither by their Writings, nor other-way, have contradicted me; but, on the contrary, confirmed what I have said in every Article, which has been no small Satisfaction to me.

Lionel Wafer, *A New Voyage and Description of the Isthmus of America* ((i.e., the Isthmus of Darien)), London, 1699

p. 37 ((1934: p. 24))

The next Morning ((in late August or early September, 1681)) we set forward, and in two Days time arrived at the Sea-side ((near the mouth of the Concepción River)), and were met by 40 of the best sort of *Indians* in the Country who congratulated our coming, and welcom'd us to their Houses. They were all in their finest Robes, which are long white Gowns, reaching to their Ancles, with Fringes at the bottom, and in their Hands they had Half Pikes. But of these Things, and such other Particulars as I observed during my Abode in this Country, I shall say more when I come to describe it.

We presently enquired of these *Indians*, when they expected any Ships? They told us they knew not, but would enquire; and there-
fore they sent for one of their Conjurers, who immediately went to work to raise the Devil, to enquire of him at what time a Ship would arrive here; for they are very expert and skilful in their sort of Diabolical Conjurations. We were in the House with them, and they first began to work with making a Partition with Hammocks, that the *Pawawers*, for so they call these Conjurers, might be by themselves. They continued some time at their Exercise, and we could hear them make most hide-ous Yellings and Shreiks; imitating the Voices of all their kind of Birds and Beasts. With their own Noise, they join'd that of several Stones struck together, and of Conch-shells, and of a sorry sort of Drums made of hollow Bamboes, which they beat upon: making a jarring Noise also with Strings fasten'd to the larger Bones of Beasts: And every now and then they would make a dreadful Exclamation, and clattering all of a sudden, would as suddenly make a Pause and a profound Silence....the Oracle...was to this Effect: That the 10th Day from that time there would arrive two Ships; and that in the Morning of the 10th Day we should hear first one Gun, and sometime after that another: That one of us should die soon after; and that going aboard we should lose one of our Guns: All which fell out exactly according to the Prediction.

The Indians fall to Conjuring.

Pawawing.

The Answer made to the Conjuring.

Of the Indian Inhabitants: their Manners, Customs, &c.

p. 167 ((1934:p.99))

The Men make also a sort of Pipes of small hollow Bamboes, and sometimes of a single Reed. They cut Notches in it, and blow it strongly, making a whining Noise, but without any distinct Notes: and they frequently entertain themselves with such Instruments, as they us'd in their *Pawawing*. They will do any thing to make a Noise, which

Their Recreation.

they love much; and they keep every one a Humming at the same time to themselves.

They Hum also when they Dance, which they do many times 30 or 40 in a ring, Men only together. They stretch out their Hands, laying them on one anothers Shoulders. Then they move gently sideways round in the same Circle; and shake all the Joints of their Bodies with a wrigling Antick Gesture, as they move along the Ring.

They pipe and drum often, even at working times; but their dancing they use chiefly when they get together to make merry....A Dancing-bout, if the meeting be large, lasts sometimes a whole Day, seldom less than 5 or 6 Hours; and 'tis usually after having a short drinking Bout: But they dont dance after they have drunk very hard.

Dancing.

10 MICHAEL ANGELO & DENIS DE CARLI

The title-page of the English translation of the account by Michele Angelo and Dionigi Carli of their journey to Congo described them as 'Michael Angelo of Gattina and Denis de Carli of Piacenza, Capuchins, and Apostolick Missioners into the said Kingdom of Congo." The book was first published in Venice in 1674, then in a French translation (Lyons, 1680), in German (Augsburg, 1692) and in English in the first edition of A. and J.Churchill's *A Collection of Voyages and Travels* (1704).

E.G. Cox (*A Reference Guide to the Literature of Travel*, i, 1935, p. 372) noted of the missioners:

> To qualify them for their arduous undertaking they were invested with some extraordinary powers, such as giving plenary indulgence, delivering a soul out of purgatory, wearing secular clothes in case of necessity, and of reading prohibited books, except Machiavelli. The first part of the account was made out of the letters of Angelo, who died in the Congo region, and the rest composed by Denis, who returned home. The account tells of Brazil as well.

Denis de Carli died in Venice in 1695.

Michael Angelo and Denis de Carli, *A Curious and Exact Account of a Voyage to Congo in the years 1666 and 1667,* in A. and J. Churchill, *A Collection of Voyages and Travels*, 4 vols., London, 1704

Vol. I, p. 621

All that follows to the End is writ by F. Denis Carli

Kingdom of Congo

Province of S. Salvador

We set out both of us for our Mission of *Bamba*, where a great Duke subject to the King of *Congo* resided; for in that Kingdom there are five Provinces. The first is that of S. *Salvador*, or S. *Saviour*, where the King of *Congo*, whose name is *D. Alvaro*, resides. It takes name of the capital City call'd S. *Salvador*, which is best seated, and in the wholesomest Air in the Kingdom, built upon a Hill. In it there are scarce any Flys or Gnats, Fleas or Bugs, as there are in the rest of the Kingdom; but it is not free from Ants, which are very troublesom. The King's Palace is almost a League in compass. Formerly it was the only House that was boarded, but the *Portugueses* who have settled there have put the Great Men in the way of adorning and furnishing their

Houses. The Cathedral is built with Stone like those of our *Lady*, S. *Peter* and S. *Anthony* of *Padua*, in which are the Tombs of the Kings of *Congo*. That of the Jesuits dedicated to S. *Ignatius* is not the meanest. Our *Lady* of *Victory* is made of Mud, but whitened both within and without; it was given to the Capuchins by King *Alphonso* the Third. The second Province is that of *Bamba*, where the Great Duke call'd *D. Theodosio* rules. The Third that of *Sondi*, where there is another Duke. The Fourth that of *Pemba*, where a Marquess resides; and the Fifth that of *Songo*, in which there is a Count who has not own'd the King of *Congo* for some Years: He resides in the Town of *Songo*, a League from the River *Zaire*.

Having provided all things necessary, F. *Michael Angelo* and I went aboard, and coasting along the Continent, in two days came to Dante, on the Frontiers of the Kingdom of *Angola*, where the *Portugueses* have a Fort. We went to wait upon the Governour, and show'd him the Letters we brought from the Lords of the Council of *Loanda*, who then govern'd the Kingdom, the Viceroy that was expected not being yet come; they were Letters of Recommendation for him to help us to *Blacks* to carry us and our Goods. During two days we stay'd there, the Governor sent out a fishing, and salted the Fish for us; and among other sorts there were Soles and Pilchards above a Span long. Our Provision being ready, and thirty *Blacks* appointed to carry us and our Equipage, Hammocks were provided for us; the Gentlemen of that City giving us to understand, that it was impossible for us to go afoot, being clad and equipp'd as we were: so that there being no other Remedy, we comply'd with the Custom of the Country.

....

p. 622

The first *Libatte* was pretty large, consisting of about a hundred Cottages, separate from one another, and without any order; It may be said they don't live in them in the daytime, for the Men go abroad a walking, to take their Diversion, to converse together, and play upon certain Instruments, which are wretched and ridiculous enough, till night, being altogether strangers to Melancholy....In this first place we baptiz'd thirty, each of us fifteen, to our great satisfaction, they being the first we had made Christians. I spoke to the *Macolonte* to prepare things to say Mass next day; and immediately he sent out several *Blacks* to cut Wood, and Palm-tree Leaves, wherewith they created a little green Chappel, as was the Altar, I having given them the height, and breadth; and then we furnish'd it, all the Missioners carrying a Chest along with them, containing all things necessary for the Holy Sacrifice. Whilst my Companion said Mass, the *Macolonte* sent notice to other *Blacks* that were at a small distance from thence, who came time

94

enough to hear the second Mass: after which we baptiz'd ten Children
of that neighbouring *Libatte*. There was a great number of People
present, the Chappel having been erected on a rising ground, to the end
they might at least see, if they could not hear the Mass. Next we
catechis'd, dividing the People into two parts, and explaining what we
said to them by the help of an Interpreter.

That done, they fell a playing upon several Instruments, a dancing, and shouting so loud, that they might be heard half a League off. I

A Musical Instrument. will describe but one of their Instruments, which is the most ingenious
and agreeable of them all, and the chief of those in use among them.
They take a piece of a Stake, which they tie and bend like a Bow, and
bind to it fifteen long, dry and empty Gourds, or *Calabashes* of several
sizes, to sound several Notes, with a hole at top, and a lesser hole four
fingers lower, and stop it up half way, covering also that at the top with
a little thin bit of Board, somewhat lifted above the hole. Then they
take a Cord made of the Bark of a Tree, and fastning it to both ends of
the Instrument, hang it about their Neck. To play upon it they use two
Sticks, the ends whereof are cover'd with a bit of Rag, with which they
strike upon those little Boards, and so make the Gourds gather Wind,
which in some manner resembles the sound of an Organ, and makes a
pretty agreeable Harmony, especially when three or four of them play
together.

Drums. They beat their Drums with open hand, and they are made after
this manner: They cut the Trunk of a Tree three quarters of an Ell long,
or more; for when they hang them about their Necks, they reach down
almost to the ground: They hollow it within, and cover it top and
bottom with the Skin of a Tiger, or some other Beast, which makes a
hideous noise when they beat it after their manner.

The Gentlemen or Gentlemens Sons, carry in their hand two
Iron Bells, such as the Cattel among us wear, and strike sometimes the
one, sometimes the other, with a Stick, which is seldom seen among
them, this Instrument being only carry'd by the Sons of Great Men,
who are not very numerous among them.

....

*A Voyage to Congo and several other Countries, chiefly in Southern-
Afric, by Father* Jerom Merolla da Sorrento, *a Capuchin and Apostolick Missioner, in the Year 1682*

....

p. 691

Dominions. The Count's Dominions are very large, and in which are many
Cities call'd *Banze*, one of the principal of which is *Chiova*, but the
greatest of all is the *Banza* of *Songo*, where the Count resides. This

Banza is always govern'd by one of the Count's near Relations or Friends, and who has only the Name of Governor, the rest having only the Title of *Mani*. There are likewise several Territories and Towns subject to these Cities, which are term'd by the Natives *Libattas*.

....

p. 694

The Count's Habit differs according to the several Feasts, and sometimes on other occasions....On the most solemn Days he puts on a shirt of the finest Linen, as likewise yellow or Crimson Silk Stockings, and a Cloak of flower'd Silk, which bears the Name of the *Spring*. When he comes to communicate with us at the Altar, he has a Cloak all white, and which drails along upon the Pavement as he walks. When the Count comes to Church, which is at least three times a week, he has a Velvet Chair and Cushion carry'd before him, being brought himself in a Net on the Shoulders of two Men, each with a Commander's Staff in his hand, one all Silver, and the other only of Ebony tipp'd: The Hat the Count then wears is cover'd first with Taffety, and next with a sort of very fine Feathers: On his Head he generally wears likewise a little silk stitch'd Cap, which can be worn only by him and some few others. Before him marches one Musician above the rest, who has several little round Bells fix'd to an Iron two spans long, wherewith he gingles, and chants to it the Glory and Grandure of his Lord: Besides this there are several other sorts of Musical Instruments made use of at Festivals, the principal whereof are those which in the Country Language have the Name of *Embuchi*, which I mention first because they belong only to Kings, Princes, and others of the Blood-Royal. There are a sort of Trumpets made of the finest Ivory, being hollow'd throughout in divers pieces, and are in all about as long as a Man's Arm; the lower Mouth is sufficient to receive one Hand, which by contracting and dilating of the Fingers forms the Sound; there being no other holes in the Body as in our Flutes or Hautboys. A Concert of these is generally six or four to one Pipe. The *Longa* (which is made of two Iron Bells join'd by a piece of Wire Archwise) is sounded by striking it with a little stick: Both these are carry'd also before Princes, and that especially when they publish their Pleasure to the People, being us'd as the Trumpet is with us. The Instrument most in request us'd by the *Abundi*, being the People of the Kingdom of *Angola. Matamba,* and others, is the *Marimba*; it consists of sixteen *Calabashes* orderly plac'd along the middle between two side-boards join'd together, on a long frame, hanging about a Man's Neck with a Thong. Over the Mouths of the *Calabashes* there are thin sounding slips of red Wood call'd *Tanilla*, a little above a span long, which being beaten with two little sticks, returns a sound from the *Calabashes* of several sizes not unlike an Organ. To

The Counts Habit.

Musick.

make a Concert, four other Instruments are play'd upon by as many Musicians, and if they will have six they add the *Cassuto*, which is a hollow piece of Wood of a lofty tone about a yard long, cover'd with a Board cut like a Ladder, or with cross slits at small distances; and running a stick along, it makes a sound within which passes for a Tenor: The Base to this Concert is the *Quilando*, made of a very large *Calabash*, two spans and a half or three in length, very large at one end, and ending sharp off at the other, like a taper Bottle, and is beaten to answer the *Cassuto*, having Cuts all along like it. This Harmony is grateful at a distance, but harsh and ungrateful near at hand, the beating of so many Sticks causing a great Confusion.

Another Instrument of this Concert is that which the Natives call *Nsambi*, and which is like a little Gittar, but without a head, instead whereof there are five little bows of Iron, which when the Instrument is to be tun'd, are to be let more or less into the Body of it. The Strings of this Instrument are made of the Thread of Palm-Trees: It is play'd on with the Thumbs of each Hand, the Instrument bearing directly upon the Performer's Breast. Tho the Musick of this Instrument be very low, it is nevertheless not ungrateful.

Over and above the great Drums us'd in the Army, there are another sort of a lesser size, call'd *Ncamba*; these are made either of the Fruit of the Tree call'd *Aliconda*, or else of hollow'd Wood with a skin over one end only: They are commonly made use of at unlawful Feasts and Merry-makings, and are beaten upon with the Hands, which nevertheless makes a noise to be heard at a great distance. When the Missioners hear any of these at night, they immediately run to the place in order to disturb the wicked Pastime. It fell often to my lot to interrupt these Hellish Practices, but the People always ran away as soon as ever I came up to them, so that I could never lay hold on any to make an Example of them. The *Giaghi* not only make use of these Drums at Feasts, but likewise at the infernal Sacrifices of Man's Flesh to the Memory of their Relations and Ancestors, as also at the time when they invoke the Devil for their Oracle.

11 a ANTHONY SEPP & ANTHONY BEHME

The original print of Anthony Sepp's letters recounting his and Anthony Böhm's voyage to Paraguay and some of their experiences there has the following title:

RR. PP. Antonii Sepp, und Antonii Böhm, der Societät Jesu Priestern Teutscher Nation, deren der erste aus Tyrol an der Etsch, der ander aus Bayrn gebürtig, Reissbeschreibung wie dieselbe aus Hispanien in Paraquariam kommen. Und kurtzer Bericht der denckwürdigsten Sachen selbiger Landschafft, Völckern, und Arbeitung der sich alldort befindenten PP. Missionariorum, gezogen aus denen durch R. P. Sepp, Soc. Jes. mit aigener Hand geschriebenen Briefen, zu mehrern Nutzen von Gabriel Sepp, von und zu Rechegg, leiblichen Brudern in Druck gegeben. Mit Erlaubnus der Obern, Nürnberg, in Verlegung Joh. Hoffmanns, 1697

Etsch is the river that becomes Adige in Italy. This work had appeared in the previous year in Brixen and Nürnberg. The greatly compressed anonymous English translation in John Churchill's collection seems to be the only version in another language. The party consisted of forty-four missionaries, among whom were natives of Spain, Italy, the Netherlands, Sicily, Sardinia, Genoa, Milan, Rome, Bohemia, Austria "and I a Tyroler, together with my faithful companion Father Anthony Adam Böhm (letter of June 24th. 1962). They sailed from Cadiz on January 17th (St. Anthony's day), 1691, and arrived in Buenos Aires on April 6th. The first letter, "from Buenos Aires on the river Rio de Plata in America", was dated April 15th, Easter Day.

Sepp thus described their arrival (translated from the original print, p. 132):

There was on the morning of today (April 6th) upon the great silver river nothing heard but the cheerful thundering of the cannon-firing, the martial sound of the trumpets, the murmuring of drums and fifes, the lively clamour of the boatmen and fishermen. Nothing else was seen but the flourishing of war-banners, standards and flags, the formations of Spanish Guardsmen, some in companies of horsemen, some of footmen, innumerable Americans with their musical instruments, and Indian women with their small children, two held by the hand and two in the arms.

Though the Jesuits had first begun their missions among the Guarani Indians in 1588, the firm establishment of their system of *reductiones* — mission villages into which the Indians were gathered in populations of a hundred or more families — dates from 1610. The number of *reductiones* by the end of the seventeenth century has been put at thirty, with a total population of at least 100,000.[1] Sepp in 1691 estimated the number of musicians as "easily three thousand" and spoke of twenty-six *reductiones* with a total population of 104,000.[2] In 1767 Charles III of Spain banished the Jesuits from Spain and her dominions; the mission organisation soon fell apart, and the buildings became ruins.

The original print of Sepp's letters has, in the course, of a section in which his daily routine is detailed (*Tag Ordnung der Patrum Missionariorum*, p. 323) this account of its musical part:

...then I go to the musicians and hear their singing. Just now I have eight trebles, six altos, innumerable tenors and six basses. After them I hear the playing of my four trumpeters, eight shawm-players and four cornettists, and I hear their reading. After that I teach the harpists, of whom I have six, the four organists and the one theorbist. Every second day I take the dancers in hand and teach them some dances which we customarily use in stage-pieces, and which were used in Spain in the churches on all the great festivals. With us it is absolutely essential to charm the unbelievers with things of this kind, to win them over with the aid of these external ceremonials of the church, and thus draw them to an internal affection for the Christian religion.

For this reason, on all festivals after Vespers and before High Mass we attire some Indian chaps from among the multitudes in splendid clothes, such as the poor Indians never see in all their days except then in the churches, where everybody assembles to arrange the aforesaid dances. We have these also in public processions, especially on the feast of Corpus Christi, when dancing is done before the Blessed Sacrament, just as David was accustomed to dance before the Ark of the Covenant.

((Original: ...darauff gehe ich zu denen *Musican*ten, höre ihr Gesang, jetzt die *Discanti*sten, deren ich 8. Altisten deren ich sechs. *Tenori*sten ohne Zahl. Bassisten 6. habe, nach dem blasen die 4. Trompetter. 8. Sallmeier. 4. Cornetisten auch ihre *Lection*.

Darauf *instruire* ich die Harpisten deren ich 6. Organisten deren 4. Theorbisten deren ich einen hab. Einen andern Tag nimme ich die Tantzer zu Handen: Lehre sie einige Täntz, wie wir in denen Comedien zu haben pflegen: Und in *Hispania* an alle

1. George Pendle, *A History of Latin America*, London, 1967, p. 59. Details may be found in Etta Becker-Donner and Gustav Otruba, eds., *Zwettler Codex 420 von P. Florian Paucke S. J.*, I, Vienna, 1959, chaps.,III-VI.
2. Original print, p. 265; see p. 107.

hohe Fest in der Kirchen gehalten werden: Hier hochstens vonnöthen, die Unglaubige mit dergleichen Sachen einzunehmen
mit denen äusserlichen Kirchen Geprängen eine innerliche
Affection zur Christlichen Religion ihnen abzugewinnen und
einzudrucken.

Darumben dann wir alle Fest Tag nach der Vesper und vor dem
Hoch-Ambt etliche Indianer Büblein über die messen schön an-
kleiden, dergleichen die arme Indianer ihr Lebtag nie gesehen als
dann in der Kirchen, allwo alle versamlet, gesagte Tänz anstellen.
Diese halten wir auch in denen offentlichen *Processionibus*, und
sonders am Fest *Corporis Christi*, allwo vor dem *Venerabile*
nicht anderst als vor diesem David vor der *Arca* etwelche zu
tantzen pflegen.))

The Swiss-born composer Johann Melchior Gletle (1626-1683),
with whose music Sepp was so desperately anxious to adorn the Vespers, High-Masses and Litanies of the missions, was Kapellmeister of the
Cathedral of Augsburg. His volume of eight masses, plus a motet, which
Sepp put first on his list of requirements, was printed in 1670 in Augsburg with this title:[1]

> Expeditionis musicae Classis III. Missae concertatae a 5 voc. con
> 5 instrum., 5 ripienis, additâ unâ ab 8 et 7 instrum. cum duplici
> Bc. Violone etc. Op. 3. Aug. Vindel. 1670

The Vespers, which contains settings of twenty-eight Vesper psalms,
had been printed two years before, with this title:

> Expeditionis musicae Classis II. Psalmi breves, breviores, brevis-
> simi:...a 5 voc...2 vel 5 instrum. concert. ad lib. et 5 voc. ripien.,
> seu chori pleni, cum duplici Bc...Op. 2. Aug. Vindel. 1668. (2
> V. 1 Va. Fag. 2C. A. T. B. ripieno. Violone = 15 Stb.)

The Litanies, which were *Classis V*, Op. 6. were printed in 1661. The
former of Gletle's two books of motets, which Sepp did not insist upon
but would have accepted if dropped from heaven, began as he noted
with a setting of *O quales cibos*.[2] It consists of nine part-books (Cantus
I and II, Altus, Tenor, Bassus, Violin I and II, "Viola Bass" and Organ),
each book having the title:[3]

> Expeditionis musicae classis I. *Motettae* sacrae concertatae
> XXXVI. XVIII. Vocales tantum absque Instrumentis: XVIII.
> Vocales ac Instrumentales simul: potissimum a 2. 3. 4. 5. cum
> nonnullis à 6: Duabus à 7: et Una à 8: quae ipsae tamen etiam à
> paucioribus concini possunt. Stylo moderno cultius elaboratae

1. As given in Eitner, *Quellen-Lexikon*, from which the title of the Vespers is also taken.
2. Hans Peter Schanzlin, *Johann Melchior Gletles Motetten*, Bern, 1954, p.24.
3. Ibid., p. 22.

ac in lucem datae à Ioanne Melchiore Gletle Bremgartensi, Ecclesiae Cathedralis Augustanae Capellae Magistro. Opus I. ((Part-book title)). Cum facultate Superiorum. Augustae Vindelicorum, sumptibus Authoris, typis Andreae Erfurt. Anno Domini MDCLXVII

The second motet-collection had this title:[1]

Expeditionis musicae classis IV. *Motettae* XXXVI. à Voce Sola. Et 2. potissimum Violinis, saepius necessariis, aliquoties ad libitum: Cum aliis quoque Instrumentis, graviori Harmoniae efficiendae, passim additis. Authore.. ((etc., as in Classis I)). Opus V. ((Part-book title)). Cum facultate ((etc., as in Classis I)). Typis Joannis Schönigkii, Anno Domini MDCLXXVII

Sepp did not in his letters go into his performance plans for the items he anticipated using if his appeal were in fact successful; it appears from his narrative that he did not train bowed stringed-instrument players. The Organ part-book of the first motet collection has the following note: In motets à 6 or 7 which call for several instruments, fewer will suffice, but at least the two violins contained in part-books 6 and 7 must be used; other instruments may be omitted in cases where they are not available, or cannot be employed because of the lack of players. ((Original: Motettis a 6. u. 7. quae pluribus Instrumentis constant, etiam pauciora sufficiunt, soli nimirum Duo Violini 6ta et 7ma Parte contenti; Instrumentis caeteris omissis, sicubi ea non habentur, aut ob paucitatem Musicorum adhiberi nequeunt.))[2] The expression 'II vel V Instrumentis Concert. ad libitum' on the title-page of the Vespers psalms implies that they could be done without instruments.

Gletle also published two volumes of non-sacred music, the former of which had the title:[3]

Musicae genialis latinis-germanico oder newe lateinische und teutsche weltliche musicalische Concert von 1-5 Stimmen, theils ohne Instrumente, theils mit 2V. ad lib. Sampt 2 Sonaten und 36 Trombeterstücklen. Augspurg 1675

A second book was published in 1684. The thirty-six *Trombeterstücklen* were intended for two tromba marinas; twelve of these were reprinted in 1932 in an edition by Willi Schuh. This instrument was used in music of the kind Gletle composed; the *Epinicion marianum* (St. Gall, 1683) by Valentin Molitor (1637-1713) has the note: "Nam Clarinis, 2. Violini. vel etiam Tubae Marinae commodissimé substitui possunt."[4]

---

1. Schanzlin, *op. cit.*, p. 23.
2. As given in Eitner.
3. Ibid., p. 23.
4. Schanzlin, *op. cit.*, p. 134, n. 206a

The "Master Kerll" whose motets Sepp said he did not particularly need was certainly Johann Kaspar Kerll (1627-1693), who was at Munich from 1656 to 1674 and was subsequently organist of St. Stephen's, Vienna. Sepp also referred to a "well known setting of *Laudate pueri*" by Father Ignatius Gletle, apparently brother of Father Paul Gletle, both sons of Johann Melchior. No composition by Ignatius Gletle seems to have survived.

Sepp's account may usefully be supplemented by some paragraphs from *Histoire du Paraguay* by Pierre-François Xavier de Charlevoix (born in St. Quentin in 1682; died in 1761), which was published in Paris in 1756. De Charlevoix had been to the north American missions and to Santo Domingo but not to Paraguay. He based his history of the Jesuit missions there on reports from missionaries in the field.

An Account of a Voyage from Spain to Paraquaria; Performed by the Reverend Fathers, Anthony Sepp and Anthony Behme, both German Jesuits, the first of Tyrol upon the River Elh, the other of Bavaria.... Taken from the letters of the said Anthony Sepp, and publish'd by his own Brother Gabriel Sepp, translated from the High Dutch original, printed at Nurenberg, 1697, in A. and J. Churchill *A Collection of Voyages and Travels,* 4 vols., London, 1704

Vol. IV, Chapter V: *Description of the Cantons or Towns inhabited by the Converted* Indians *in* Paraquaria

p. 658

Their Marriage Agreement consists only in two Articles, *viz.* The Woman promises to fetch what Water the Husband wants, from the River, in lieu of which he engages to furnish the Kitchen with Fuel. We allow them no Musick nor Dancing at their Weddings, but so soon as they are Married, and have heard Mass, the Bridegroom goes his ways, and the Bride hers; and if the Missionary has presented them with a fat Cow, a little Salt, and a few Loaves, they invite the Parents to Dinner, and so make the best Chear they can......

Let us now take a view of the Churches. Each Canton has a very handsome lofty built Church and Steeple, with 4 or 5 Bells; one, and sometimes two Organs, a high Altar, richly gilt, besides two or four Side Altars; a richly guilt Pulpit, divers painted Images, done by the *Indians*, and that tolerably well; Eight, Ten and sometimes more Silver Candlesticks; Three, Four or Five Silver Chalices; Three or Four Pair of Silver Offering-Vessels; Three Silver Crosses, and a large Silver *Ciborium.* The

Sepp
1691

Chalices are not gilt here, but of the natural Colour of Silver, as they use them in *Spain*; all the *Antipendia*, and other Ornaments belonging both to the Altar and the Priest's Vestments, are as Rich and neatly kept as any in *Europe*.

Every *Saturday* we Sing the Litany of our Lady, and every *Sunday* a Sermon, and high Mass, when our Musicians entertain the Congregation with their Musick, which they begin to perform tolerably well.

I don't question but that several of our Friends, such as Father *Glette* ((*sic*)), and my two Brothers *Paul* and *Gabriel Sepp*, when they hear you read this Passage will be apt to ask you, who it is that Composes these Psalms, Litanies, Hymns and Masses; who is it that has taught the *Indians* to Sing, who to play on the Organs, and to sound the Trumpets and Hautboys? Unto which I answer, that the same Missionaries, who taught these poor Wretches the Rudiments of the Christian Religion, to say Our Father, to bake Bread, to Paint, cast Bells, Organs and Trumpets, and to make Clock-works; the same I say have instructed them in Musick; which was first introduced here by some *Netherland* Fathers, who with incredible Labour taught these indocible People to Sing, and composed certain Pieces, not according to Art, but such as their natural Inclination led them to: The same was improved afterwards, by a certain *Spanish* Missionary, but after the old way, without a Base, without Measure; of Double, or Triple Notes, they know not the least; nay, even not the *Spaniards* themselves to this Day, as I observed whilst I was at *Cadiz* and *Sevil*. Thus I saw my self obliged to begin with them, quite after another and new Method, and to teach, old Gray Hair'd Fellows, the *Ut, Re, Mi, Sol, La* again. By which means I have (tho' with incredible Labour) instructed Six Trumpets (of whom each Canton has Four), Four Organists, Three Theorbists, Thirty Hautboys, and Fifty Voices (besides other Instruments) to Play and Sing most of my Compositions; which has got me such a Reputation with the other Missionaries, that they send continually to me some of their Flocks, with Presents of Hony, Preserves, and Fruit, to court my Friendship, and to have them instructed in Musick; and, to Speak without Vanity, has purchased me the singular Esteem of the *Indians*.

Upon this occasion I can't but intreat you dear Fathers *Ignatius* and *Paul*, and other Friends who have been formerly my School-fellows, to have pity of a poor Missionary at so vast a distance, and of so many Musicians under my Care; to send me over some Mission Pieces, which I desire should be no other than the *Vespere, Missae, Breves, Breviores, Brevissimae*, as also the *Litany* of the Composition of Mr. Melchior Glettle, Director of the Mission in the Cathedral of *Augsburg*; and these I don't desire to be new ones, but others tho' half torn will serve my Purpose as well; for I intend to have them copy'd by the

Indians, which they do very well, and with great exactness, all the
Books we send to the other Cantons being transcrib'd by them.

In requital of this Kindness, I will oblige my self and sixty
Missionaries besides, that we will say sixty Masses for him, who will be
at the charge of Buying them, and twenty more for him who will take
the trouble to send them, tho' as to the refunding of the Mony there is
no great difficulty; for what ever is laid out upon this Account is
therein fully repaid by our Father *Procurator* here to the Father *Procurator* at *Munichen*; which had I known it before I left *Germany*, I
would have provided my self with several Things in *Germany* for my
and the other Missionaries use, which will stand us in great stead now in
Paraquaria, and would not have amounted to above 10 or 15 Crowns
there; a slender Addition to the Sum of 80000 Crowns bestowed upon
that Mission, whereof I was an unworthy Member....

....

p. 661

A Missionary in these Parts, must submit to all Functions, the
Indians being so Stupid, that they are not capable of undertaking the
most frivolous Thing, without a plain Direction. Whence it came that it
was a Question among the first Missionaries sent hither, Whether these
People were capable of receiving the Sacrament or not.

But as Stupid as they are at Inventing, so happy they are in
imitating, provided you give them a Model; thus if you shew one of
these *Indian* Women a Piece of Bone-Lace, she will unrip some part of it
with a Needle, and will make another after it, with so much exactness,
that you shall not know one from the other. We have two Organs, one
brought from *Europe*, the other made here so exactly, after the First,
that I my self could scarce discern the difference. I have a *Missal* Printed at *Antorff*, which is imitated in Writing by an *Indian*, with that
nicety, that they are scarce distinguishable. We have Trumpets and
Watches made here, not inferiour to those of *Nurenburgh* and *Augs-
burgh*, and some Pictures, excellently well Copy'd. ((Original: Die
Trompetten sind auch denen Nürnbergischen gantz gleich: die Uhren
geben dem weltberühmtisten Augspurgerinnen nichts nach: etliche Ge-
mählde scheinen *Rubens* zu seyn.)) In short they will imitate any thing
very nicely, provided thay have the Model constantly before their Eyes,
without which they cannot advance one Step, their Intellects being so
Stupid, that they can't form to themselves in the least any Idea of a
Thing, unless it be before them.

Paragraphs 3 to 6 of the foregoing appear to correspond to the
following twelve paragraphs of the original, beginning at page 251:

Alle Samstag haben wir ein gesungenes Hohe Ambt von U.L. Frauen und Litaney. Alle Sonntag Hoh-Ambt und Predigt: so pflegen mir meine Musicanten alle Tag unter der heiligen Mess zu *musiciren*, so sie, GOTT sey gedancket, nunmehr nicht gar übel machen. Es wird mich mein *Reverentissim. & amantiss. P. Ignatius, P. Paulus Glettle,*[1] und alle andere *Patres & Magistri Musici, quos omnes in Domino amplector, & peccatori meo abstringo: vere omnium amicus & in Christo JESU servus infimus, quibus has literas velut cuilibet seorsim scriptas communicari unice desidero, ut me in hac parte adjuvare possint, ubi desideria & preces meas ex his intellexerint: supplico enim non meo solum sed & omnium pauperculorum musicorum Indorum nomine, qui si ex omnibus Reductionibus in unum computantur, facile tria millia constituunt.*

Es werden, sage ich diese *Reverendi Patres* und Herren Brüder, *Paul* und *Gabriel Sepp*, fragen: wann sie so viel Aembter Litaneyen, Vesperen und Messen halten, wer *componi*rt ihnen dann die *Psalmos, Litanias, Hymnos, offertoria?* wer die Messen und so viel Motteten? und wer hat diese Indianer singen gelernet? wer die Orgel schlagen? wer die *Cornett* blasen und Schallmeyen, Fagott, &c. *Reverendi Patres*, wer diese Arme Verlassne hat das Christliche Leben gelehret, wer das Heilige Vatter Unser beten, wer Brod bachen, Kleider machen, kochen, mahlen, Glocken Giesen, Orgel, Cornet, Schallmeyen, Trompeten, *Harpan*, und was noch mehr, wer sie hat gelehrt rechte Schlag-Uhren samt den viertel und gantzen Stunden zu machen, dieser hat sie auch die *Musicam* und alle andere Künsten und *Opificia* und Handwerken gelernt, nemlich die erste *Patres Missionariis*, unsere Heil. Vor-Eltern, und sonders etlich Niederländische *Patres*, deren Gedächtnuss, Mühe und Arbeit allhier annoch *in Benedictione est*. Diese, sag ich, hatte die Indianer singen gelehret mit höchster Müh und Arbeit: dann wie es ihre *Compositiones* geben, seynd die keine *Musici ex professo* gewesen, haben nur was weniges in der Phanthasen gehabt, und dieses wenige, was sie gewust, mit höchster Mühe und Arbeit denen Indianern so offt vorgesungen, biss sie es endlichen in ihren harten Schedel hineingebracht, und sie noch bis heutigen Tag *per traditionem* alle Männer und Weiber diese in der Kirch an Sonntägen alle *choro pleno* singen. Nach diesem kame ein Spanischer *Pater*, der was mehrers verstunde, brachte diese Kunst noch weiters fort: *componi*rte *Missas, Vesperas, Offertoria, Litanias,*[2] aber alles dieses aus dem alten Testament und Arca Noe her: so doch neu seyn muss, weilen wir nichts anders und bessers haben. Kein eintzige Mess oder Psalm hatte einen Orgel-Bass, so *utique* das Fundament: sondern an statt des Sing-Bass blasen sie den

1. Orig.: *Glettee*
2. Orig.: *Litanais*

Fagott, welcher in etwas das Fundament ersetzet. Weilen im Sing-Bass, als in einer Stimm bissweilen Pausen sich einfinden: schweiget der Fagott auch, und müssen die arme Indianer ohne Bass und Fundament fortsingen, welches zweiffels ohne nicht gut in denen Ohren lauten kan. Und dieser Ursachen schlagen die Indianer zu keiner Mess oder Psalm das *acompangamento*, nemlichen sie haben keines; und wann sie schon eins hatten, müssen sie es erst lernen.

O wie wünschte ich jetzt einige *Instruction* von denen *Reverendis Patribus Glettle*, Seidner, und andern genommen zu haben. Es hat mir *Rvdus*[1]*P.* Christoph Brunner, er wird gewiss schon gestorben seyn zu Alten Dettingen vor meiner Abreiss einen *modum Componendi*, auff 2. *Octav*-Blädlein kurtz zusammen geschrieben, wann ich diesen nit hätte, wäre es aus mit mir, bediente mich also dessen und fangte an zu *componi*ren ein Mess à 14. *Vesperas; zweyerley: de confessore & Beatissima Virgine.* item à 14. zwey kurtz Litaneyen à 16. Ich muss die Warheit bekennen: der liebe Gott hilffet mir augenscheinlich, es wäre nicht müglich in einen Jahr eine so bitere, schwehre Sprach zu lernen, in der ich doch das andere Monat nach meiner Ankunfft schon Kinderlehr gehalten, alle *Sacramenta*, ausgenommen das Beichthören, *administri*ret, nicht müglich wäre es, neben andern oben angezognen *Spiritualibus* und *temporalibus Negotiis*: auch noch so viel tausend Noten abschreiben, geschweigen *componi*ren, doch, Gott sey gedanckt, hab ich dieses gethan. Der Herr Vatter *Melchior*, Gott tröste seine Seel, hat in der Mess und Vesper tapffer herhalten müssen, dann weilen ich diese fast auswendig gekennt, und die *Species* gleich in meiner Ankunft noch frisch waren, fallte mir bald da, bald dort ein Vers ein, jetzt aus dieser Mess das Amen. Jetzt das *Sanctus*, jetzt das *qui tollis &c*, ebnermassen bald aus den *Brevibus*, bald aus den *Brevioribus*, jetzt aus den *Brevissimis*. Die gröste Mühe ware, alles in ein Thon zu bringen, unter so viel Stimmen auszutheilen, erwarte auf diesen ein Antwort. O werthiste, allerliebste Ehrwürdige *Patres*! *P. Ignati, P. Paule*, und alle andere, sie erbarmen sich doch eines armen verlassenen, *olim* unwürdigen Mitbruder, *Connovitii, Condiscipuli*, jetzt aber in der eussersten Welt unter denen wilden Heyden wohnenden, biss auf blutigen Schweiss arbeitenden *Missionarii*, sie erbarmen sich doch umb Christi Jesu willen meiner und meiner armen so viel tausend Musicanten, schicken mir, begehre keine andere *Autores*, nur alleinig die *Missas, Vesperas Breves, Breviores, Brevissimas*, und auch um Mariae lieb, die *Litanias* ihres Herrn Vattern, Herrn Capellmeister der Thumkirchen zu Augspurg Herr Melchior *Glettle*. Die *Motteten*, deren die erste *arcc. O quales cibos*, traue ich mir nicht zu begehren, doch solte ich sie empfangen, wäre es mir

---

1. Orig.: *Rudus.*

eben, als brächte sie ein Engel von Himmel in *Paraquariam*. Aber hier werden sie mir gleich sagen: Mein lieber *Pater Antoni*, wir von grund unsers Hetzens wolten sie gern überschicken; aber wer zahlet uns diese. Erstlich *obligire* ich mich, und 6. andere *Patres Missionarii*, 60. heilige Messen zu lesen, für jenen, er seye geistlich oder weltlich, der die Unkosten machen wird. Für den *Pater* aber, der sie mir schicket, umb seine Mühwaltung 20.

Zum 2. begehre ich nicht, dass diese neu; sie mögen alt und zerrissen, verschmutzt seyn wie sie wollen wann sie nur noch leselich, dann die Indianer-*Musicant*en schreiben schon schön Noten, ich sage nicht als Auspurger, sondern Antorffer Truck, und müssen wir ohne das diese Bücher für so viel *Reductiones* für ein jede abschreiben lassen, so hier gar kein *difficultaet*.

Es sagt mir wiederum einer, wohin muss ich aber dieses Paquet *dirigi*ren, dass es *in Paraquariam* gewiss komme, ich sag, es ist zu *Genua*, oder Rom, so ist es schon *in Paraquaria*, liget wenig daran, lang oder kurtz, nacher Rom dem *Patri Procuratori* auffgegeben, wäre es am besten. Dieser gebe es dem *Procuratori Paraquariae*, so jetzt nacher Rom geschickt wird, oder ist keiner alldorten, dem *Procuratori Indiarum*, so allzeit zu Rom sich auffhaltet.

Oder noch besser, wann ein *Pater* aus der *Provinz* sollte mit dieser *Mission in Paraquariam* geschickt werden, nimmet er dieses mit sich und bringet es nacher *Genuam*: hat er es schon *in Paraquaria*, biss hieher in die *Reductiones* der Indier kommet alles zu Wasser, und kostet keinen Heller. Sollte, sag ich, ein oder zwey *Patres* hieher geschickt werden, alles wäre sehr leicht auch wegen der Bezahlung: ja sie kunten noch mehrer dergleichen ihren und allen hiesigen *Patribus Missionariis*, die mich wegen der *Music* also plagen, liebes und Gutes erweisen, noch einem oder den andern *Authorem* mit sich bringen. Mit der Bezahlung, sage ich, wär es leicht: auff diese Weiss, dem *Patri Procuratori* zu München wird alles *refundirt* von dieser Provintz, er gebe wenig oder viel aus für einen *Patre*. Welches wann ichs gewust hätte, da ich annoch mich in der Provintz befunden, und zugleich auch gewust hätte, dass in *Paraquaria* dergleichen Sachen so hoch vonnöthen, und alle höchstens verlangten, hätte ich gleich zu München viel Sachen eingekaufft für *Paraquaria*, und mit mir getragen, mit dem ich gewisslich das gröste Werck dieser Provintz und allen *Missionariis* erwiesen. Gestalten was wäre *Paraquariae* daran gelegen wann es 10. oder 15. Reichsthaler mehrer, und zwar wegen einer so nothwendiger Sach, ausgeben hätte? über die 80. tausend die ohne dessen diese *Mission*, mit der ich gekommen, gekostet.

Es sagt mir aber der *Pater*, so *in Paraquariam* geschicket wird: Es seye zu München der Tax schon geschlagen, was man einem gebe biss auf Genua. Freulich, die Reiss belangend, aber nicht, was ihm nothwendig vonnöthen, welches, wann ers in Teutschland kauffen kan fur *Paraquaria*, ist es besser, er kauffe es alldorten, als in Hispania siebenmal so theur, oder aus Abgang muss ers gar gerahten.

Genug hat mich mein *Procurator* dessentwegen gefiltzet, und muss ichs auf heutigen Tag noch hören, dass ich so gar keinen eintzigen *Auctorem Musicor.* mit mir gebracht: indeme er doch alles gerne würde der Teutschen Provintz gut gemachet haben. Dieses das sie die *Reverend. Patres Procuratores* zu München und *Super.* glauben, solte ihnen genug seyn zur Prob, was ich sagen will.

Also wird die *Music* gesetzet hier *in Paraquaria*: dass der *Procurator* so mit uns gekommen, eine Orgel in Niederland gekauffet für *Bonos Aëres* um tausend Thaler, so er doch nicht gesehen, ob das Werck gut oder böss, ja so gar noch nicht *in Paraquariam* gekommen. *Item*, kauffte er mir allerhand *instrumenta Musica in Hispania*, so erschröcklich theuer, und dannoch nichts nutz seyn, *respective* der Teuschen, als ein Spinet, *Clavicordium*, *Trompa Marina*, Schallmeyen, so alles er gar gern bezahlet.

Jam Reverendi in Christo Patres, nihil amplius super est, quam egeno & pauperculo suo Patri Antonio in hoc tam desiderato negotio succurrere per Christi & Magnae Matris amorem negraventur: obstringent certe non me solum, neque tot Patres Missionarios, sed tot Indorum millia maximo hoc beneficio, quod hae viginti sex Reductiones animas DEO & Ecclesiae Romanae mancipatas, Orco ereptas in hunc diem vivas numerant, centum nempe & 4. millia. O veniant petitae Litaniae per Magnae Matris amorem! Veniant Missae: & dictae Vesperae! adjungantur dictae Mottetae: Et tandem Mottetae Domini Kerll, ubi est cantio illa: plorate ululate Christo sepulto voce sola non indigeo. Quia hae cantantur in Lingua Hispanica, & non Latina: veniant, inquam, omnia ista, & ne per terrestre vel maritimum iter patiantur aliquid: componantur in cistula lignea, &c.

Die *Musici* haben meine Feder ein wenig aufgehalten, aber alles dieses, Gott weiss, wie ichs vonnöthen, sollte ich diese guldene Bücher bekommen: Als Herr *Glettle* auch *in America flori*ren müsste, nicht anderst, als ich ihme in Europa allezeit höchstens geschätzet, auch der Ursachen, weilen er mich einer unseglichen Mühe und Arbeit, so ich in *componi*ren habe, entheben würde. Was mich kostet die Indianer in unser Europaeischen Music zu *instrui*ren, ist dem lieben Gott allein bekannt. Alle *Missionarii*, der eine von da, der andere von dorten, auch über die hundert Meil weit, schicket mir seine Musicanten, dass ich sie unterweise in dieser Kunst, welche ihnen gantz neu, und von der alten Spannischen, so sie annoch haben, wie Tag und Nacht voneinander geschieden. Sie wusten nicht um unsere *Mensur*, *Statuta* oder *Tact*, nichts um die unterschiedliche Trippel, nichts umb die Zieffer 76. 43.

&c. Die Spannier auch noch biss heutigen[1] Tag, wie ich zu *Sevilia* und *Gadiz* gesehen, haben keine Faselen, noch doppelte *Noten*, weit minder dreyfache. Ihre *Noten* seynd alle weiss, Gantze, halbe und *Coral-Noten*, nemlichen uhralte *Music*, dergleichen *Scarteke*n die *Corregent* gantze Kästen voll in der teutschen Provinz haben, und zum Einbinden neuer *Auctores* tauglich seyn. Muss also mit diesen meinen gestandnen, barte-ten Eissgrauen Capell-Buben von der *Scala Musica, Ut, Re, Mi, Fa, Sol, La*, gantz auf ein neues anfangen[2], so ich wegen der Liebe Gottes gar gerne thue.

  Dieses Jahr hab ich schon *instru*irt, und gleichsam zu so viel Meister gemacht. Sechs Trompetter, unterschiedlicher *Reduction*, ein jedes Dorff hat 4. Trompetter, drey gute Tiorbisten, 4. Organisten. Zeigte diesen noch kein *partitur*, weilen dieses ihnen noch zu schwehr, sondern nur gewisse *Arien, Praeambula* und *Fuga*: O wie so schwehr kommt mich dieses an. Schallmeyer 30., Cornetisten[3] 18., Fagotisten 10. hab ich dieses Jahr so weit gebracht, dass sie alle meine *Composi-tiones* blasen und singen können. *Discanti*sten habe ich schon unter-wiesen über 50. so nicht üble Stimmen, in meiner *Reduction* hab ich 8. Indianer-Büblein, setzte ihnen das so berühmte *laudate Pueri, ab CC. R. P. Ignatii Glettle*, so ich fast auswendig gekönnt, auf das Papier, lehret sie solches, singen es mit solchen *Garbo* und Manier, dass es von diesen armen, nackenden, unschuldigen Indianer-Büblein in *Europa*, kaum wird geklaubt werden, alle *Patres Missionariis* seynd voll der Freuden, dancken dem höchsten Gott, dass er einmal, nach so langen Jahren, einigen Mann geschickt, der die *Music* auch in einigen guten stand brächte: Zur Danckbarkeit schicket mir der eine da, der ander dort ein Fässlein Hönig, Zucker, *Americani*sche Frücht zu. In was für Ehr mich die Indianer halten, wie sie mich lieben, wil die geistliche Geschämig-keit der Federn zu schreiben nit Erlaubnuss geben. Bin alles höchstun-würdig, der grösseste Sünder, unmitzeste Knecht aller Diener in Christo.

TRANSLATION

  Every Saturday we have a sung High Mass of Our Blessed Lady and Litany, every Sunday High Mass and Sermon. My musicians are so accustomed to providing music for me every day during High Mass that, God be praised, they now do so not at all badly.

  I wish particularly to ask my most Reverend and most beloved Fathers Ignatius Glettle and Paul Glettle, and all the other Fathers and

1. Orig.: heuntigen
2. Orig.: aufangen
3. Orig.: Corretisten

Music-Masters, all of whom I embrace in the Lord, and bind with my sin — I who am truly a friend of them all and in Christ Jesus their lowly servant — to whom the contents of this letter, as well as any other particular writings, are communicated, that they may find it possible to help me in this matter, in which they understand my wishes and my prayers from these letters. What I ask is not only for myself, but is asked also in the name of all the impoverished Indian musicians, who if those from all our communities are counted together easily amount to three thousand persons.

It may be, I say, that these Reverend Fathers the brothers Paul and Gabriel Sepp will ask, that if so many services of Litanies, Vespers and Masses take place, then who composes for them the Psalms, Litanies, Hymns and Offertories? Who composes the Masses and so many Motets? Who has taught these Indians to sing, to play the organ, to blow the trumpet and shawms, the bassoon, and so on? Reverend Fathers, those who taught these poor forsaken people to live the Christian life, to say the Lord's Prayer, to bake bread, to make clothes, to cook, to mill, to cast bells, to make an organ, a cornett, shawms, trumpets, harps and many more such things, and to make accurate clocks which chime the quarter-hours and all the hours, they have also taught them music and every other art, artifice and craft. I mean the first missionary fathers. our saintly forerunners, particularly certain Netherlands fathers, whose trouble and toil are here still kept in blessed remembrance. These, I say, have with the greatest trouble and toil taught the Indians to sing. As concerns their compositions, these were not the products of professional musicians, but they had only the few they had improvised, and the few that they wished to teach the Indians they sang to them, with the greatest trouble and toil, so often that they were finally driven into those hard skulls, and still to the present day, through oral transmission, every man and woman in church on Sundays sings them all in full choral sound. After them came a Spanish father, who had more understanding of the art and advanced it farther; he composed Masses, Vespers, Offertories and Litanies, though all in a style as ancient as the Old Testament or Noah's Ark — still, they must be regarded as new so long as we have nothing else better. Not a single Mass or Psalm has an Organ continuo, and therefore obviously lacks its foundation. Instead of the sung bass-part they play this on the bassoon, which to some extent takes the place of the continuo foundation. But where rests appear in the bass singing-part, as in any voice-part, the bassoon ceases to sound, and the poor Indians must go on singing without the bass-foundation, which doubtless cannot sound well in their ears. These are the reasons why the Indians do not play accompanying continuo parts in any Mass or Psalm, simply because they have none, and if they did possess some they would first have to learn them.

O how I wish now that I had taken some instruction from those Reverend Fathers Glettle, Seidner and others! The Reverend Father Cristoph Brunner, who certainly must be dead by now, did in Old Dettingen before my departure write down on two octavo pages a short summary of a method of composing — if I did not have this it would be all over with me — so I made use of this and began to compose a Mass for fourteen parts, Vespers of two kinds (for a Confessor and for the Blessed Virgin Mary) also for fourteen parts, and short Litanies for sixteen parts. I must confess to the truth, that the dear God obviously helped me, for it would not otherwise be possible to learn in one year a language so harsh and difficult, in which only the second month after my arrival I held children's classes and administered all the sacraments except the hearing of Confession — this would not have been possible, in addition to other spiritual and temporal business already mentioned, and in addition to copying so many thousands of notes, let alone composing them: nevertheless, God be thanked, I have done these things. Herr Melchior ((Glettle)) the father, God rest his soul, must have suffered severely during our Mass and Vespers, since although I have known his settings almost by heart, and their style was still fresh in my mind right at my arrival, a Verse came into my mind only occasionally, now here, now there, now the Amen of one Mass, now the *Sanctus* of another, now a *qui tollis*, and so on, and similarly these were sometimes from the short settings, other times from the shorter, or from the very short ones. The greatest trouble was to bring them all into the same key, and to distribute the music among so many voices — and about this I am still waiting for the answer. O most worthy, exquisite and venerable Fathers, Father Ignatius, Father Paul and all the others! Take pity on a poor, forsaken, unworthy former co-brother, co-novice and co-disciple, now living however in the uttermost part of the world, amongst these savage heathens, a missionary working so hard as to be in a state of bloody sweat, take pity, if it be the will of Christ Jesus, on me and on my so many thousand poor musicians, and send me — for I desire the music of no other composers — solely and only the Masses, short, shorter and very short Vespers, and also, for the love of Mary, the Litanies of your father, the choirmaster of the Cathedral Church of Augsburg, Herr Melchior Glettle. The motets, the first of which has the text *O quales cibos*, I dare say I do not require, though I should accept them if they were brought to me, as if an angel from heaven should bring them to Paraguay. But at this point those Fathers could simply just say to me: my dear Father Anthony, from the depth of our hurried lives we will with pleasure send these things over, but who will pay us for them? In the first place (I answer), I undertake, as do six other missionary fathers, to say sixty holy Masses for each person, be he priest or layman, who shall defray those costs. But for the father who should send them to me, we would say twenty Masses for his trouble.

In the second place, I do not require that these books of music be new; they may be old and torn, they may be as dirty as you wish so long as they are readable, since the Indian musicians already write beautiful notes — I don't say as good as those of Augsburg printers, but as good as those of Andorf, and not having books for so many communities we must have one copied for each, but about this at any rate there is no difficulty.

Again, some other person may say to me, but where must I send this parcel so that it gets safely to Paraguay? I say, send it either to Genoa, or to Rome, and that way it is already in Paraguay, or will get there after more or less delay, though it would be best to deliver it to the Father Administrator in Rome. He would give it to the Administrator of Paraguay, who just now has been sent to Rome, or if he is not there to the Administrator of the Indies, who is constantly staying in Rome.

Or better still, if a father from the Province should be sent out to the Mission in Paraguay, he could take it with him and bring it to Genoa; he has then already got it to Paraguay, since everything comes by water to this point in the Indian communities, and does not cost a cent. Should it happen, I say, that one or two fathers are sent here, everything would be very easy also in the matter of payment; indeed they could bring with them still more things of the same kind by one composer or another, and thus show their charity and goodness to all those missionary fathers hereabouts who bother me so much about music. As to the payment, I say, it would be easy, and could be done in this way: the Father Administrator at Munich would refund the full amount from this Province, for he pays out that much, more or less, to any one father. If I had been aware of this payment problem, when I was still there in the Province, and if I had known at the same time that there was such acute need in Paraguay for things of this kind, and that they were so ardently desired, I would have bought right there in Munich many things for Paraguay, and brought with me things with which I certainly could demonstrate how very important is the work being done in this Province by all its missionaries. What would it matter if for Paraguay's sake, and to provide something so essential, there should be spent ten or fifteen thalers, over and above the eighty thousand thalers which this Mission to which I belong has otherwise cost?

But the father who is being sent to Paraguay might say to me: it may be that the cost of what one takes to Genoa would have to be paid in advance at Munich. Yes, this is true, if it is something that relates to his travel, but not if it is something absolutely necessary for his work here, and something which he can buy in Germany to bring to Paraguay, so that it is better to buy it right there, since in Spain it is seven times dearer, and to buy it at the time of departure must be quite advantageous.

My Administrator has already been niggardly enough to me, and must I at this stage still be told that I did not even bring with me the music of a single composer, since then all the expense would willingly have been made good by the German Province? If this is what the Reverend Father Administrators at Munich and the Superiors believe, what I am now going to say will be proof enough for them.

This is how our music was provided for here in Paraguay: the Administrator who came with us bought in the Netherlands an organ for Buenos Aires for a thousand thalers, but he did not look to see whether the workmanship was good or bad, and even so it has not yet arrived in Paraguay. He also bought for me in Spain various musical instruments, all of which he willingly paid for, although they were frightfully expensive and even then not so useful compared to such German instruments as a spinet, clavichord, tromba marina or shawm.

Now, Reverend Fathers in Christ, nothing more remains that may prevent you from helping, for the love of Christ and his great Mother, your needy and impoverished Father Anthony in this so desired business. It is certainly not myself only, nor so many father missionaries, who are concerned with this very great favour, but so many thousands of Indians, for these twenty-six communities number truly one hundred and four thousand souls, rescued for God and the Roman Church, snatched from the mouth of hell, and alive at this day. O may the Litany-prayers come to us, for the love of our great Mother! May the Masses come, and the aforementioned Vespers! And may there be added the aforementioned Motets! The motets of Master Kerll, however, which include a setting of *Plorate, ululate Christo sepulto* for solo voice, I do not require, because they are sung with Spanish text and not with Latin text. May all these come, I say, and lest they should suffer any damage on their land or sea journey, let them be packed in a wooden chest, &c.

The musicians have somewhat detained my pen, so may I receive all these things — God knows how much I need them — which are contained in those golden books. It is right that Herr Glettle should flourish in America also, exactly as in Europe, where I have always treasured him most highly, and also for the good reason that this would relieve me of the unspeakable trouble and work which composing entails for me. What it has cost me to instruct the Indians in our European music is known to the dear God alone. All the missionaries, one here, another there, for a hundred miles around, send me their musicians so that I may instruct them in this art, which seems to them a completely new one, as different as day is from night from the way of the old

Spanish teachers which they still retain. They know nothing about time-signatures or a regular beat, nor about the different triple metres, nor about such indications as 7-6 or 4-3 in figured bass. The Spaniards, as I observed in Seville and Cadiz, even to this day have no solmisation and no quarter-notes — much less triplets. Their notation is all in white notes — whole notes, half-notes and plainsong note-forms, to wit, very ancient music, in worthless old books like those that the choir-directors in the German Province have whole chests-full, and which are useful only for binding the work of more recent composers. This is why I have to begin from the beginning with my bearded, hoary choir-chaps the musical scale *ut, re, mi, fa, sol, la,* which I quite willingly do for the love of God.

This year I have already instructed, and so to speak formed into so many masters, the following: six trumpeters for various communities (each village has four trumpeters); three good theorbo-players; four organists (these of course do not play continuo parts from the score, since this is still too difficult for them, but they play only certain arias, preludes and fugues - and O dear, with what difficulty have I got them to this point!); thirty shawm-players, eighteen cornettists, ten bassoonists. I have brought these this year to the point where they can play and sing all my compositions. Also I have already this year trained more than fifty treble-part singers, whose voices are not at all bad, and in my own community I have eight Indian choir-members. For them I have set down on paper the well-known setting of *Laudate pueri* by the Reverend Ignatius Glettle, which I knew almost by heart, and they have learnt it so well and sing it with such panache and style — this would hardly be believed in Europe of these poor, ill-clad, innocent Indian chaps — that all the missionary fathers are delighted and thank the highest God that He has at last, after so many years, sent one man who has brought music into such a good situation. In their gratitude they send me, one from here and another from there, a jar of honey, or sugar, or American fruit. How much the Indians hold me in honour, and how much they love me, the clerical modesty of my pen will not allow me to write, since I am the least worthy, the most sinful and the most negligible wretch among all workers together in Christ.

11b. PIERRE FRANÇOIS–XAVIER DE CHARLEVOIX

R. P. Pierre François-Xavier de Charlevoix, de la Compagnie de Jésus, *Histoire du Paraguay*, 3 vols., Paris, 1756

Vol. I, p. 257 ((in margin: 1610))

De la Musi-
que.

      On a pu comprendre, par ce que j'ai dit du goût naturel qu'ont ces Indiens pour la Musique, que les Missionaires ne pouvoient pas manquer d'en profiter, pour engager les Infideles, que la curiosité ou quelqu'autre sujet conduisoit dans les Réductions, à se faire Chrétiens, & ceux qui l'étoient déja, à s'affectionner au Service divin. C'est pour cela qu'on a mis en chant toute la Doctrine Chrétienne, & on s'en est bien trouvé. Un goût même si décidé suppose, ou indique de grandes dispositions; & c'est encore ce qui a déterminé à établir dans chaque Bourgade une Ecole de Plain-chant & de Musique. On y apprend à toucher toutes sortes d'instrumens, dont l'usage est permis dans les Eglises; & on a été étonné de voir que sur la simple inspection de ceux qu'on avoit fait venir d'Espagne, ils ont appris d'eux-mêmes à les faire dans la perfection, & qu'il leur a très peu coûté pour les savoir toucher comme les Maîtres. Ils ont appris à chanter sur les notes les Airs les plus difficiles, & on seroit presque tenté de croire qu'ils chantent par instinct comme les Oiseaux. Mais ces Musiciens, en inspirant aux autres de la dévotion, en paroissent eux-mêmes pénétrés; ce qui prouve encore qu'ils ne font pas de grands efforts d'application, & que comme l'effet naturel de la Musique est de réveiller les sentiments que chacun a dans le coeur, elle ne trouve en eux, ni dans ceux qui les entendent, rien qui ne les porte à la piété. Ces Musiciens sont vêtus, quand ils chantent à l'Eglise, aussi-bien que ceux qui servent à l'Autel, d'une maniere très propre & fort décente.

Des Fêtes so-
lemnelles.

      Les Fêtes solemnelles sont célébrées avec le plus grand appareil, surtout celle du Titulaire de l'Eglise, & celle du S. Sacrement. On envoie faire, pour la premiere, des invitations dans les Bourgades les plus proches, & il s'y fait un grand concours. Les Officiers y viennent à cheval, revêtus de leur Uniforme; & la Fête commence la veille par une très belle marche, où l'Alferez, qui porte le grand Etendart, est monté sur un Coursier très bien enharnaché, & sous un magnifique baldaquin. Après qu'on a traversé en bon ordre les principales rues au son des Tambours & des autres instrumens de guerre, on se rend à la grande porte de l'Eglise, où l'on met pied à terre, & l'Alferez va prendre la place qui lui est préparée dans une chapelle. On chante alors les premieres Vêpres, après lesquelles on fait danser les Enfants dans la grande Place, où tout le monde est rangé avec beaucoup d'ordre. Cela fait, la Cavalerie retourne à l'endroit où elle avoit commencé sa marche, & le soir on allume des feux de distance en distance, & toutes les rues sont illuminées. Le lendemain on va à la grand'Messe, de la même maniere qu'on étoit allée aux premieres Vêpres. A midi on régale les Etrangers, & on donne à tout le monde un coup de vin. Au sortir des secondes Vêpres, où tout se passe comme aux premieres, il y a une course de bague: les Missionaires y assistent avec tous les Chefs & les Officiers, pour y tenir tout le monde en respect, distribuer les prix aux Vainqueurs, & donner le signal de la retraite.

Mais rien n'est comparable à la Procession du S. Sacrement; & l'on peut dire que, sans richesse & sans magnificence, elle forme un spectacle qui ne le cede en rien à tout ce qu'on voit ailleurs de plus riche & de plus magnifique. D. Antoine de Ulloa nous apprend en général qu'on y voit de fort belles danses, & beaucoup au-dessus de celles qui se font dans la Province de Quito: que les Danseurs ont des habits fort propres, & que la pompe en égale celle des plus grandes Villes: mais qu'on y remarque plus de décence & plus de dévotion.[1] J'ai dit qu'on n'y voïoit rien de précieux: mais toutes les beautés de la simple nature y sont ménagées avec une variété qui la représente dans tout son lustre. Elle y est même, si j'ose ainsi parler, toute vivante; car sur les fleurs & les branches d'Arbres, qui composent les Arcs de triomphe sous lesquels le S. Sacrement passe, on voit voltiger des Oiseaux de toutes couleurs, qui sont attachés par les pattes à des fils si longs, qu'ils paroissent avec toute leur liberté, & être venus d'eux-mêmes pour mêler leur gazouillement au chant des Musiciens & de tout le Peuple, & bénir à leur maniere celui, dont la Providence ne leur manque jamais.

De la Procession du Sacrement.

Toutes les rues sont tapissées de Stores bien travaillés, & séparés par des guirlandes, des festons & des tapis de verdure dans une très belle symmétrie. D'espace en espace on voit des Lions & des Tigres bien enchaînés, afin qu'ils ne troublent point la Fête, & de très beaux Poissons qui se jouent dans de grands bassins remplis d'eau. En un mot toutes les especes de Créatures vivantes y assistent, comme par députation, pour y rendre hommage à l'Homme-Dieu dans son auguste Sacrement, & reconnoître le souverain domaine que son Pere lui a donné sur

1. The reference is to Jorge Juan y Antonio de Ulloa, *Relacion Histórica del Viage a la America Meridional*, 4 vols., (Madrid, 1748). Samuel Claro, in "La musica en las misiones Jesuitas de Moxos", Universidad de Chile, Instituto de Investigaciones Musicales, Colleccion de Ensayos No. 17, Santiago de Chile, 1969, p. 22, n. 47, quotes the following passage (from Vol. III, Book I, Chap. XV, p. 233): "Las Iglesias tienen su Capilla de Musica, compuesta de crecido numero de Instrumentos de todas especies, y de Cantores: celebrase en ellas el Culto Divino con la pompa, y seriedad, que en las Cathedrales; y del mismo modo se hacen las Processiones publicas; entre las quales se particulariza la del *Corpus*, à que acompañan el Governador, Alcaldes, y Regidores con las galas reservadas para tales Dias, y las Milicias en cuerpo de Tropa, quedando para alumbrar la demàs gente, que toda và con buen orden, y mucha reverencia. Disponense para ella Danzas muy lucidas..."

toutes les Créatures vivantes. Partout où la Procession passe, la terre est couverte de nattes & jonchée de fleurs & d'herbes odoriférantes. Tous, jusqu'aux petits Enfants, travaillent à cette décoration, dans laquelle on fait aussi entrer les chairs des Animaux nouvellement tués, toutes les choses dont on se régale dans les grandes réjouissances, les prémices de toutes les récoltes, pour les offrir au Seigneur, & les grains qu'on doit semer, afin qu'il y donne sa bénédiction. Le chant des Oiseaux, le rugissement des Lions, le frémissement des Tigres, les voix des Musiciens, le Plain-chant du Choeur, tout s'y fait entendre sans confusion, & forme un concert, qui est unique.

....

p. 350

((Among a party of forty-two Jesuit missionaries who arrived in Paraguay in 1628 were two French priests, Nicholas Henard from the diocese of Toul, who had been a page to Henry IV, and Noel Berthold from Lyons, whose name was changed by the Spaniards to Emmanuel Alvarez. A letter from Berthold is paraphrased in the following paragraph.))

Dans une de ces Lettres, qu'il écrivit en débarquant, il dit que l'on remarquoit déja une grande différence entre les Indiens des Réductions & les autres; que ceux-ci lui parurent des Bêtes plutôt que des Hommes, & que ceux-là n'avoient absolument plus rien de barbare, pas même dans les manieres; qu'il fut fort étonné d'en entendre un qui lisoit au Réfectoire du Collége, pendant la table, en Espagnol & en Latin, aussi-bien que s'il eût parfaitement entendu ces deux Langues, & que dans les Fêtes qu'ils donnerent à l'occasion de leur arrivée, ils exécuterent des Ballets avec une Musique à deux choeurs dans le bon goût de France; que c'étoit un Frere Jésuite, François de Nation, qui avoit été leur premier Maître, & que comme une des choses qui avoient le plus contribué à réunir & à fixer ces Indiens, étoit le Chant & la Musique, on disoit que ce bon Frere avec son Violon avoit rendu à cette Eglise autant de services que bien des Missionaires; que ces nouveaux Chrétiens couroient après lui comme après leur Orphée, & que ce fut ce qui acheva de déterminer les Fondateurs de la République Chrétienne des Guaranis à leur faire apprendre la Musique, & à jouer de toutes sortes d'instrumens; enfin, que les Infideles, lorsqu'ils les entendoient chanter & jouer des instrumens, & qu'ils les voïoient peindre, demeuroient de quatre heures entieres immobiles & comme en extase.

TRANSLATION

It will be understood, from what I have said earlier about the natural taste these Indians have for music, that the missionaries could not fail to take advantage of this to persuade the uncoverted, who were led by curiosity or some other motive to visit the *reductiones*, to become Christians, and to cause those who were already converted to acquire a love of the divine service. It was for this reason that the whole of Christian doctrine was set for singing, and this was found to be well worth while. So decided a talent as this presupposes or indicates great predisposition, and this led to the decision to establish in each village a school of plain-chant and music. The pupils learned to play all the kinds of instruments whose use is permitted in church, and it was astonishing to observe that simply by inspecting the instruments which had been sent from Spain they learned by themselves to make them to perfection, and that it took very little effort for them to acquire the ability to play them like masters. They learned also to sing the most difficult tunes from notation, and one was almost tempted to believe that they sang instinctively as birds do. But these musicians, in inspiring devotion in others, seemed themselves to be permeated with it, which proves again that they did not have to make great efforts of application, and that since the natural effect of music is to lay bare the feelings which each one of us has in his heart, it aroused nothing in them, nor in those who listened to them, which did not lead them to piety. These musicians are robed, when they sing in church, as well as those who serve at the altar, in a very fitting and highly seemly manner.

The festivals of first rank are celebrated with the greatest ceremonial, above all that of the patron saint of the church, and that of Corpus Christi. For the former occasion invitations are sent to the nearest villages, and there is a great assembly. The army officers come on horseback, decked out in their uniform, and the festival begins on the evening before, with a very splendid procession, in which the *Alferez*, who carries the great standard, is mounted on a finely caparisoned charger, under a magnificent canopy. After proceeding in good order through the principal streets, to the sound of drums and other warlike instruments, they arrive at the great door of the church, where they dismount, and the *Alferez* goes to take the place prepared for him in a chapel. First Vespers are then sung, after which it is arranged that the children dance in the great square, where all the people are gathered in good order. This done, the cavalry returns to the place where it had begun the procession, and in the evening fires are lit at a certain distance from each other, and all the streets are illuminated. On the next day the procession goes to High Mass in the same fashion as it went to First Vespers. At midday strangers are greeted, and everyone is given a cup of wine. At the end of Second Vespers, where everything is done in the same way as at First Vespers, there is running at a ring. The missionaries attend, as do all the chiefs and the officers, in order to impress on everyone the dignity of the occasion, to distribute the prizes to the winners, and to give the signal for dispersal.

But nothing can compare with the Corpus Christi procession. It can be said that this, although lacking both wealth and magnificence, nevertheless makes a spectacle which is in no way inferior to anything one may see elsewhere, be it the richest and the most magnificent. Don Antonio de Ulloa has informed us in a general way what very beautiful dances can be seen there ((i.e., in Paraguay)), which are much superior to those done in the Province of Quito; that the dancers wear highly decorative clothes, and that the pomp involved equals that seen in the greatest towns, except that here one notices more propriety and more devotion. I have said that there is nothing very precious to be seen; nevertheless, all the beauties of simple nature are deployed with a variety which shows it off in all its lustre. Nature herself, if I may dare to speak so, is altogether alive. For on the flowers and on the branches of trees which make up the triumphal arches under which the Blessed Sacrament is carried one may see flying here and there birds of every colour, which are attached by their feet to threads so long that they seem to have their full liberty, and to have come of their own accord in order to mingle their chirping with the singing of the musicians and of all the people, and in order to bless in their way him whose Providence never fails them.

All the streets are carpeted with well worked tapestries, separated, in a beautiful symmetry, by garlands, strewn leaves and carpets of greenery. At intervals one sees lions and tigers, securely chained so that they do not disturb the festivities, and very beautiful fish disporting in large bowls full of water. In a word, all kinds of living creatures are present as though forming a deputation, in order to pay homage to God made man in his revered Sacrament, and to recognise the sovereign power which his Father has given him over all living creatures. Everywhere the procession passes the ground is covered with straw mats and strewn with flowers and aromatic herbs. Everyone, down to the smallest child, works at this decoration, which also includes the flesh of newly killed animals, all those things with which people enjoy themselves at great rejoicings, the first fruits of all the harvests, in order to offer them to the Lord, and the seeds which are to be sown, in order that he may give them his blessing. The song of the birds, the roaring of the lions, the growling of the tigers, the voices of the musicians, the plainsong of the choir — all this can be heard without confusion, and makes a unique concert.

p. 350

In one of these letters, written on disembarkation, he says that a great difference was remarked upon already between the Indians of the *Reductiones* and other Indians. The latter seemed to be beasts rather than men, and the former retained nothing of their former barbarity, not even in their manners. It was most astonishing to hear one of them read in the refectory of the college during a meal, in Spanish and in Latin, just as well as if he had perfectly understood those two languages. At the festivities they held on the occasion of the arrival of the missionaries they performed ballets with music for two choirs in the best French manner. There was a Jesuit brother named François de Nation who had been their first teacher. Since one of the things which had contributed most to unite and stabilise these Indians was singing and music, it was said that this brother with his violin had performed as good service to this church as many missionaries combined. These new Christians ran after him as after their Orpheus, and it was this that decided the founders of the Christian Republic of the Guaranis to have them taught music and playing all kinds of instruments. It was also said that the unconverted, when they heard the singing and the playing of instruments, and when they saw pictures being painted, remained for four hours on end motionless and as though in ecstasy.

12 JEAN CHARDIN

Le Chevallier Jean Chardin (Sir John Chardin), born in France in 1643, was a Huguenot who had a remarkable career and died near London in 1715. Sent by his father when he was twenty-five to the East to engage in the diamond trade, he returned to Paris in 1670 and left again for the East in the following year. In 1681 he went to London and ten days later was knighted by Charles II, who sent him to the Netherlands in a diplomatic capacity. In his *Journal du voyage du Chevalier Chardin au Perse et aux Indes Orientales*, published in Amsterdam in 1686, he announced his intention of publishing three further volumes. The last of these, which was to have contained a history of Persia and his diaries of the years 1675-7, did not appear. The 1711 three-volume *Voyages*, from which these extracts are taken, comprised the other two of the projected volumes and the 1686 volume with additions. An English translation of the 1686 publication (described as 'The First Volume') was printed in London in the same year.

Voyages de monsieur le chevalier Chardin, en Perse, et autres lieux de l'orient, 3 vols., Amsterdam, 1711

Vol. I, p. 133

Il y a une habitation de Missionaires Capucins à *Tifflis*, comme je l'ai dit. Le Préfet des Missions, que cet Ordre a en *Georgie,* & de celles qu'elle espere d'y avoir, & dans les païs circonvoisins, y fait sa résidence. Il y a treize ans qu'on les envoya de *Rome....*

....

p. 134

Il vint d'abord\beaucoup de peuple à leur Eglise de *Tifflis*, attirez par la nouveauté du service, & d'une petite musique de quatre ou cinq voix,, mélées avec un luth & une épinette; à présent, il n'y vient plus que cinq ou six pauvres gens, à qui ces Missionaires font gagner quelque chose....

....

p. 142

((At Tiflis the Prince invited M. Chardin to the marriage of his niece at the Palace))
....Lors qu'on commença les santez, les Instrumens commencérent de sonner. Ils étoient mêlez de voix. Le concert en plaisoit beaucoup à l'assemblée. Elle en paroissoit ravie: pour moi, je n'y trouvois rien

d'agréable, il me sembloit au contraire rude & malconcerté. Le Prince qui s'en divertissoit fort, & en qui la gayeté operoit, fit dire au Préfet de faire apporter son épinette. Lui & son compagnon penserent enrager de la fantaisie du Prince. Ma présence étoit la principale cause de leur déplaisir, parce qu'ils apprehendoient, que je ne fisse une rélation desadvantageuse pour eux, de la lâche complaisance qu'ils avoient témoigné en cette rencontre, & qu'un Préfet des Missions se fût prostitué jusqu'à faire le métier d'un violon devant un Prince Mahometan, dans une assemblée d'Infidéles & d'Héretiques, de Clercs & de Séculiers, qu'on pouvoit appeller, en l'état où le vin les avoit mis, une troupe d'yvrognes. Quand l'Epinette eut été apportée, on la posa sur un carreau au milieu de la sale. Le Préfet fut obligé d'en jouer; & le Prince lui ayant fait dire de chanter & de jouer tout ensemble, il se mit à chanter le *Magnificat*, le *Te Deum*, le *Tantum ergo;* & puis des chansons, & des airs de Cour, en Italien, & en Espagnol, parce que l'air des hymnes ne réjouïssoit pas assez le Prince. L'épinette étoit fort mal accordée. Le Préfet en jouoit par dépit, & étant tout blanc, & tout cassé d'âge, & de fatigues, on peut juger que son concert étoit un fort méchant divertissement. Il fit pourtant celui du Prince pendant deux heures. Durant ce tems-là, le premier Maître d'hôtel, qui étoit Mahometan de naissance, s'approcha de moi & me demanda, si l'usage des instrumens étoit permis en nôtre Religion? Je lui dis qu'il l'étoit. Il me repliqua, que la créance Mahometane le défendoit bien expressément. Nous eûmes un entretien de demie heure sur ce sujet, dans lequel ce Seigneur me confirma ce que j'avois apris il y a long-tems, que les Instrumens de Musique sont défendus par Mahomet; & qu'encore que l'usage en soit universel dans toute la Perse, il ne laisse pas d'être illicite. Il me dit encore, que les Instrumens étoient sur tout prohibez dans la Religion, n'y ayant que la voix de l'homme avec laquelle Dieu vouloit être loué. Durant cet entretien un Evêque Georgien se mit à discourir sur le même sujet avec le Pere *Raphaël* ((Raphaël of Parma, the Prince's doctor)). Je ne sai pas tout ce qui y fut dit, car je n'entendois pas leur langage, & ce Pere ne me le voulut pas expliquer. Il me dit seulement, que cet Evêque se scandalisoit de voir le Préfet divertir l'assemblée en un festin, de la même sorte dont il prétendoit louër Dieu à l'Eglise. Le Pere *Raphaël* ajoûta, qu'il avoit un sensible déplaisir de l'autorité que le Viceroi avoit prise sur eux, d'obliger leur Préfet à joüer du lut, & à chanter par tout où il lui en prénoit envie; mais que leur sureté dépendoit si entiérement de ses bonnes graces, qu'ils n'osoient presque lui refuser aucune chose. Nous nous retirâmes à minuit......

.....

p.221 ((At Isfahan))
Lors que quelque Grand traitte le Roi, il l'invite seul, lui laissant le choix de la Compagnie qu'il veut avoir. Le Roi se rend sur les huit ou

neuf heures du matin au Palais où il est invité, qui est meublé le plus somptueusement qu'il se peut. Dès qu'il y est entré, l'Hôte lui fait un présent qui est toûjours fort considerable. La salle où le Roi est introduit se trouve couverte d'une magnifique collation de confitures seches & liquides, de biscuits & de masse-pains, de sorbets, & de toutes sortes de liqueurs, aigres & douces. On met devant sa personne, & devant les principaux Seigneurs qu'il a amenez, de grandes & riches cassolettes, qui brûlent jusqu'à tant qu'on en soit entêté, & qu'on les fasse emporter. Cependant les Musiciens, & les Danseuses de la Cour, sont dans un lieu proche, attendant que le Roi en veuille prendre le divertissement. Les Musiciens du Roi sont toûjours, non seulement les plus habiles du Royaume à chanter & à toucher des instrumens, mais ce sont aussi d'ordinaire les meilleurs Poëtes du païs. Ils chantent leurs propres piéces, comme on le disoit d'*Homere* & des autres Poëtes Grecs de son tems. Elles sont, pour la plûpart, à la loüange du Roi, & sur plusieurs actions de sa vie, que la flatterie est ingenieuse à exalter quelque dignes de blame ou d'oubli qu'elles soient. Les chansons rouloient ce jour-là sur la rehabilitation du premier Ministre, si j'ose me servir de ce mot. J'en vis une toute pleine de pointes assez fines & assez spirituelles. Le refrain des couplets étoit:

    Lui à l'écart, tous les hommes ont paru égaux. Le Soleil cher-
    choit au ciel sans succès un autre astre, pour être l'astre Polaire.

Allusion ingenieuse au titre d'*Ivon medary*, qu'on donne au premier Ministre, qui signifie *le Pole de la Perse*....

    ....

Vol. II : *Contenant une Description générale de l'Empire de PERSE: & les Descriptions particulieres des Sciences & des Arts, qui y sont en usage; du Gouvernement Politique, Militaire, & Civil, qui s'y observe; & de la Religion que l'on y exerce.*
Section : *La Description générale de la PERSE*

    ....

Chapter XII : *Des Exercises & des Jeux des Persans.*

    ....

p.43

    La *Lutte* est l'exercice des gens de moindre condition, & presque seulement des gens de néant. On appelle le lieu où l'on montre *à lutter Zour Koue ((sic))*, c'est-à-dire *la maison de la force*. Il y en a en toutes les maisons des grands Seigneurs, & particulierement des Gouverneurs de Provinces, pour exercer leur monde. Chaque ville a de plus sa troupe de *Lutteurs* pour le spectacle. On appelle les *Lutteurs, Pehelvon*, mot qui veut dire *brave, intrepide*. Ils font leurs *Exercices* pour divertir;

car c'est un spectacle, comme je l'ai dit, & voici comme ils les font. Ils se mettent nuds, avec des chausses seulement, faites de cuir fort justes, huilées et grasses, & un linge à la ceinture aussi gras & huilé. C'est afin que l'adversaire y ait moins de prise, & qu'il ne prenne pas par les habits, parce que s'il y touchoit sa main deviendroit glissante, & perdroit de sa force. Les deux *Lutteurs* étant en présence sur l'arene unie, un petit *tambour* qui joüe toûjours durant la *lutte* pour animer, donne le signal. Ils commencent par se faire mille bravades en Rodomonts: puis ils se promettent bonne guerre, & se donnent les mains. Cela fait, ils se frapent les fesses, les cuisses, & les hanches, à la cadance du *tabourin*: puis ils se redonnent les mains & se refrapent comme auparavant trois fois de suite. C'est-là comme pour les Dames, & pour se mettre en haleine: après cela, ils se joignent en faisant un grand cri, & s'efforçant de renverser leur homme. Il faut, pour être victorieux, l'étendre tout plat en terre sur le ventre tout de son long, autrement c'est n'avoir rien fait.

....

Section: *La Description des Sciences & des Arts liberaux des Persans.*

....

Chapter VII: *De la Musique.*
p.113
LE mot de *Musique* est *Mousiki* en *Persan*, tout comme en *Grec*, & les *Persans* connoissent la *Musique*, comme vous voyez, non seulement entant que partie de la *Mathematique*, qui considere les *nombres sonores*, mais aussi comme *Art liberal*, qui enseigne à manier sa *voix*, & à *toucher des instrumens* avec *régle* & *mesure*. Ils ont divers Auteurs qui en ont traité, entre'autres un *Abou Aloufa*, fils de *Sahid*, dont j'ai apporté le livre avec moi, qui traite de la *Musique*, pour le *chant*, & pour les *instrumens*, dont on joüe avec la bouche & les doigts, qui est la *division* que l'Auteur en fait; mais à mon grand regret je n'y entends rien, ayant manqué de lire le livre sur les lieux, avec quelqu'un qui m'en fît entendre le sens. C'est un petit Ouvrage, qui n'est que de quelques trois heures de lecture. Ce que j'y découvre seulement est que les *Persans* ont *neuf tons*, qu'ils ont des *tablatures* pour le *chant* & pour les *instrumens*, beaucoup plus amples que nous n'en avons, & qu'ils apprennent cet Art par une *methode*, qui a bien des *régles*, & de bien grandes, & de bien embrouillées, à ce qui me semble. J'en ai donné cinq exemples en la planche suivante. Les figures qui sont marquées *A.B.C*, sont des premieres du livre, & par consequent les plus simples. Il y en a trente-neuf de la façon d'*A.B.C*, & avec des explications dont je n'entens point les termes: celle qui est marquée *C*, est suivie de trente-cinq autres figures, aussi dans la même *methode*: & celle marquée *D*, est

suivie de treize, dont la penultiéme est un *cercle* une fois plus grand, avec quarante-quatre points dans le tour, dont huit sont rouges. J'ai pensé que les gens Savans en l'*Art* de la *Musique* pourroient juger par les seules figures, quelle est la methode *Persane* pour cette Theorie, en attendant ce que j'en pourrai découvrir avec le tems, s'il plaît à Dieu que j'aye quelque jour le loisir d'y étudier. Outre ces *Tablatures* il y en a de faites en échiquier, dont les plus grandes sont divisées en trois cens six *compartimens*, les uns marquez de *Notes*, les autres blancs. Je trouve en un endroit de ce Traité que L'Auteur dit, *que la Musique est une ville qui a quarante-deux quartiers, chacun de trente-deux ruës*, & à la fin du livre il y a une grande *Table* en figure de *Globe*, divisé en *quatre cercles*, coupez par *quarante lignes*, ce qui fait *cent soixante Notes*. Leurs *Notes* de *Musique* ne sont pas des *syllabes* sans sens & sans signification, mais ce sont, ou des noms de *villes* du Païs, ou des noms des *parties du corps humain*, ou des plus ordinaires choses de la *nature*; & quand ils enseignent cet *Art*, ils disent pour marquer les *modes, allez de cette ville à celle-là*, ou, *allez du doigt au coude*: les noms des *quarante-huit tons divers*, sont les noms de *ville*, à cause, disent-ils, que ces divers *tons* sont affectez & particuliers en ces *villes*. Ainsi il y a, comme il me semble, beaucoup d'embarras & de confusion dans leur *Theorie*; cela vient sans doute de ce que la *Musique* est peu en usage chez eux; car autrement ils la réduiroient en une *methode* plus courte & plus facile. Leurs habiles & doctes *Musiciens* sont tous aux gages du Roi, & ils n'excédent pas le nombre de dix à douze à ce qu'on m'a assure. J'ai donné dans la même Figure joignante un petit *Air Persan* sur lequel on jugera aussi de la nature de leurs petits *Airs*. En voici les autres paroles.

Celle qui tient mon coeur m'a dit languissamment,
pourquoi étes vous morne & défait?
Quelles levres de sucre vous ont mis dans leurs chaînes?
J'ai pris un miroir, je le lui ai presenté,
En disant, qui est cette beauté qui resplendit dans ce miroir?
La langueur de vôtre teint est l'ambre qui tire la paille.
Pourquoi vos yeux brûlent-ils ce que vos appas attirent?
Maudit soit ce compagnon qui se pâme si vîte.
Apportez des fleurs odoriferantes, pour faire revenir le
coeur à mon Roi.

Leur *Chant* est clair, ferme & gai, comme on represente le *Chant Dorien*: ils aiment les *voix fortes* & *hautes*, le *fredon* & les *grands roulemens*: ils disent que pour bien chanter il faut faire rire & pleurer par l'harmonie de la voix. *Perdeh* est le terme *Persan* qui signifie *Air de Chanson*, & ils distinguent les *Airs* par des noms de leurs anciens Rois, & par des noms de Provinces. Ils n'ont pas de *Chants à parties*, mais il font *chanter* les *bonnes voix* l'une après l'autre. On *chante* d'ordinaire chez eux avec le *Luth* & la *Viole*: les hommes ont les plus belles *voix*;

mais il n'y en a gueres qui sachent bien *chanter* par la raison que le *Chant*, comme la *Danse*, passent pour deshonnêtes en *Perse*; l'un & l'autre sont des Arts qu'on ne fait point apprendre à ses enfans, mais qui sont releguez parmi les femmes prostituées & les Baladins; de maniere que c'est une indécence parmi eux que de *chanter*, & que l'on se rendroit méprisable en le faisant. Cependant le peuple a une telle pente au *chant*, qu'en plusieurs professions, ils *chantent* tout le jour quoi que fort lentement, pour s'animer & s'exciter. Il ne faut pas s'étonner après cela, que la *Musique* ne soit pas plus débrouillée, & pas plus courte chez eux. Les *Persans*, comme les *Arabes*, appellent les *Chanteurs Kayné*, mot qu'on dit qui vient de Caïn, parce qu'on prétend en *Orient* que les filles de *Caïn* inventerent le *Chant* & la *Musique*.

Leurs *Instrumens* de *Musique* sont en grand nombre. Ils ont premierement la *Timbale*, & le *Tabourin*, dont le fonds est de cuivre ou de laton; après ils ont le *Tambour de basque*, dont ils *joüent* fort adroitement, & une sorte de *Tabourin* long, qu'ils portent attaché à la ceinture sur le devant, incliné de côté, dont ils touchent les deux bouts avec les mains, une main à un bout une à l'autre. Ils ont des *Timbales* de trois pieds de diametre, & si pesantes que même un chameau ne les peut porter, ils les font trainer sur des charrettes: on diroit d'un muid coupé en deux. Après cela ils ont des *Cornets droits*, qui leur servent de *Cors* & de *Trompettes*, qui sont proportionnez à ces *Timbales*, & qui sont de merveilleusement grands *Instrumens*: les moindres sont plus longs qu'un homme n'est haut. Il y en a de sept à huit pieds, faits de cuivre ou de laton, d'une grosseur inégale, car le fust est fort étroit à un pied de l'embouchure, d'où il s'élargit vers l'embouchure jusques à deux pouces de diametre, mais le bas est large de près de deux pieds. Le *Joüeur* de cet *Instrument* a peine à le tenir élevé, & il plie sous le faix; l'on en entend le bruit fort loin, qui est rude tout seul & sourd, mais mêlé avec d'autres *Instrumens*, il fait assez bien, servant de *Basse*. Ceux qui en sonnent le remuent continuellement pour varier les sons ou pour se délasser. Outre ces *Cors*, où l'on mettroit aisément la tête, ils en ont d'autres, faits les uns comme des *Cors de chasse*, d'autres comme des *Clairons*. Ils ont après cela le *Hautbois*, la *Flute*, le *Fifre*, le *Flageolet*, mais il s'en faut beaucoup, qu'ils n'en *joüent* avec tant d'*harmonie* qu'on fait chez nous. Ensuite ils ont les *Instrumens à corde*, *Rebec*, *Harpe*, *Epinette*, *Guitarre*, *Tetracorde*, *Violon*, & une maniere de *Poche*; le *Tamboura*, qui est une *Coucourde* ou *Callebasse* au bout d'un manche, dont ils se servent comme de *Luth*, & un autre *Instrument* qu'ils appellent *Kenkeré*, dont vous voyez la figure dans la planche joignante marquée F, telle qu'elle est dans mon Livre de *Musique Persan*. Vous observerez, que les cordes de leurs *Instrumens* ne sont pas des *cordes à boyau*, comme aux nôtres, à cause que chez eux c'est une impureté legale de toucher aux parties mortes des animaux: leurs *cordes d'Instru-*

mens sont, ou de *soye cruë retorse*, ou de *fil d'archal*. Ils ont après cela cette sorte d'*Instrumens*, que le Pere *Mersenne*, dans son Livre de *Sons*, appelle *Cymbale*, qui sont deux *bassins* de *laton* en *timbre* dont on *joüe* en les frappant l'un contre l'autre, & d'ordinaire c'est en les tenant élevez au dessus de la tête, & les remuant de tous côtez. Les Danseuses mettent à la main des *Os*, dont elles se servent, comme les *Bohemiennes* font des *Castagnettes*, qui rendent un *son* clair & fort: je pense que les *Castagnettes* ont été faites sur ces *Os*—là. Les Chanteurs en animant les Danseuses s'en servent aussi, & ils savent pareillement faire *claquer* leurs doigts si fort, qu'on diroit qu'ils ont des *Os*, ou des *Castagnettes* à la main. Ils font une maniére de *Carillon*, avec des porcelaines, ou des coupes d'airain, de diverses grandeurs, rangées par ordre, sur lesquelles on *touche* avec deux petits bâtons, longs & menus; cela fait une *harmonie* plus agréable que le *Carillon* d'Horloge, & beaucoup plus agitée.

Il en est en *Orient* des *Instrumens* de même que de la *Musique* : c'est aussi une indécence d'en *joüer*, & d'apprendre à en *joüer*, & même c'est pire; car la Religion en proscrit l'usage: les Ecclesiastiques & les gens dévots ne les veulent pas seulement entendre, & c'est la cause que l'*Art* n'en est pas poli ni avancé comme en nos Païs. Les *Joüeurs d'Instrumens* sont pauvres en *Perse*, & mal habillez: il n'y a que ceux que le Roi entretient, qui meritent d'être écoutez. La Bande en est assez bonne, on l'appelle les *Tchalchi bachi,* comme qui diroit, *La Troupe capitale des Joüeurs d'Instrumens & Chanteurs*; les autres ne savent pas grand' chose, comme je l'ai observé. Ils vont joüer dans les maisons pour ce qu'on veut leur donner; & lors que le Roi donne quelque grand emploi à un Seigneur, ou lors qu'on circoncit publiquement un enfant dans quelque grande maison, ils vont joüer à la porte, pour avoir quelque chose.

La *Danse* en *Perse* est encore plus deshonnête, & plus contraire à la Religion que le *Chant*, & que les *Instrumens*, car elle est même tout-à-fait infame, & ne s'exerce que par les femmes protituées, & les plus publiques. C'est comme parmi les *Romains*, qui souffroient cet *Art* dans les personnes dévouées à la Turpitude, mais qui le condamnoient dans les autres. Ainsi les hommes ne *dansent* point; il n'y a que les femmes, mais quand les femmes *dansent,* il y a toûjours quelques hommes auprès de la principale Actrice, l'animant de son *chant*, & quelquefois de ses gestes. La *Danse Persane*, comme par tout l'*Orient*, est une représentation: il y des endroits Comiques & enjoüez, & il y en a d'autres en plus grand nombre graves & recueuillis: les Passions y sont représentées dans toute leur force, mais ce qu'il y a de détestable, sont les *postures* lascives & deshonnêtes à voir, les jouissances & les impuissances dont ces représentations sont pleines, & où ils réussissent d'une maniere fort opposée à la vertu; car il ne se peut rien concevoir de plus touchant. Une *danse* dure quelquefois trois à quatre heures sans finir; l'*Heroïne* en fait seule les principaux actes, les autres au nombre de quatre à cinq se joignent à elle de tems en tems. D'ordinaire après la *danse*, les Femmes & les *Musiciens*, se mettent à faire les *sauts perilleux*. Ces gens-là ne représentent point dans un lieu exprès pour le public, comme nos *Comediens*, mais on les fait venir chez soi, & outre le présent de celui qui les mande, c'est la coûtume qu'à la fin de la *danse*, une vieille qui est comme la Mere de la bande, ou la principale actrice, va tendre la main à tous ceux de l'assemblée pour avoir quelque chose. Comme ces filles gagnent bien plus à se prostituer qu'à *danser*, elles s'éforcent de toucher les gens, & elles sont fort aises, qu'on leur donne assignation, ou qu'on les tire dans un cabinet, chose qui a le même air parmi ces peuples-là que chez nous de se lever de table, & d'aller au Buffet boire un coup de vin, quand on est en débauche.

TRANSLATION

Travels of Sir John Chardin in Persia and other places in the Orient.

(I.133) There is a house of Cistercian missionaries at Tiflis, as I have said. The Prefect of the missions that this order has and hopes to have in Georgia and the surrounding countries resides here. They were sent from Rome thirteen years ago....

(I.134) At first many people came to their church at Tiflis, attracted by the novelty of the service and of the small-scale music for four or five voices mingled with a lute and a spinet; at present only five or six poor people come who have gained something from the missionaries.

(I.142)...As soon as the toasts began the instrumentalists began to play. Voices were mingled with them. The ensemble gave much pleasure to those present, who seemed enraptured by it; as for me, I found nothing agreeable about it; on the contrary it seemed to me rough and ill synchronised. The Prince, who enjoyed it very much, in an access of gaiety sent word to the Prefect to have his spinet brought. He and his companions seemed enraged at the Prince's fancy. My presence was the chief cause of their displeasure, because they were afraid that I would tell the story to their disadvantage, of the slack compliance they exhibited at this encounter, and of how a Prefect of Missions had prostituted himself so far as to play the fiddler before a Mohhamadan Prince, in an assembly of infidels and heretics, of clergy and of seculars, which could be termed, in the state to which wine had brought them, a gang of drunkards. When the spinet had been brought, it was placed on a dais in the middle of the room. The Prefect was obliged to play it, and the Prince having had him told to sing and play at the same time, he began to sing the *Magnificat*, the *Te Deum* and *Tantum ergo*, and then songs and *airs de cour* in Italian and Spanish, because the church-tunes did not sufficiently delight the Prince. The spinet was very out of tune. The Prefect played under protest, and being altogether hoary and broken down with age and tiredness, it can be imagined that his performance made decidedly bad entertainment. However, he entertained the Prince for about two hours. During that time, the Chief Steward, who was Mohhamadan by birth, came to me and asked if the use of instruments were permitted in our religion. I told him it was. He replied that the Mohhamadan faith forbad it quite expressly. We had a half-hour's discussion on this subject, in which that gentleman confirmed something I had learnt a long time before, that musical instruments were forbidden by Mohhamad, and that although their use was universal throughout Persia, it was nevertheless unlawful. He told me further that instruments were above all prohibited from religious use, since it was only with the human voice that God wished to be praised. During this interview a Georgian bishop began to discourse on the same subject with Father Raphael ((Raphael of Parma, the Prince's doctor)). I do not know everything that was said since I did not understand their language, and the Father was not willing to explain. He told me only that the Bishop was scandalised to see the Prefect diverting the company at a banquet in the same manner as he presumed to praise God in church. Father Raphael added that he felt a definite displeasure at the authority the Viceroy had taken over them in obliging their Prefect to play the lute and to sing anywhere that he had the inclination to ask him, but that their safety depended so completely on his good will that they hardly dared refuse him anything. We left at midnight.

(I.221) Whenever some noble entertains the Shah, he invites him only, leaving to him the choice of the company he wishes to have. The Shah arrives about eight or nine o'clock in the morning at the place to which he is invited, which is furnished as sumptuously as possible. As soon as he has arrived there the host gives him a present which is always a very sizeable one. The hall into which the Shah is brought is laid with a magnificent collation of dried fruits and fruit-syrups, biscuits and cakes, sherbets and all sorts of liqueurs, bitter and sweet. They put before him, and before the principal noblemen he has brought with him, large and rich scented braziers, which burn enough to make one giddy, as long as they keep bringing them in. Meanwhile the court musicians and dancers wait in a nearby place until the Shah wishes to be entertained. The Shah's musicians are always not only the most skilled in the kingdom in singing and playing instruments, but they are also usually the best poets in the country. They sing their own compositions, as is said of Homer and other Greek poets of his time. These are for the most part in praise of the Shah and about various exploits of his life, which flattery is ingenious enough to exalt, however worthy of blame or of oblivion they may be. The songs on that day revolved around the rehabilitation of the prime minister, if I dare use that word. I noticed one replete with rather delicate and witty points. The refrain of the couplets was:

Apart from him, all men have seemed equal.
The Sun searched the sky without success for another star to be the Polestar,

an ingenious allusion to the title *Eivan medary*, given to the prime minister, which signifies 'the Pole of Persia'.

Vol. II: *Containing a general description of the Persian Empire, and particular descriptions of the sciences and arts which are in use there, of the political, military and civil government which is in force there, and of the religion which is practised there.*

Section: *General description of Persia.*
Chapter XII: *Of the exercises and games of the Persians.*

Wrestling is the exercise of people of the lowest order, and almost exclusively of people of no substance. The place to which one goes to wrestle is called *Zour Koue* ((properly *Zurkhane*)), that is, 'the house of strength'. They exist in all the great nobles' houses and particularly in those of the provincial governors, to provide exercise for their people. In addition, each town has its team of exhibition wrestlers. Wrestlers are called *pahlevân*, a word which means 'brave', intrepid'. They do these exercises to entertain, for it is a show, as I have said, and this is how they do it. They are naked except for knee-breeches made of very close-fitting leather which is oiled and greasy, and a cloth around the waist also greasy and oiled. This is so that the opponent has less grip and cannot take hold by the clothes, because if he touches them his hand will become slippery and lose its power. Both wrestlers being present in the arena, a little drum which is played continuously during the wrestling to enliven it, gives the signal. They begin by putting on a thousand vainglorious boasts; then they mutually promise a fair fight and shake hands. That done, they slap their buttocks, their thighs and their hips in time with the drum; then they shake hands again and slap themselves as before three times in succession. This is as if for the benefit of the ladies, and to put themselves in form; after that they come together uttering a great shout, and striving to throw their man. To be victorious one must stretch him quite flat on the ground, full length on his stomach, otherwise nothing has been accomplished.

Section: *Description of the sciences and liberal arts of the Persians.*
Chapter VII: *Of music.*

The word for music in Persian is *Mousighi*, just as in Greek, and the Persians regard music, as you see, not only as part of mathematics, which has to do with the numerology of sound, but also as a liberal art which teaches how to manage one's voice and to play instruments with correctness and rhythm. There are various writers who have dealt with it, among others one *Abou Aloufe*, son of *Shid*, whose book I have brought back with me. It deals with music for voice, and for instruments played by the mouth and by the fingers, which is the division made by the writer; but to my great regret I understand nothing of it, having missed reading the book on the spot with someone who might have told me what it meant. It is a small work, only about three hours' reading. What I make of it is only that the Persians have nine modes, that they have tablatures for singing and for instruments that are much more elaborate than we have, and that they learn this art by a method which has many long and perplexing rules, as it seems to me. I have given six examples on the following plate ((see Illustration E)). The diagrams which are marked A, B and C are the first in the book and consequently the simplest. There are twenty-nine of the same kind as A, B and C, with explanations whose terminology I do not understand at all. The one that is marked C is followed by thirty-five other diagrams, also using the same method, and that marked D is followed by thirteen others, the penultimate of which is a circle as big again, with forty-four points on its circumference, eight of which are red. I have thought that people knowledgeable in the art of music would be able to deduce from the diagrams alone what is the Persian method for this theory, in anticipation of what I may be able to discover in time, if it please God that I should have some day the leisure to study it. Apart from these tablatures, there are some that are made in squares, the largest of which are divided into three hundred and six sections, some marked with notes and the others blank. I find in one place in this treatise that the author says that music is a town that has forty-two neighbourhoods, each one with thirty-two streets, and at the end of the book there is a great diagram in the shape of a globe, divided into four circles, sectioned by forty lines, which makes one hundred and sixty notes. Their musical notes are not syllables without sense or significance, but they are either names of towns within the country or names of parts of the human body or of the more ordinary things in nature; and when they teach this art, they say in order to indicate the modes: 'go from this city to that one', or,'go from the finger to the elbow'. The names of the forty-eight different modes are town-names because, they say, these different modes are much used in and special to those towns. Thus there is, as it seems to me, much fuss and confusion in their theory; this results no doubt from the fact that music is so little in use among them, for otherwise they would have reduced it to a shorter and easier method. Their skilled and learned musicians are all in the Shah's employment, and their number does not exceed ten or twelve, as I have been assured. I have given in an adjoining illustration on the same plate a little Persian tune by which one may judge also the nature of their little tunes. Here are its other words:

> She who holds my heart has said to me languidly: why are you
> gloomy and pale? What sugar-lips have put you in their chains?
> I have taken a mirror, I have given it to her, saying: who is this
> beauty who shines in this mirror? The languor of your colour-
> ing is the amber-colour of straw. Why do your eyes burn him
> whom your allurements draw? Cursed be this companion who
> pines away so quickly. Bring fragrant flowers to make the heart
> of my Shah revive.

Their singing is clear, strong and happy, as Dorian singing is said to have been; they like strong and high voices, trills and long roulades; they say that to sing well one must laugh and weep through the music of one's voice. *Pardeh* is the Persian term which signifies song-tune, and they distinguish tunes by the names of their ancient kings, and by the names of provinces. They do not have polyphonic songs, but the good singers sing one after the other. Usually they sing with the lute and the viol; the men have the most beautiful voices, but there are hardly any who are able to sing well, for the reason that singing, like dancing, is regard-ed in Persia as disreputable; both are arts which one would not teach to one's own children but which are relegated to women prostitutes and street entertainers; thus they consider it indecent even to sing, and anyone who does so makes himself reprehensible. However, people have such an inclination for singing that in several occupations they sing all day, though very slowly, in order to amuse and enliven themselves. Since this is so, one need not be surprised that their music-theory is not as straightforward and concise as it might be. The Persians, like the Arabs, call singers *Kayné*, a word which in the Orient implies that the daughters of Cain invented singing and music.

Their musical instruments are very numerous. They have first of all the kettle-drum and the small drum whose bowl is of copper or brass. Next they have the tambourine which they play most skilfully, and a sort of long drum which they carry attached to their belt in front, sloping to the side, and which they play on both ends with the hands, one hand at each end. They have kettle-drums three feet in diameter and so heavy that even a camel cannot carry them, and they are moved on little carts — as one might say a large vat cut in two. Next they have straight cornetts which serve as horns and trumpets, which are in proportion to those kettle-drums and which are marvellously large instruments; the smallest are larger than a man's height. There are some seven or eight feet long, made of copper or brass, and unequal in diameter throughout, since the bore is very narrow at one foot's distance from the *embouchure*, and from there it becomes larger towards the *embouchure* up to two inches diameter; but the lower end is nearly two feet broad. The player of this instrument has trouble in holding it up, and he bends under the weight; its sound, which can be heard at a great distance, is rough and dull when solo, but it does well enough when mingled with other instruments, when it serves as bass. Those who play it move it constantly to vary the sound and to ease the strain. Apart from these horns, in which one could easily lay one's head, there are other kinds, some made like hunting-horns and others like our high trumpets. Then they have the oboe, the flute, the fife, the flageolet, but these are so very inadequate that they do not play them with as much harmony as is done with us. Next they have stringed instruments: rebec, harp, spinet ((probably *santur*)), guitar, tetrachord, violin and a sort of kit; the *tamboura*, which is a gourd or calabash at the end of a neck, which they use as lute, and another instrument which they call *Kongereh*, whose diagram you see in the adjoining illustration marked F, just as it is in my book on Persian music. You will observe that the strings of their instruments are not gut, as ours are, because with them it is a contamination in law to touch dead parts of animals; their instruments' strings are either of twisted raw silk or of spun brass. They have in addition the kind of instruments which Father Mersenne, in his *Livre de Sons*, calls cymbals[1], which are two bowls or basins of brass that are played by striking one against the other, usually while holding them raised above the head and moving them in all directions. The female dancers hold bones in their hands, which they use as gypsies do castanets, and which give a clear strong sound; I believe that castanets were made in imitation of such bones. The singers also use them for exciting the dancers, and they can equally well snap their fingers so loudly that one would say they had bones or castanets in their hands. They make a kind of carillon with porcelain or with brass vessels of various sizes arranged in order, which they strike with two small sticks that are long

1. Mersenne used and illustrated the term *Cymbales* in Propositions XXIV and XXVI of the *Livre Septiesme: Des instrumens de percussion* in his *Harmonie Universelle*, iii, Paris, 1636; reprint, Paris, 1963.

and thin; this makes more agreeable harmony than a clock carillon, and
is much more lively.

In the Orient it is the same with instruments as with music itself
— it is likewise improper to play them and to learn to play them, and
even worse, for religion forbids their use. The ecclesiastics and pious
people do not wish even to hear them, and this is the reason why the
art is not polished and advanced as in our country. The players of
instruments are poor in Persia and badly clad; only those whom the
Shah maintains are worth hearing. Their ensemble is quite good: thev
are called the *Chahichi-Bashi,* as if to say *The principal ensemble of
instrumentalists and singers*; the others do not know much, as far as I
have observed. They go to play in houses for whatever people care to
give them, and when the Shah gives some high appointment to a nobleman, or whenever an infant is publicly circumcised in some great house,
they go and play at the door, in order to earn something.

The dance in Persia is even more disreputable, and more contrary to their religion than are singing and instrument-playing, since it is
indeed completely infamous and is engaged in only by the most noto-
rious women prostitutes. It is as it was among the Romans, who tolerat-
ed this art in people sunk in depravity but condemned it in others. Thus
men do not dance, only women, but when women dance there are
always several men near the principal actress exciting her with their
singing and sometimes with their gestures. Persian dance, as in all of the
Orient, is a representation; there are comic and enjoyable passages, and
there are others, in greater number, that are serious and contemplative;
the passions are represented in all their power; but what is detestable to
see are the lascivious and disgusting posturings, the raptures and frustra-
tions of which these representations are full and in which they succeed
in a manner strongly inimical to virtue, for it is not possible to conceive
of anything more affecting. A dance lasts sometimes three or four hours
before finishing; the heroine performs the principal episodes alone, and
the four or five others join her from time to time. Usually after the
dance the women and musicians engage in dangerous leaps. These
people do not perform in a place made expressly for the public as our
actors do, but they are called to people's homes, and apart from their
reward from the person who called them, it is the custom that at the
end of the dance an old woman who is, as it were, the matron of the
group, or the principal actress, puts out her hand to each person in the
company in order to receive something. As these young women earn
much more from prostitution than from dancing, they make every
effort to move the audience, and they are well pleased if they are given
an assignation, or are led into a private room, a thing which for those
people means no more than for us to leave the table and go to the
sideboard to drink a glass of wine at a drinking-party.

13 ENGELBERT KAEMPFER

Engelbert Kaempfer was born at Lemgo in 1651, studied at Danzig, Thorn and Cracow and after a visit to Sweden was made secretary to a Swedish embassy going to Russia and Persia. The embassy arrived in Ispahan on March 29th, 1684. When it returned to Sweden Kaempfer decided to visit the 'courts, states and nations of the east'. His travels took him to Java, from where he went to Japan as physician to the mission that the Dutch East India Company sent each year to the trading post on the artificial island of Dejima, off Nagasaki. Through this foothold the Netherlands had uninterrupted relations with Japan for some two hundred years, the only European country to do so. After a two-year stay in Japan Kaempfer returned to Europe via Batavia, and practised medicine in Lemgo, dying in 1716.

Kaempfer's manuscripts and drawings, together with his botanical collection and other materials, were bought after he died by Sir Hans Sloane, and were later acquired by the British nation for the British Museum. The *History of Japan* was first published in English, translated by Johann Caspar Scheuchzer, son of a noted Swiss geographer, from the 'High-Dutch', i.e., German, in two folio volumes in 1727. A French and a Dutch translation from the English were published in the Hague in 1729 (Amsterdam, 1732). The original German manucript text was published in Lemgo in 1777-79, edited by Christian Wilhelm Dohm, and was reprinted in Stuttgart in 1964. A three-volume reprint of the English text was published in Glasgow in 1906, and in 1929 a complete facsimile of the original print of 1727 was published in Kyoto, Japan.

In the *Amoenitates exoticae* Kaempfer printed Persian technical terms in Persian script, followed by a trancript in italics, sometimes with a Latin case-ending. The Persian script is omitted in these extracts, and the transcripts are printed in the form Kaempfer gave them. In the English translation the spelling of his transcripts has been changed where necessary to conform to a usual current spelling. E.C. Cox, in his *Reference Guide to the History of Travel* (vol. i, Seattle, 1935, p. 252), listed Kaempfer, *Travels in Persia, and in other countries of the East,* 2 vols., London, 1736; this was presumably a translation of the *Amoenitates exoticae.* It has not been used for the present anthology, which has a new translation of the extracts quoted.

Engelbert Kaempfer, *Amoenitatum exoticarum politico-physico-medicarum fasciculi V, quibus continentur variae relationes, observationes & descriptiones rerum Persicarum & ulterioris Asiae, multa*

attentione, in peregrinationibus per universum Orientem, collectae,
Lemgovia ((= Lemgo)), 1712

Fasciculus I, Relatio II: *Coronatio Regis Solymanni.*

....

p. 38

His paulo ante undecimam peractis, illico nomine Serenissimi
mandatur; *Primo,* ut Regia foris ac intus excubiis muniatur, Majestatis
praesentiae debitis; *Secundo*: ut theatrum Musicum dies viginti inde-
finenter personet, ad numerum scilicet annorum, quos agebat Rex. Est
illud theatrum pergula quaedam lignea, longa & praealta, supra exter-
num fornicem *Kaisarièh,* seu palatii mercatorii, exstructa, ad orientale
latus fori maximi, adjacentis Regio Palatio instar vestibuli. In illo occu-
pantur & stipendia sua merentur quadraginta tubicines, qui post
mediam noctem, & sole oriente, nec minus in Regiis conviviis & solen-
nitatibus publicis, pro honore Serenissimi horrendo sonitu dissonos
boatus & clangores edunt. Vix genus buccinae in Europa & Asia in-
venio, quod hic, sed indocta bucca, inflari non viderim; pulsantur
ibidem loci tympana quoque discrepantis soni & figurae; a quibus per-
gulae illi nomen *Nachora-chonèh,* id est, tympanorum domus, imposi-
tum est....

*Novissima
a Corona-
tione man-
data.*

*(Vide figu-
ram suo
loco).*

....

Relatio VI: *Primates Aulae togati, quibus in Regio Consessu locus est.*

....

p. 87

Tsjahehtsjì basjì, i.e. *supremum Musicum,* cui, velut Capellae
magistro, omnes obtemperant, qui in solenni Convivio, cum id Regi
volupe est, Choro Musico serviunt tubis, tympanis, cymbalis, nolis,
chordis & voce humana modulando. Pari modo saltatrices, cantatrices,
lusores, recitatores historiarum, actores, Poëtae, histriones, luctatores,
eum in finem stipendiis gaudent, ut, jussi, conviviis praesto sint, & lusus
per artem suam moveant. Sed qualis farinae homines in censum hic
nostrum non veniunt.

*Director
Musica.*

....

Relatio VIII: *Antistites spirituales. Aedificia sacra.*

....

p. 106

Muwasin, Cantores, qui preces publicas mane, meridie & vesperi,
vel soli, vel una cum sociis, ejulant, & quam possunt voce altissima
declamant, constituti in summitate turrium. quae a veteribus eum in

Cantores.

finem templis primariis adstructae sunt. Malunt *Isphahani* ex templorum tectis decantare; indignantibus vicinis, quod ex turribus declamator possit uxores illarum conspicere.

p. 109

. . . . Series Imamorum haec est, sed Persis calculatoribus, qui *Abubakerum, Osmannum* & *Omerum* a Turcis praemissos, ex catalogo Pontificum suorum relegarunt: 1. *Mortusa Aali,* 2. *Hasen,* 3. *Hossein,* 4. *Sein elaabediin,* 5. *Mahhamed Backiir,* 6. *Djaäfer tsadik,* 7. *Musa kasìm,* 8. *Resaa,* 9. *Mohhamed Takhì,* 10. *Ali nachi,* 11. *Hasen askerì,* & 12. *Mahhamed mehdì.* Ex his unus Resà intra fines Persicos sepultus est, videlicet in metropoli Corasanorum *Masjhèd.* Haec civitas florem & celebritatem suam quam maxime sacris debet exuviis, ad quas adorandas peregrinatores confluunt Musulmanni, sed praesertim Persiani Sjijaitae; qui post *Aali,* dilectum Mahhamedis generum, & *Dsjaferì* suum plus videntur sanctitatis reponere in uno *Resaa,* quam in ceteris Imamis omnibus: Inprimis credunt coecos fiducia adorationis hic posse recuperare visum. Nam non raro Sacerdotes, ut advenarum fidem concilient, supponunt, qui visus orbitatem simulet, quo ipso, fictis precibus recuperato, turbam concitant admiratorum, qui patientem per plateas cymbalis tympanisque comitantibus circumducunt, velut in triumphum & laudem opitulatoris sui....

....

p. 116

Professores.
Studia.

.... Magno in hac gente honori ducitur docere; & in magna celebritate versatur, qui frequenti auditorum corona cingitur. Hanc laudem multi sic ambiunt, ut etiam clam data pecunia sibi emercari discipulos soleant, velut eruditionis suae tubicines....

....

Relatio IX: *Officinae Domus Regiae. Officiales Aulae minores.*

....

p.130

Nagaraan choneh; quod Tympanorum domum sonat. Pergula est

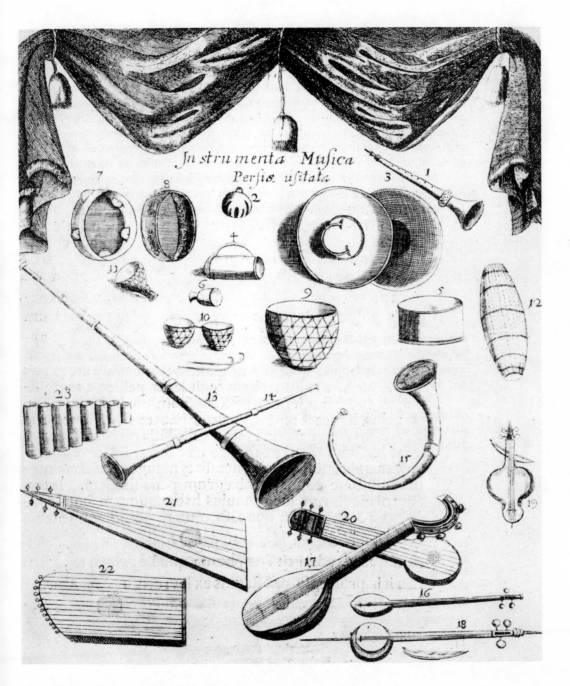

F. Persian instruments, from no. 13

Theatrum musicum. (Figuram vide suo loco)

praealta & longa, ad septentrionalem fori maximi faciem, non procul a Regio Palatio fabricata; ex qua in honorem Majestatis quotidie cum occasu solis, & duabus horis ante ortum, varia, inque terris nostris ignota buccinarum & tympanorum genera incondito strepitu resonant. Praeterea in auspiciis novilunii & festis religiosis, tum etiam in conviviis Regiis sine intermissione instrumentis plauditur, donec festivitas terminaverit. Adsunt tympanistae, tubicines, cymbalistae, numero quadraginta, qui stipendia sua recipiunt ex censu *Khawaal*. Hoc vocabulum significat voluptuarium genus hominum, veluti scorta, choraulas & quoscunque facientes quaestum in lupanariis; iniquum enim reputant, si ejus generis reditus in seria collocentur. Chorum hunc, cum in Aulis Asiaticis, tum in singulis Persiae civitatibus primus instituisse dicitur *Tamerlanes*, hodiernae Monarchiae Persarum, ac magni Mogolis conditor. Collegii inspectionem habet *Mesjeldaar basji*.

....

Relatio XI: *Attributa Aulae potiora.*

....

p. 158

Series feriarum haec est:

Primus Mensis, Muhharrèm, dies primores dones esse lugubres & nefastos jubet, ob *Hosseinii*, filii Aali, trucidationem, factam hujus Mensis die decimo.... Sub vesperam denuo in diversoria, compita & areas publicas tumultuose confluunt, & congestis cremiis ac lucis materia, ignes construunt, quos circa choreas instituant parentales. Nec mora, tripudiare incipiunt, subinde *Hosseinii* nomen, voce non tristi aut ejulante, sed indignantium simili, exclamant, alterne & quasi per choros: dum ad numerum hujus soni in gyrum velut metro acti, pectus pugno, terramque pede importune quatiunt....

....

p. 162

Festorum cultus in eo reponitur, ut ex foris publicis tympana, tubae, cymbala, a nocte media ad usque meridiem personantia, diem ceteris reddant illustriorem; populus vero ab opere cessans, in templis, foris & areis publicis magno strepitu & frequentia conveniat, invicem gratuletur, propalam laetetur, ludat, nugetur, catervatimque accumbens Nicotianam sugat, cum alternatis sorbilium exiguis haustibus: Poëtas idem, & dramatum actorus audiat, concionum religiosarum & ambituum, si qui habendi veniunt, sedulus adsit comes vel spectator; & diem denique in publico emensus, intra parietes quoque laetus quisque cum suis partem noctis exigat.

p. 216

Relatio XVI: *Admissio hospitum coram Serenissimo, quam vulgo vocant* Audientiam.

Principum Nuncios moris est, Regiae Majestatis alloquio non admitti, nisi publico totius Curiae in Consessu, quem Persae vocant *Medsjilès*. Solennis hic aulicae Universitati actus est, qui sumptuoso convivio & publica cum festivitate celebrari aliquoties intra annum vertentem solet.... Omnia illo in actu incredibilem prae se ferunt magnificentiam, & accedentem hospitem stupore afficiunt, cum in immanes statim belluas, superbo amictu exornatas, incidit, velut elephantes, rhinocerotes, leones, tigrides; nec non in equos, auro, unionibus, gemmis micantes, orbis totius generosissimos;....quin & aures abripiunt peregrinae chordarum, cymbalorum, tympanorum levi digito expressae consonantiae, quas & vox humana intersonat; & gustum aureis vasis, multorum millionum pretii, expositae invitant dapes & cupediarum Regales lautitiae....

Vita legatorum in Aula Persica. Admissionis scena.

....

p. 220

Trigesimo Martii anno 1684 Isfahanum appulsi, Regalis alloquii copiam haud citius trigesimo Julii impetravimus....Hortus est ita dictus, trans pontem urbis orientalem, in littore fluminis *Senderuut*, quo ipsa urbs ab hortis & oppidulis suburbanis disjungitur. Una igitur hora ab orto sole conscendendos obtulit equos duodecim, centurio quidam praetorianus eques, Mahhammandari vices in deductione praestiturus. Hunc secuti ductorem, sequenti ordine incessimus: In acie equitabant una cum tympanista gemini tibicines; mox pedites sequebantur satellites duodecim, viridi holoserico induti; tum Secretarius Legationis equo vectus, manu, fronte tenus elevata, Literas gestans sui Principis, panno obvolutas aureo....

Horti admissionis topographia.

Hortus Schadès abaad.

....

p. 228

Imum atrii, velut maximum proscenium, ad cisternae utrumque latus duo referebat triclinia, utrobique ab invicem trium intercapedine passuum remota; tum duo alia ad frontispicii cancellos, adeoque ex opposito Regis & in transversum locata.... Transverso ordine sedebant Musici utrinque ad introitum quindecim, adeoque interrupta serie in duos divisi choros: qui alternata vice tibiis, cymbalis & variis chordis peregrinum consonabant melos; cui & tympana levi compuncta digito, rarius & vox quaedam humana intercinebat. De concentu si judicium expectas? Strepitus potius quam concentus erat, nullis harmoniae regulis adstrictus, non inconditus tamen & ingratus; verum si vocem cantoris excipio, sat suavis, & submissus adeo, ne colloquia & agenda in

In infimo.

Senatu quicquam interpellaret, sed peregrina quadam varii stridoris dulcedine considentium aures & animos demulceret....

....

p. 248

Prandium.

....Saltatrices quoque ac cantrices aberant; eo consilio repulsae, ne his Princeps illecebris denuo in corporis noxam impingeret. Aberant gladiatores luctatores, comoedi, quos alioqui & consimiles agyrtarum globos invitare voluptas, vino lacessita, non raro solita erat. Cum prandii exordio quoque Musicorum cessabat studium, instrumentisque reconditis, non in fidibus amplius, sed in patinis decertabat; exemplo ceterorum, qui solis omnes intenti missibus, alto prandebant silentio sepulti....

....

Fasciculus IV, Relatio IX: *In Palmetis hospitantium occupationes.*

....

p. 738

Lusus & recreationes.

Qua vero in frugali rerum affluentia, ne quid externae laetitiae messem destituat, en praesentes etiam actores, poëtas, saltatrices, modulatores, & si quid aliud ad convivii hilaritatem desideraveris. Modo vides *Sjaaïr* seu vatem arguto rhythmo illustris heroinae *Leilì*, ejusdemque rivalis *Medsjnuun* amores & exilia decantantem; modo *Khisseh choon*, seu oratorem, qui Persarum Herculis *Rustàm*, filii *Saal*, robur, facinora & bella, vel *Behraam, Jesdegardi* filii in jaculando excellentiam atque ceteras dotes exclamat. Alium audis ex ordine religiosorum pauperum *derviisj*, qui *Aälì* sui, & ceterorum Imamorum atque religionis antistitum miracula recitat; aut *Omar* injustam ad *chalifatum* irruptionem demonstrat & diris execratur. Illis vero absentibus *Raiisj deh*, seu pagi sui senior, *Taäriife* seu Elogia praeclarorum virorum, aut provinciae suae chronica & priscorum in ea Principum res gestas & bella repetit. Nunc *mola* aliguis, sive religionis aut musarum sacerdos Rosarium *Sjeich Saädi*, aut *Diwaani Chodsja Hafès Sjirasì*, aliorumque acuta epigrammata praelegit, & meditabundo distinguit silentio. Nunc graves conciones *takhliidsjì*, seu histrio aliquis, aut *hokkehbaas*, seu praestigiator opportuna lusus & risus vicissitudine interpellat. Haec inquam otii diurni deliciae sunt.

Chorea.

Inclinante sole, ubi membra laxata dies algidior reficit, de agendis etiam tripudiis cogitatuur. Atque, ut ut omnis ad numeros se movere ruricola haud perfunctorie peritus sit, adsunt tamen, qui exactius possunt ejusdem artis in utroque sexu professores circumforanei, *rakkaas* dicti; qui mediterraneis egressi urbibus, hominibus plena hoc tempore nemora frequentes invisunt, & ludis praestigiisque variis instructi, hamis pendentibus discurrunt. His igitur, si adsint, sparta committitur ducendi choreas; quas ipsi alioquin, si absunt, neutiquam omittunt. Mireris spec-

tacula & lepidos motus, quos illi tripudiando edunt. Non enim Sarmata-
rum ad gravitatem alterno pede terram quatiunt, ut Poëta loquitur; nec
ad Gallici moris levitatem vesani discurrunt; sed testudineo gradu, nudis
pedum plantis, huc illuc diu se proripiunt, dum arguto corporis motu
pulsus chordarum & mensuras excipiunt, & nullo non membrorum arti-
culo facete exprimunt. Mox resupini miris flexibus totum corpus tor-
quent, brachiis nunc super humum distentis, nunc extensis super verti-
cem, velut lamentantium dolores, non gestientium laetitiam expressuri.
Demum, tympanis concitatius tactis, protinus exsultantes, in velocissi-
mos motus rapiuntur, ac in gyros varios, imumque summo versi ac
circumvoluti, saltatricum officia histrici leporis vicissitudine permiscent.

    Musica vero, quae tripudiantium membra diriget, hem, quam   *Musica.*
peregrina est! quam grate dissonans & instrumentorum varietate
delectabilis! Primas inter instrumenta tribuimus tibiis gingrinis *Surnaì*,
(Fig. 1.) quae grunniente sono prae ceteris aures affatim implent. Illis
assonant *(Fig. 2.)* tinnientes nolae vulgares, nostratibus similes; vel
etiam cymbala perampla *Sindsji* dicta *(Fig. 3.)*, patinarum, quibus in
mensis utimur, figuram referentia, sed minori disco, majori margine, &
gibba facie manubrio instructa, quo teneri & ad invicem collidi valeant.
Pro basi servit tympanum, vel oblongi dolioli figura *denbaal, (Fig. 4.)* ab
Indis mutuatum, vel ex Europa translatum *dohùl, (Fig. 5.)* quo militares
copias abducimus, vel praegrande ejusdem figurae aliud, ob magnitudinem haud portabile. Haec omnia non bacillis, sed digitis solum, mani-
busve utrinque leniter pulsantur, ita sonum redditura submissiorem, &
reciproca alterni lateris dissonantia gratiorem. Utramque paginam in
agresti choro absolvere videntur tympana *donbèk (Fig. 6.)* levis structurae, cocta ex argilla, figura & capacitate ollarum fictilium, nisi quod
fundus in brevem appendicem producitur, qua pulsantis axillam gestata
replent, oris vero hiatu vesica vel membranula tensa obducto. Hoc vel
solo genere. quasi ruricolis vernaculo, festivitates suas celebrant palmi-
colae, sociatis plausibus & volarum collisionibus, quibus concinentes
convivae saltantium in scena vigorem & metra promovent. Civili
symphoniae interdum subsonat cythara tetrachordoides *Tsjaartaar*, vel
sola, vel aliis organis polychordoidibus conspirans. Nec raro circum dul-
cisonum ingreditur tympanum quoddam *def* appellatum, *(Fig. 7.)* mag-
nitudine, figura & levitate ad assem simile cribello, quatuor in ambitu
spithamarum, cujus aperto altero, unum saltem tegit latus pellicula
tenuissima, ex qua sonus irritatur saltem submisso digitorum ictu. Ora
ejus, lignea & tenuis, quatuor habet vel quinque paria orbiculorum, ex
palmari intervallo suis quaeque axillis per transversum infixa, ex sonoro
aere facta, subcava & exiguae magnitudinis, quae concusso tympano
strepitum mutua collisione edunt cymbalorum pene similem. Interdum
orbiculorum loco annulos habet, quorum sonus confusus est & remis-
sior: hoc casu, mutato nomine appellatur *Daireh (Fig. 8).* Hujusmodi

instrumentum saltem unicum quavis admittit symphonia, quod e primis tractat, si fuerit in proscenio, praesultans ex levi censu *Kawalî*, frequentius autem & extra tripudium chori phonascus, qui, eodem utraque manu comprehenso, fauces cantu hiantes & gesticulationem ab aliorum intuitu defendit: dum interea non modo diversos submissosque sonos ex pellicula pulsata elicit, sed severiori motione interdum mixtos quoque tinnitus & clangores ex infixis orbiculis excutit. Hic igitur praecentor raucisona & quam potest altissima voce melos suum modulatur; cui per choros, junctis organis, respondent convivae circumsidentes, vel in circo tripudiantes, si choreae ducantur. Nonnunquam hilaritate acta concinit universa multitudo, vocibus autem ut indoctis, ita instrumentis quoque indocte tractatis, & nullis unquam harmoniae regulis (etiam in Choro Aulico) respondentibus, sed per tonos, quos vocant, unisonos & octavos omne melos absolventibus, Qualiscunque symphonia fuerit, concors tamen, submissa & modesta est, gratiam pariens singularem varietate mensurae, quae per tot modulorum genera in concitatiores semper triplas jugi pulsu ac spiritu devolvitur, non agrestes modo & indoctas aures demulcens, sed & artis musicae bene gnaros, haud injuria mirantium, id plebejam hanc gentem in variandis mensuris praestare, quod nostri in scholis longa artis industria edocendi sunt. Sunt plura Persis instrumentorum genera, quibus in conviviis & privato otio demulcendis auribus, vel in militia etiam, & in foris urbium ad intimandas temporum festivitates utuntur. Ex *thabl* seu tympanis aciem ducit *Kuus*, *(Fig. 9.)* tympanum grande, aeneum, nostrati simile, sed ad moderandum strepitum nerveo reticulo constrictum, cui pulsando duo serviunt bacilli, extremitatibus incurvatis. *Nagharèh*, *(Fig. 10.)* ejusdem stucturae & aeris tympana sunt gemina, exiguae molis, valido nexu invicem copulata, & ab unico tractanda artis tympanizandi perito. *theblebaas*, *(Fig. 11.)* i.e. tympanum falconum, parvulum est, aeneum, in appendicem productum, reticuloque densisssime munitum, ita dictum, quod falcones in aucupio emissi, ejus sono revocentur; inde singula ephippiis (ad sinistrum latus) affixa gestantur a nobilibus atque ipso Rege. Adest & aliud genus tympani *(Fig. 12.)* ligneum, majusculum, figurae ovatae oblongioris, inprimis familiare Multhanis in hoc regno habitantibus, & ut mihi videtur exoticum, utraque simul nuda & inermi manu pulsandum, hinc dextra, illinc sinistra. Ex *Nefiir*, sive buccinis, prima horrisona est *Kharahnà*, *(Fig. 13.)* duarum orgyiarum longitudinis, figura similis instrumento acustico. Altera *(Fig. 14.)* subtilioris toni, generis nomen retinet, recta, gracilima, orgyjam longa. Tertia *Sjach Nefür*, *(Fig. 15.)* i.e. buccina cornuta, grandis pariter & aenea est, in figuram cornu ingentis arcuata. Ex *Uud*, seu Chelidibus, quae nervis resonant (ex intestinis ovium elaboratis) communissima est *trichordos* *(Fig. 16.)* colli longissimi, ventris exigui ovati, ponticulo membranaceo. Sunt, quae chordis quatuor, quinque & pluribus instruuntur; ex quarum

censu palmaris est *Tsjehesdeh*, *(Fig. 17.)* magnitudinem & figuram utcunque nostratium referens, nervis dotata octo, vel novem, geminis semper in unisono conspirantibus, postremis etiam tribus, si nervos novem
habeat. Ex Violis, quas vocant, principem locum vendicat tribus & ali-
quando chordis quatuor instructa, *Kamaantsjèh* dicta, *(Fig. 18.)* nam
scite tractata organorum quodcunque genus soni submissa dulcedine
antecellit; arcu plectitur pilis armato equinis, dum ima pars humi reponitur instar violae *di gamba*, quam vocant. Manubrium ei gracile est &
cono simile, verticillis pro fidium numero instructum, obesis adeo capi-
tibus, ut manum tendentis impleant. Venter rotundus est, spithamalis
diametri, ponticulo obductus membranaceo; Imam faciem stylus termi-
nat ferreus, artificiose sculptus, sesquispithamalis longitudinis. Tota
cum stylo machina quinque longitudine spithamas exhibet, concha mar-
garitifera aureisque filis pretiose vermiculata, digno suavitate sua artifi-
cio. Est & alius structurae Pandura, quatuor intenta chordis, *(Fig.19.)*
fortasse exotica, quae pari situ deposita, arcu quoque plectitur; collum
ei compressum est & breve, venter duplicatus, superiori parte oblongior,
amplior & apertus, ima minor, rotundus & ligneo ponticulo clausus.
Cithararum, quemadmodum Testudinum, varietates sunt, diverso chordarum numero discrepantes, ex quibus unicam saltem ob figurae inso-
lentiam hic delineavimus *(Fig. 20.)*. Sambucarum *Tsjeng* communissima
est, & ab indocto facile tractabilis, sex chordis instructa, *(Fig. 21.)*
figurae triangularis amblygoniae; Rarior est altera multis pollens chordis, *(Fig. 22.)* utcunque quadrata,çutraque bacillis incurvis, vel pennis
plectenda, a nostratibus figura & tractandi arte parum differentes.
Omitto machinam octo tubulorum *Musicaar* dictam *(Fig. 23.)* ore in-
flandam; omitto tibias, utriculos, arundines, crepitacula, ne historiae
telam moremur.
....

TRANSLATION

Engelbert Kaempfer, *Five fascicles of political-physical-medical exotic
delights, in which are contained various relations, observations and descriptions of things of Persia and further Asia, collected with much
assiduity in travels through the whole Orient*, Lemgo, 1712
Fascicle I, Relation II: *Coronation of Shah Soliman.*

p. 38
    These things having been completed shortly before eleven, it
was commanded on the spot in the name of the Most Serene One: *first*,
that the palace should be defended within and without by guards,
devoted to his majesty's protection; *second*, that the assemblage of
musical instruments should perform incessantly for twenty days — ac-

*Newest
commands
at the
Coronation.*

(See the
illustration
in its place)[2].

tually the number of years in the Shah's age.[1] That assemblage is in a
certain wooden gallery, long and very high, constructed above the outer
archway of the Ghaiserièh, or trading palace, which is at the eastern side of
the largest quadrangle, and is adjacent to the royal palace after the
manner of an entrance-court. In it are employed and earn pay forty
trumpeters, who after midnight and at sunrise, and in addition at royal
banquets and public ceremonies, in honour of the Most Serene One give
forth with horrendous din discordant bellowings and clangours. Rarely
do I find in Europe and Asia the kind of straight trumpet as here, but I
have not observed them to be blown with unlearned breath; in the same
place drums are beaten, of different sound and shape; from this the
name *Naghareh khanèh*, that is, the house of drums, is applied to the
building....

Relation VI: *The leading civil officers of the Court, for whom there is a
place in the royal assembly.*

p. 87

*Director
of Music.*

The Chahichì-Bashì, that is, the highest-placed musician, to
whom, as to a Kapellmeister, all submit who in a ceremonial banquet,
when that is the Shah's pleasure, serve in the musical ensemble, performing on trumpets, drums, cymbals, bells, stringed instruments and
the human voice. In the same manner female dancers, female singers,
jesters, reciters of tales, actors, poets, mimics, wrestlers are so pleased at
the prospect of their payments that when they are commanded they are
on hand for banquets, and produce entertainments with their skill. But
men of such a kind do not come into our listing here.

p. 106

Singers.

Relation VIII. *Spiritual priests, sacred buildings.*
Muwasin are singers who wail public prayers in the morning, midday
and evening, either alone or with associates, and who proclaim them in
the loudest voice they can, stationed at the tops of turrets which were
first added to the most important of the ancient mosques, at their ends.
In Isphahan they prefer to sing from the roofs of the mosques, to the
indignation of the neighbours, because from the turrets the announcer
can gaze at their wives.

---

1. Kaempfer noted (original text, p. 43) that Shah Soliman was born in 1646.
2. The reference is to a large folded-in plate opposite page 170, captioned *Frons Palatii Regii
cum parte Fori maximi*; above part of the surrounding buildings can be discerned a long gallery,
from which long straight trumpets are being played.

p. 109

.... This is the festival-list of Imams, but as calculated by the Persians, who leaving Abubaker, Osmann and Omar to the Turks, remove them from the catalogue of observances of their pontiffs:
1. *Mortesa Aali*; 2. *Hasan*; 3. *Hossein*; 4. *Zeinolaabediin*; 5. *Mohhamad Backiir*; 6. *Djaäfar sadegh*; 7. *Musa kasèm*; 8. *Resaa*; 9. *Mohhamad Taghi;* 10. *Ali naghi*; 11. *Hasen asgheri*; and 12. *Mohhamad mehdi*. Out of these *Resà* alone is buried within the Persian boundaries, namely in Mashhad, the city of the inhabitants of the province of Khorasan. This community owes its prosperity and fame chiefly to the sacred relics, which the Muslim pilgrims flock to worship, but especially the Persians of the Shiite sect, who, after *Aali*, the beloved son-in-law of Mohhamad and his family *Dsjaferi*, seem to invest *Resaa* alone with more sanctity than all of the other Islamic holy ones; in particular they believe that faith in worship in this place can restore sight to the blind. For often the priests, in order to secure the confidence of strangers, bring along someone who simulates loss of sight, and when he has been cured by false prayers, they incite a crowd of admirers, who lead the recovered one in triumph around the streets with accompanying cymbals and drums, in praise of his healer....

p. 116

... Among this people teaching brings great honour, and he who *Professors.* is continually accorded the crown of approbation of his listeners basks in great celebrity. Many canvas for this fame, to the extent that they *Studies.* are accustomed to purchase disciples for themselves by secretly giving them money, as if to personal trumpeters of their erudition.

Relation IX: *Officers of the Royal Household; lesser officials of the Court.*

p. 130

Naghareh khanèh is the name which signifies the house of the *The assemblage* drums. It is a very high and long gallery, at the northern end of the *of musical in-* largest quadrangle, not far from the royal palace. From it are sounded *struments.* every day at sunset and two hours before sunrise, in honour of his *(See the* majesty, various sorts of trumpets and drums unknown in our coun- *illustration* tries, with a disorderly din. Besides this, musical instruments are played *in its place)* without intermission for the divinings connected with the new moon and for religious festivals, and likewise for royal banquets. The players include female tambourinists, trumpeters and female cymbalists to the number of forty, who get their stipends from the payroll of the *Gha-*

waal. This word signifies a category of pleasure-providing men, comparable to prostitutes, singing dancers and suchlike who make their living in the brothels; for they think it improper if people of this sort were to be brought in from outside. It is said that this dancing group, both in Asian courts and also in each community of Persia, was first instituted by Tamerlane, founder of the current monarchy of the Persians and of the great Mogul. The *Majlesdaar bashi* has the oversight of this guild.

Relation XI: *The more important activities of the Court.*

p. 158

This is the series of festivals: In the first month, *Muhharrèm*, the first ten days are ordered to be mourning-days with no business transacted, on account of the assassination of *Hossein*, son of Aali, which was committed on the tenth day of this month.... In the evening again they gather noisily in the inns, at cross-roads and in public open spaces, and having collected brushwood and combustible materials they build fires around which they organise dances in honour of their forbears. Then without delay they begin to dance, and continually call out the name of *Hossein*, with a voice neither sad nor wailing, but like indignant people; they do this alternating as it were in responding choirs; while moving to the measure of this sound in their circular motion as though driven by the rhythm, they violently strike their breasts with their fist and the ground with their feet....

p. 162

The cult of festivals works out in this way, that they render the day more illustrious than others with the sounding of drums, trumpets and cymbals from the market-squares from midnight until midday; the populace abandoning work gathers in the mosques, market-squares and public open spaces with great noise and commotion; there is mutual congratulation, public rejoicing, games, frivolity, with masses of people lying down smoking tabacco, alternating with small sips of water; there may likewise be poets and actors of plays to be listened to; and if some come to hold religious meetings and prayer-circuits these are sedulously attended by adherent and onlooker alike; and in a short everyone spends the day in public, and also passes part of the night rejoicing with his own people within the walls of his house.

Relation XVI: *Admission of guests into the most serene presence, which is commonly called the* Audience.

p. 216

    It is the custom that the messengers of princes are not allowed to have converse with his royal majesty, unless in a public assembly of the whole court, which the Persians call *Madjlès*. This ceremonial is a presentation of the whole courtly community, which is customarily celebrated several times in the course of a year with sumptuous banqueting and with public festivity.... Everything in this presentation exhibits an incredible magnificence, and affects the approaching guest with stupor, as there suddenly burst upon him enormous animals decorated with superb covering, such as elephants, rhinoceroses, lions, tigers, not to speak of horses, the finest in the whole world, glittering with gold, large pearls and gems.... not to mention that there breaks upon the stranger's ears the combined sounds, articulated with lightness of finger, of stringed instruments, cymbals and drums, among which the human voice also sounds; while with golden vases, of the value of many millions, the banquets spread before him and the royal splendours of its delicacies entice his taste....

The life of the ambassadors at the Persian Court.

The scene of the Admission.

p. 220

    Having been brought to Isfahan on the thirtieth of March in the year 1684, it was not any sooner than the thirtieth of July that we achieved the opportunity of a royal conversation... The garden so called is across the east bridge of the city, by the bank of the river Zendeh-Rude[1], by which the city proper is separated from the gardens and the small suburban towns. Accordingly, at one hour after sunrise twelve horsemen were led by a certain centurion-horseman of the royal bodyguard, forewarned to escort us in the place of the Maghammdar. Following this leader, we proceeded in the following order: in a single line there rode a pair of reed-instrument players together with a drummer; then followed twelve attendants on foot, clothed in green silk; then the secretary of the legation borne on a horse, with his hand, raised to his forehead, bearing the letters of his prince, which were covered all around with a gold cloth...

Topography of the garden of admission.

The garden Schadès abaad

p. 228

    At the furthest point of the open court, as though at the greatest width of a proscenium, were placed two couches, one on either side of the chest, removed from each other by a distance of about three

At the furthest point.

---

1. Kaempfer explained (p. 165) his transcript *Sendeh ruud* (elsewhere *Senderuut*) as meaning 'river of life'; this is apparently the river that is today called *Zaaindeh-Rude*.

paces, while two others were located in a position facing the gratings, at a point opposite to the Shah and crosswise... Fifteen musicians sat in a crosswise position on both sides, and thus in a broken row divided into two groups; these in turn sounded together a strange tune with reed-instruments, cymbals and various stringed instruments; drums struck with a light finger, and less often the human voice, joined in with them. Perhaps you expect my opinion about this ensemble? A noise rather than an ensemble, it was unencumbered by any rules of harmony, but nevertheless not confused nor disagreeable; in truth if I except the singer's voice, it was pleasant enough, and subordinated to the extent that it did not disturb the conversations or the proceedings in the assembly, but rather with a certain strangeness in its varied but low-level sound caressed the ears and spirits of the seated company with its sweetness.

Of meals.

p. 248

... Female dancers also, as well as female singers, were absent, barred by this consideration, that the Prince by their enticements might continually come in contact with them to the detriment of his person. Also absent were public fighters, wrestlers, comedians and similar bands of vagrants, whom otherwise it was the frequent and customary delight, stimulated by wine, to invite. With the beginning of the meal the activity of the musicians also ceased, and their instruments having been removed, it was no longer with strings but with dishes of food that they were involved; after the example of the rest, one and all interested in the provisions, they ate their meal sunk in a deep silence....

Fascicle IV; Relation IX: *Activities of sojourners in the palmgroves.*

Games and re-creations.

p. 738

In cases where there was a more frugal material situation, lest anything should be left out of the harvest of outward rejoicing, there were also at hand actors, poets, female dancers, musicians and whatever else you might desire for the gaiety of the gathering. Sometimes you see a *Shaer*, or bard singing with lively rhythm about the loves and exiles of the illustrious heroine *Leili*, and of her rival *Medsjnuun*; sometimes a *Ghesseh khaan*, or orator, who proclaims the strength, infamies and battles of *Rustàm*, the Hercules of the Persians and the son of *Saal*, or the excellence in javelin throwing and the other endowments of *Bahram*, son of *Jasdegerd*. Another time you will hear a member of the order of religious paupers called *derviish* who recites the miracles of *Aàli* himself, and of the rest of the Imams and high priests of their religion; or else he holds forth about *Omar*'s unjust usurping of the *khelafate* and curses him with fearful things. If all these should fail to appear a *Raiise-Deh*, or senior man of his district, retails the *Taäriife* or eulogy of its distinguished men, or the chronicles of his province and the great deeds and wars of its ancient princes. At one time some *molà*, or priest of religion or of the muses, reads out the Golestan of *Sheikh Saädi*, or pointed epigrams from the *Diwaan*[1] of *Khajeh Hafèze Shirazi* or of some others, separating them with a meditating silence. At another time a *taghlidchi*, a kind of actor, or a *hoghebaaz*, a juggler, interrupts these serious speeches with a welcome change to games and laughter. These are in my opinion the delights of the day's leisure.

Dance

As the sun goes down, when the cooler time of day restores relaxed limbs, thoughts also turn to organising dances. And, since every contryman is by no means skilled in the accomplishment of moving to the rhythms, there are therefore on hand around the square professors of both sexes, called *raghaas* who are more exactly capable in that art; these, having emigrated from Mediterranean towns, often visit the groves which at this time are full of men, and being trained in games and various acrobatics, run around with hanging hooks. To them, therefore, if they are present, are entrusted the ropes for leading the dances, which, even if they are absent, the people nevertheless do not omit. You would be astonished at the sights, and the elegant movements which they produce in their dancing. For they neither shake the earth with the weight of their alternating feet, as the poet says about the Sarmatians; neither do they run around madly with the lightness of the Gallic manner; but they move with tortoise-like step, with the soles of their feet naked, hither and thither for a long time, while with a lively movement of the body they follow the pulses and rhythms of the stringed instruments, and with every articulation of their limbs they express good humour. Then lying on their backs they bend their whole body with astonishing twistings, with their arms now extended along the ground and now stretched up above the top of their head, as though about to express the sorrows of mourners, not the gladness of merry-makers. At length with the drums being struck more quickly, they are caught up, continuously exulting, in the most rapid movements and in varied gyrations, and finally turning and rolling around in extreme fashion they combine the routines of female dancers with dramatic changeableness of humour.

1. Poetical works

How strange the music which regulates the limbs of the dancers! How agreeably dissonant and how delightful in the variety of its instruments! We assign first place among the instruments to the small reed instruments *Surnai (Fig. 1)*, which more than any others fill one's ears to satiety with their grunting sound. With these are sounded the ordinary small tinkling bells *(Fig. 2)*, similar to those of our country, or even very large cymbals called *Sindsj (Fig. 3)*, which correspond in shape to the plates we use at our tables, but with a smaller diameter and a larger rim, and with a protuberance furnished with a handle with which they can be held and struck against each other. A kettle-drum serves as foundation, either the *danbaal (Fig. 4)*, with the shape of an oblong cask, an instrument borrowed from the Indies, or the *dohùl (Fig. 5)*, imported from Europe, where we use it to lead military forces, or another very large one of the same shape, not portable on account of its size. All these are struck not with sticks but only with the fingers or hands lightly on both sides, thus giving out a rather quiet sound, and one made pleasanter by the comparative difference in sound of the alternating sides. The drums *donbak (Fig. 6)* seem to be an essential element in the rustic sung-dance; they are light in construction, made of baked potter's clay in the shape and size of earthenware pots, except that the bottom is prolonged into a short appendage by which they are carried under the arm of the player, the opening of the mouth being covered with a bladder or stretched small skin. With this, or with the only kind which is like the one common among peasants, the palm-tree cultivators celebrate their festivals, with united cheering and hand-clapping, in which the company joins to stimulate the energetic rhythms of the parading dancers. Sometimes the fourstringed lute *Chartaar* is the supporting instrument in a civic ensemble, either alone or in concert with other multistringed instruments. Often the kind of tambourine called *daf (Fig. 7)* is brought into the sweetly sounding ensemble; in size, shape and lightness at the axis it is similar to a small sieve, four spans in circumference, whose one open side is covered by a very thin small skin, whose sound is excited by a gentle blow of the fingers. Its rim, made of wood and thin, has four or five pairs of little disks, fixed crosswise at a hand's-breadth distance each by its axis, made of sonorous material, somewhat concave and very small in size, which when the tambourine is shaken give out by their mutual concussion a sound almost like that of cymbals. Sometimes instead of disks it has rings, whose sound is diffused and more relaxed; in that case its name is changed and it is called *Daireh (Fig. 8)*. Every kind of ensemble includes at least one instrument of this sort; frequently the instrument is used by the *Kawali*, at stage front with dancing; but more often it is a matter of the music- and dance-director, standing apart from the dancing, holding an identical instrument in each hand and hiding the performer's gesticulation and throats wide open in song from the view of others. Meanwhile, he not only produces various quiet rhythmical sounds from the struck skin, but also sometimes combines this with a more definite motion to produce jinglings and clangings from the attached disks. The song-leader accordingly performs his tune in as penetrating and loud a voice as possible; to this the company responds by groups, the instruments joining in, the company either sitting around in circles or dancing if the sung-dances are initiated. Sometimes, when hilarity has taken over, the whole crowd sings together, but as though with unlearned voices, with the instruments also handled in an unlearned way, and observing none of the rules of harmony (like those in a court choir), but all the time with the tones that are called unisons and octaves. Of whatever kind the ensemble may be it is unfailingly harmonious, quiet and unassuming, emanating a special charm by the variety of its rhythm, which through so many kinds of tunes that are always in quick triple movement is performed with combined precision and spirit. They do not play down to the boorish and unlearned sort of listener and they are in addition completely knowledgeable in the art of music, so that people wonder with some justice how these ordinary people can excel in the performance of varying rhythms, which our people are taught in schools only by long application to this art. There are more kinds of Persian instruments that are used at parties and for pleasant listening in private, also in military service, and in the market-places of cities for announcing the seasonal festivals. Among the *thabl* or kettle-drums, the *Kuus (Fig.9)* is used to lead a battle-line; it is a large kettle-drum, made of bronze, similar to ours but constricted by a net made of string in order to moderate the sound; it us beaten with two sticks whose extremities are curved. *Nagharèh (Fig. 10)* are an identical pair of kettle-drums of the same shape and capacity, of very small size, attached to each other by a strong link and played upon with a skill unique in the art of drumming. A *theblèbaas (Fig. 11)*, that is, a falcon's drum, is very small, made of bronze, extended into an appendage, and furnished with a very close net; its sound is said to be used call back falcons sent up for bird-catching. Single ones attached to saddles on their left side are carried by nobles and by the Shah himself. Another kind of kettle-drum *(Fig. 12)* is also found: it is made of wood, and somewhat larger, of an oval-oblong shape, and is particularly associated with the Multhani[1] who live in this kingdom. An exotic instrument, as it seems to

1. Kaempfer has explained (p. 174) that more than thousand Indians from the region of 'Multha-nia' (now in Pakistan) were among the non-indigenous groups living in Persia.

me, it is played by each naked and unequipped hand at the same time, or at one time by the right and another by the left. Among the *Nefiir*, or trumpets, the first in horribleness of sound is *Gharahnà (Fig. 13)* of the length of two outstretched arms with the shape of the acoustic instrument. Another *(Fig. 14)*, also called by the generic name, has a more subtle sound, is straight and very slender, of the length of two outstretched arms. A third, *Shakhe Nafiir (Fig. 15)*, that is, curved trumpet, is equally large and of bronze, bent into the shape of an immense horn. Among the *Uud*, or lutes, which sound with strings made from the intestines of sheep, the most common is a three-stringer *(Fig. 16)*, with a very long neck, a slightly ovoid body and a small belly-cover of skin. These exist with four, five or more strings; the most highly esteemed is *Chahzadeh (Fig. 17)*, corresponding generally in size and shape to ours, equipped with eight or nine strings, which are always tuned in unison in pairs, the lowest being triple if it has nine strings. Among so-called Viols, the one named *Kamaantchèh (Fig. 18)*, which is furnished with three and sometimes four strings, claims the chief place; skilfully played it excels any other kind of instrument in the quiet sweetness of its sound. It is played with a bow furnished with horse-hair, while its lowest part rests on the ground in the manner of violas *da gamba* as they are called. The head is slender and shaped like a cone, provided with tuning-pegs for the number of strings, the heads being large enough to fill the hand of one tuning it. The body is round, a span in diameter, and covered with a small skin; the instrument terminates at the bottom in an iron spike, artfully shaped, of the length of a span and a half. The whole contrivance, including the spike, extends to five spans in length; it is magnificently inlaid with mother-of-pearl and gold threads with a craftsmanship worthy of its elegance. There is also a Pandura of different construction, provided with four strings *(Fig. 19,)* which is decidedly exotic; it is held in the same position and also played with a bow. Its neck is narrow and short, its belly double, more oblong, fuller and open in the upper part, smaller in the lower, and covered by a small wooden belly. Among the stringed instruments in the manner of short-necked lutes there are different kinds, varying in the number of strings; we have depicted here only one of them *(Fig. 20)*, on account of the unusualness of its shape. Among zithers, the *Chang* is the commonest, and is easily handled by an uninstructed person; it is provided with six strings and has the shape of an obtuse-angled triangle *(Fig. 21)*. Less common is one furnished with many strings, but quadrangular *(Fig. 22)*; it is played either with curved sticks or with quills, and is less different than the other from ours in shape and manner of performance. I omit the contrivance with eight small pipes called *Musighaar (Fig. 23)*, blown into by the mouth; I omit reed-instruments, bagpipes, rustic reed-pipes, rattles, lest we hinder the progress of our history.

14 *ENGELBERT KAEMPFER*

The History of Japan, giving an Account of the ancient and present State and Government of that Empire;..Written in High-Dutch by Engelbertus Kaempfer, M.D. Physician to the Dutch Embassy to the Emperor's Court; and translated from his Original Manuscript, never before printed, by J.G.Scheuchzer, F.R.S. and a Member of the College of Physicians, London, 2 vols., London, 1727

Book III (Of the state of Religion in **JAPAN**), Chapter III: *Of the Sintos Rebi, that is, their fortunate and Holidays, and the Celebration thereof.*

....

p.216

....The worshippers, having first wash'd and clean'd themselves, put on the very best cloath they have, with a *Kamisijno*, as they call it, or *a garment of Ceremony*, every one according to his ability.....All this being done, they strike thrice the bell, which is hung up over the door of the *Mia*, for the diversion of the Gods, whom they believe to be highly delighted with the sound of Musical Instruments, and so retire....

Devotions of the Japanese how perform'd.

....

Book V (The Author's two Journies To the Emperor's Court at JEDO, the City of his Residence), Chapter V: *Of the great Numbers of people, who daily travel on the Roads.*

....

p. 433

....Some of these form themselves into a society, which is generally compos'd of four persons, clad in white linnen, after the fashion of the *Kuge*, or persons of the holy Ecclesiastical Court of the *Dairi*, or Ecclesiastical Hereditary Emperor. Two of them walking a grave, slow, deliberate pace, and standing often still, carry a large barrow adorn'd and hung about with Fir-branches, and cut white paper, on which they place a large bell made of light substance, or a kettle, or something else taken out and alluding to some old romantick history of their Gods, and Ancestors. Whilst a third, with a commander's staff in his hand, adorn'd out of respect to his office, with a bunch of white paper, walks or rather dances before the barrow, singing, with a dull heavy voice, a song relating to the subject they are about to represent. Mean while the fourth goes begging before the houses, or addresses himself to charitable travellers, and receives and keeps the money which is given them out of charity. Their day's journies are so short, that they can easily spend a whole summer upon such an expedition.

Pilgrims to Isje.

152

p. 434

*,ging Order
Nuns.*

To this shav'd begging tribe belongs a certain remarkable religious order of young Girls, call'd *Bikuni,* which is as much as to say, *Nuns....* They are, in my opinion, by much the handsomest girls we saw in Japan.... They particularly watch people of fashion, who travel in *Norimons,* or in *Cango's,* or on *Horse-back.* Assoon as they perceive some body a coming, they draw near and address themselves, tho' not all together, but singly, every one accosting a gentleman by herself, singing a rural song: if he proves very liberal and charitable, she will keep him company and divert him for some hours....

p. 435

Jammabos.

Having thus given an account of these *Bikunis,* it will not be improper to add a few words of another religious begging order of the *Jammabos,* as they are commonly call'd, that is *Mountain-Priests,* or rather *Jammabus,* that is *Mountain-Soldiers,* because at all times they go arm'd with swords and scimiters.... They commonly live in the neighbourhood of some famous *Cami Temple,* and accost travellers in the name of that *Cami,* which is worship'd there, making a short discourse of his holiness and miracles, with a loud course voice, mean while to make the noise still louder, they rattle their long staffs loaded at the upper end with Iron rings to take up the Charity-money which is given them; and last of all they blow a trumpet made of a large shell ((Original, ed. Dohm: einem grossen Schnekenhorn))....

p. 436

Further Account of Beggars.

There are many more beggars, travellers meet with along the roads.... Others of this tribe, who make up far the greater part, sit upon the road all day long upon a small course mat. They have a flat bell, like a broad mortar, lying before them, and do nothing else, but repeat with a lamentable singing-tune the word *Namanda,* which is constracted from *Namu Amida Budsu,* a short form of prayers, wherewith they address the God *Amida,* as the patron and advocate of departed souls. Mean while they beat almost continually with a small wooden hammer upon the aforesaid bell, and this they say, in order to be the sooner heard by *Amida,* and I am apt to think, not without an intent to be the better taken notice of by passengers too.

....

Not to mention numberless other common beggars, some sick, some stout and lusty enough, who get people's charity by praying, singing, playing upon fiddles, guitars and other musical instruments ((Orig.: Singen, Violinen- und Zitterspielen)), or performing some juggler's tricks, I will close the account of this vermin with an odd remarkable sort of beggar's musick, or rather chime of bells, we sometimes, but rarely, met with in our journey to court, and which is from the number of bells call'd *Fatsio Canne*, the chime or musick of eight. A young boy with a sort of wooden roof or machine pendant from his neck, and a rope with eight strings about it, -from which hang down eight bells of different sounds, turns round in a circle, with a swiftness scarce credible, in such a manner, that both the machine which rests upon his shoulders, and the bells turn round with him horizontally, the boy in the mean while with great dexterity and quickness beating them with two hammers, makes a strange odd sort of a melody. To encrease the noise, two people sitting near him beat, one upon a large, the other upon a smaller drum. Those, who are pleas'd with their performance, throw them some *Sennis*, or farthings, upon the ground.

....

Book V, Chapter XII: *Description of the City of* Jedo, *its Castle and Palace, with an account of what happen'd during our stay there; our Audience and Departur.*

....

p. 534

.... The Emperor, who hitherto sat among the Ladies, almost opposite to us, at a considerable distance, did now draw nearer, and sate himself down on our right behind the lattices, as near us as possibly he could. Then he order'd us to take off our *Cappa*, or Cloak, being our garment of Ceremony, then to stand upright, that he might have a full view of us; again to walk, to stand still, to compliment each other, to dance, to jump, to play the drunkard, to speak broken Japanese, to read Dutch, to paint, to sing, to put our cloaks on and off. Mean while we obey'd the Emperor's commands in the best manner we could, I join'd to my dance a love-song in High German. In this manner, and with innumerable such other apish tricks, we must suffer ourselves to contribute to the Emperor's and the Court's diversion....

Second Audience in the inner Palace.

....

.... The rooms, where we were admitted to audience, were fill'd behind the skreens and lattices with crowds of spectators, who wöuld fain have oblig'd us to shew them some of our European customs and ceremonies, but could obtain nothing excepting only a short dance at *Bengo's* house (who came home himself a back way) and a song from each of us, at the youngest Counsellor's of State, who liv'd in the Northern part of the castle.

....

p. 536

Visit the
Counsellors
of State.
And other
chief Officers
of the Crown.

On *Friday* the 30th of *March* ((1691)), we rode out again be-
times in the morning, to make some of our remaining visits.... After this
manner ((smoking, eating and drinking)) we were entertain'd for about
an hour and a half, when they desir'd us to sing a song, and to dance,
the first we refus'd to comply with, but satisfied them as to the last....

p. 537

Visits made to
the Governors
of Nagasaki

On the 31st of March, we rode out again at ten in the morning,
and went to the houses of the Governors of *Nagasaki*, two of whom
were then absent and upon their government.... The person that treated
us in the absent Governor's name, and the other gentlemen who were
then present in the room, entertain'd us likewise very civilly, and we
could not but take notice, that everything was so cordial, that we made
no manner of scruple of making ourselves merry, and diverting the
Company each with a song....

Chapter XIV: *Our Second JOURNEY to COURT.*

....

p. 574

On the 17th of *March* ((1692)), we had our audience of the
Governor.... The rest of the audience was taken up with examining our
hats, with making us write, paint and sing. We were also desir'd to
dance, and to shew them more of our customs and ceremonies, but we
refus'd it....

....

p. 587

.... The Emperor sate behind the middle skreen on a place, which was
somewhat rais'd above the level of the room.... We made our obeisances
first according to the fashion of the Japanese, but were soon commanded to come nearer the skreens, and to do it after the European manner.
The obeisances made, I was order'd to sing a song. I chose one, which I
had formerly compos'd for a lady, for whom I had a peculiar esteem
((orig.: Ich sang demnach eben die Arie, die ich zu Ehren meiner alten
und mir in allen Ehren treu gewesenen Florimene im vorigen Jahre
alhier gemacht hatte)), and as at the latter end I extolled her beauty
and other excellent qualities, in a poetical stile, above the value of
hundred thousands and millions of pieces of money, I was ask'd, by
order of the Emperor, what the meaning of it was: upon which I
return'd in answer, it was nothing but a sincere wish of mine, that
heaven might bestow millions of portions of health, fortune and prosperity upon the Emperor, his family and court....

15 AMÉDÉE FRÉZIER

Amédée François Frézier (1682-1773), engineer and navigator, sailed on November 23, 1711, from Saint-Malo, his native town, to the Pacific, which he was the first Frenchman to map adequately. In 1719 he went to Santo Domingo, of which he did the first exact map in 1724. His *Relation du Voyage de la Mer du Sud* was printed in Paris in 1716, and in Amsterdam in 1717; a Dutch translation was published in Amsterdam in 1718.

Monsieur Frezier, Engineer in Ordinary to the French King, *A Voyage to the South-Sea, and along the Coasts of Chili and Peru, in the years 1712, 1713, and 1714*, London, 1717

Part II: *Containing the Voyage along the Coasts of* Chili *and* Peru.

p. 62

The Manner of their Assemblies consists in carrying into a good *Assemblies of* Indians Plain, chosen for that Purpose, a great Quantity of Liquor; and when they have begun to drink, the Eldest, or he who on some other Account is to make a Speech to the rest, undertakes to lay before them the Matter in hand, and delivers his Opinion with much Solidity; for they are said to be naturally eloquent: After which, the Resolution is taken by the Plurality of Votes, and publish'd by Beat of Drum; three Days are allow'd to consider on it, and if in that Time no Inconveniency be found, the Project is infallibly put in Execution, after confirming the Resolution, and settling the Means to bring it to Effect.

Those Means are within a very small Compass; for the *Caciques* furnish their Subjects with nothing to make War: They only give them Notice, and every Man brings with him a Bag of Meal, either of Barley or *Indian* Corn, which they put into Water, and live upon it many Days. Each of them has also his Horse and Arms always in a Readiness; so that they form an Army in a Moment, without any Expence; and, to prevent any Surprize, there is always, in every *Caziqueship*, on the highest Eminence, a Trump, or Instrument made of a Bull's Horn, which can be heard two Leagues about. As soon as any Accident happens, the *Cacique* sends to sound that Horn, and every Man knows what is in Agitation, to repair to his Post.

....

Their Manner of Fighting is, to form Squadrons in Files of 80, or 100 Men, some arm'd with Pikes, and others with Arrows intermix'd; when the foremost are broken, they succeed one another so quick, that it does not appear that ever they gave Way. They always take care to secure a Retreat into the Bogs, or Morasses, where they are safer than in the best Fortress. They march to Battle in a very fierce Manner, by Beat of Drum, with their Weapons painted, their Heads adorn'd with Plumes of Feathers; and before they engage, the General commonly makes a Speech; after which they all beat with their Feet, and give hideous Shouts, to encourage one another to fight.

When they are obliged to fortify themselves, they make Palisadoes, or else only entrench themselves behind great Trees: Before them, at certain Distances, they dig Pits, the Bottoms whereof they set full of Stakes upright, with Briars, and cover them with Turf, to impose upon their Enemies. Unhappy those who fall into their Power! for they tear them, draw out their Hearts, which they cut in Pieces, and wallow in their Blood like wild Beasts. If it happens to be a Man of any Note, they put his Head upon the Point of a Pike, afterwards drink out of the Skull, and at last make a Dish of it, which they keep as a Trophy; and of the Leg Bones they make Flutes for their Rejoycings, which are only dismal Drunken Bouts, and last as long as the Drink they have brought. This Debauch is so pleasing to them, that those who are Christians, celebrate, or rather prophane, the Festivals of their Religion in that Manner.

Festivals.

I was Witness of a Festival the Slaves of an *Encomienda*, belonging to two *Spaniards* of the Name of *Peter*, kept on the Day of the Name of their Masters, in the Village of *Talcaguana*, near which we lay at Anchor.....

When they had eaten, they mounted on a Sort of Scaffold made like an Amphitheatre, the Standard being in the Middle, and the others with their long Canes by it. There, being adorn'd with Feathers of Ostriches, Flamenco's, and other Birds of sprightly Colours, stuck round their Caps, they fell to singing to the Sound of two Instruments, made of a Piece of Wood, with only one Hole bored through it; blowing in which, either stronger or more gently, they form'd a Sound more or less sharp, or flat. They kept Measure alternatively with a Trumpet made of a Bull's Horn, fastned to the End of a long Cane. the Mouth of which had a Pipe, that sounds like a Trumpet. ((Original: dont l'embouchure avoit une anche qui a le son de la trompette.)) They fill'd up this Symphony with some Strokes of a Drum, whose heavy and doleful Sound was answerable enough to their Mien; which, in the Height of their Exclamations, had nothing in it that was gay. I observ'd them attentively on the Stage, and did not, during the whole Festival, see one smiling Countenance among them.

The Women gave them *Chicha* to drink, being a Sort of Beer, of which more hereafter, with a Wooden Instrument about two Foot and a half long, consisting of a Handle-Cup at one End, and a long Beak at the other, with a winding Channel cut along it, to the end the Liquor may run out gently into the Mouth through a little Hole bored in the Bottom of the Cup or Dish at the Head of the Channel. With this Instrument they make themselves as drunk as Beasts, singing without Intermission, and all of them together; but in so unartificial a Tone, that three Notes would suffice to express the Whole. ((Music-Notation II))

The Words they sing have also neither Rhyme nor Cadency, nor any other Subject than whatsoever occurrs to their Fancy: Sometimes they recount the History of their Ancestors: sometimes they speak of their Family, and sometimes say what they think fit of the Festival, and of the Occasion of celebrating it, &c.

....

p. 95

At the Foot of the Fortress, in a little Gut, or narrow Space, is the Borough or Town of *Valparaiso*, consisting of about a hundred poor Houses, without any Order, and of several Heights; it also stretches out along the Sea, where the Stores of Corn or Granaries are. As little as the Place is, there are, besides the Parish, two Monasteries; the one of *Franciscans*, and the other of *Augustins*. Of 150 Families there may be in the Place, there are scarce 30 of them Whites; the rest are Blacks, Mulatto's, and Mestizo's..... *Valparaiso Town.*

....

This Festival among the *Spaniards* is one of the first Class; they kept it with as much, nay, I dare say, more Veneration, than those of the most sacred Mysteries of our Religion: For solemnizing of it, there were Illuminations on the Eve, and Fireworks, consisting of some Sky-Rockets, made in Canes instead of Cartridges, and several Volleys of Chambers. The three next Days a private Person entertain'd the Publick with a Bull Feast, which I thought did not much satisfy my Curiosity. We saw nothing there that was worth looking at, but only a Man astride on one of those mettled Animals, with Spurs, the Rowels whereof were four Inches Diameter, after the Country Fashion. That Engagement was perform'd in a Place hemm'd in with Scaffolds, fill'd with as many People as there were Inhabitants, who are much delighted with that Sport. The three next Days they acted Plays in the same Place, before the Gate of S. *Francis*'s Church, by Candle-light, in the open Air. It would be hard to relate the Subjects, so much they vary'd *Festival of the Rosary.*

and changed; to speak properly, they were no other than Interludes of Farces, mixed with Dancing of several Sorts, well enough perform'd, and even fine, after the Manner of the Country, bating the Symphony, which consisted in only one Harp, and some Guitars; but that which made their Recitative ridiculous, and no way edifying, was an impertinent Mixture they made of the Praises of *our Lady of the Rosary*, with downright Buffonry, and Obscenities not clean couch'd.

....

p. 203

Arrival at
Lima

That Way I enter'd on the 2d of *October* 1713, in order to stay at *Lima* till a Ship sail'd for *France*. Two Days after my Arrival there, they celebrated the Feast of S. *Francis* of *Assisium*, which is none of the least in the Year; for the *Spaniards* being posses'd and infatuated by the Friers, especially the *Franciscans* and the *Dominicans*, look upon the Founders of those two Orders as the greatest Saints in Heaven. The Veneration they pay them extends even to the Habits of their Orders, much beyond other Monastical Habits.

.....

The Festival began at the Evensong of the Eve, by a Procession of the *Dominicans*, in which ten Men carry'd the Figure of S. *Dominick*, going to visit his Friend S. *Francis*. He was clad in rich Gold Stuffs, and glittering with small Stars of Silver, strew'd upon him, that he might be seen at a Distance.

.....

The next Day there was a long Sermon, and Musick, where they sung *Spanish* Motetts. The Monastery was open'd to the Women, and at Night another Procession carry'd S. *Dominick* home: Then, tho' it was Day, there was another Fire-work, and a Giant came down by a Rope to attack a Castle, and fight a Serpent with three Heads.

....

p. 238

Customs and Manners of the Spaniards *of* Peru.

Before we leave *Peru*, it will be proper, in this Place, to say something of what I could observe of the Manners of the *Creolian Spaniards*, that is, those born in that Country. To begin with Religion, I must observe, that, like those in *Europe*, they value themselves upon being the best Christians of all Nations; they even pretend to distinguish betwixt themselves and us by that Qualification; so that among them it is a very usual Way of speaking, to say a Christian and a *French* Man to signify a *Spaniard* and a *French* Man: But, without diving into the

Interior of either, they have nothing of the outward Practice of th
Church Discipline, by which they may merit that Pre-eminence.....

....

Next to the Rosary follows the Devotion of Mount *Carmel*, which is no less beneficial to the *Mercenarians*, than the former ıs to the *Dominicans*.

That of the immaculate Conception is next; the *Franciscans* and the *Jesuites* have gain'd it such Reputation, that they mention it at commencing all Actions, even the most indifferent. Praised be, say they, when a Sermon begins, at Grace, and at Candle-lighting, in every House, praised be the most Holy Sacrament of the Altar, and the Virgin *Mary*, our Lady, conceiv'd without Blemish or original Sin, from the first Instant of her natural Being. They add to the Litanies, *Absque labe concepta, Thou who art conceiv'd without Blemish*. In short, this Sentence is foisted in at all Times, when it can neither serve for the Instruction, nor the Edification of the Faithful; and the Expressions in the Hymns they sing, in Honour of that Opinion, are so singular, that it will not be ungrateful to see some Staves of them here with the Notes.

In them may be observ'd an Application of the 6th Verse of the 18th *Psalm*, according to the Vulgate, *In sole posuit tabernaculum suum, He placed his Tabernacle in the Sun*; by which it appears, that the Author of that Hymn was not well vers'd in the Language of Holy Writ, which the *Spaniards* seldom learn; for if he had consulted the *Hebrew*, he would certainly have perceiv'd, that the Meaning of that Passage is, that God has placed the Throne of the Sun in the Heavens, *Soli posuit solium suum in eis*, He placed the Throne for the Sun in them, that is, in the Heavens, which does not suit with their Subject.
((Music-Notation III))

p. 255

Their Manner of Dancing is almost quite different from ours, where we value the Motion of the Arms, and sometimes that of the Head. In most of their Dances, their Arms hang down, or else are wrapp'd up in a Cloak they wear; so that nothing is seen but the Bending of the Body, and the Activity of the Feet. They have many Figure Dances, in which they lay by their Cloaks, or Mantles; but the Graces they add are rather Actions than Gestures.

The Men dance almost after the same Manner, without laying aside their long Swords, the Point whereof they keep before them, that it may not hinder them in rising or coupeeing, which is sometimes to such a Degree, that it looks like kneeling. I could wish I had been skill'd in Choregraphy, to represent some of their Dances. I will, nevertheless, here insert the Tune of one of those that are common with them, as the Minuet is in *France*: they call it *Zapateo*, because, in Dancing, they alternatively strike with the Heel and the Toes, taking some Steps, and coupeeing, without moving far from one Place. By this Piece of Musick may be discern'd what a barren Taste they have in touching the Harp, the Guitarre, and the *Bandola*, which are almost the only Instruments used in that Country. The two last are of the Species of Guitarres, but the *Bandola* has a much sharper and louder Sound. It is to be observ'd, that the Bass is made in *France*, to the Humour of the Harp. ((Music-Notation IV))

16 JEAN BAPTISTE DU HALDE

The French Jesuit Jean-Baptiste Du Halde (1674-1743) was secretary to Father Latellier, confessor to Louis XIV. His *Description géographique, historique, chronologique, politique et physique de l'empire de la Chine et de la Tartarie chinoise* (Paris, 1735), for which he drew upon reports and memoirs of Jesuit missionaries to China since the sixteenth century, was the main source of information on that country for Europeans until late in the eighteenth century. There was a copy in the library of the Earl of Macartney, leader of the embassy which is the subject of the following section of this anthology.

E. G. Cox (*Reference Guide to the Literature of Travel*, I, 335) remarks: "The whole is, for the most part, a collection of pieces on several subjects, transmitted by the Jesuits residing in China to those of their order at home in France, and is reduced to one body by Du Halde, who added what he saw fit from other Relations and printed works. Lowndes ((i.e., William T. Lowndes, *Bibliographer's Manual of English Literature*, rev. Henry G. Bohn, 11 vols., London, 1857-1865, originally printed in 1834)) asserts that Du Halde failed to exercise a sound judgment and a scrupulous examination into the truth of many facts and opinions which he admitted into the work. Others have regarded it as the completest and most valuable history of the Chinese Empire which had appeared up to the time of its publication."

The occasional quotations from the original French given in the course of some of the extracts below were taken from the print of 1736 published by Henri Scheurleer in The Hague.

A Description of the Empire of China and Chinese-Tartary, together with the Kingdoms of Korea, and Tibet: from the French of P. J. B. Du Halde, Jesuit ((translated by R. Brookes)), 2 vols., London, 1738, 1741

Vol. I, p. 464
Declaration of the Emperor Ngay ti, *for reforming* Music.
At present, three great Abuses prevail among us; Profuseness in Entertainments, and Apparel; an Itch after Numbers of vain Ornaments, and a Passion for the tender effeminating Music of (┆ ┆)*Chin* and *Wey*. Prodigality ruins Families in the third Generation: and by it the whole Empire becomes poorer. The Itch for vain Ornaments, occasions Multitudes of People to attend only very useless Arts, and to neglect Agriculture; and effeminating tender Music inspires Licentiousness. To pretend, while these subsist, to introduce Plenty and Innocence into a State, is to seek a pure limpid Stream from a muddy Fountain. *Con-*

fucius had a great deal of Reason to say, that the Music of *Chin* should be avoided, because it inspired a Loosness of Manners.

By these Presents, we discharge our Band of Music, and all the Officers attending on it. As for the ordinary Music in the Ceremonies of *Tyau*, and the musical warlike Instruments, we do not pretend to alter them; these are approv'd of in our (*) *King*, but no Officers are appointed for these Purposes. *We will* that it be enquired into, to which of the other Officers it will be proper to commit the Management of these Matters.

The Emperor Kang hi, *who pigned himself upon being a lover of Music, makes the following Remark upon this Declaration.* Music has the Virtue to calm the Heart, and for that the wise Man loves it. Besides, in diverting himself with it, he may exercise himself in governing well, by an easy and just Application of the Government in Music. But with Regard to wanton Music, that admits of no Comparison. *Ngay* was in the right, to retrench such a number of needless Expences.

A Gloss. The Emperor saved, by this Reformation, the Pensions and Entertainment of above 440 Persons.

(I I) These are the Names of a Country, formerly two petty Kingdoms.
(*) Old Books that regulate these Affairs

Vol. II, p. 124

Of their MUSIC

Music

If you will believe the *Chinese*, they are the first Inventors of Music, and they boast of having formerly brought it to the highest Perfection: But if what they say be true, it must have strangely degenerated, for it is at present so imperfect that it scarcely deserves the Name, as may be judged by two or three of their Airs, which I have pricked down to give the Reader some Idea thereof. ((Music-Notation V))

Indeed in former times Music was in great Esteem; and *Confucius* himself undertook to introduce the Rules belonging to it into every Province whose Government he was intrusted with. The *Chinese* at this Day greatly bewail the Loss of the ancient Books which treated of this Art.

Nature of their Music.

At present Music is seldom used but at Plays, Feasts, Marriages, and on such like Occasions ((see Illustrations J 1-2)). The Bonzas employ it at Funerals; but when they sing, they never raise and fall their Voice a Semi-tone, but only a third and a fifth, or an Octave, and this Harmony is very charming to the Ears of the *Chinese*: in like manner the Beauty of their Concerts does not consist in the Variety of Voices, or the Difference of Parts, but all sing the same Air, as is the Practice throughout *Asia*. They like the *European* Music well enough, provided there be only one Voice to accompany the Instruments ((1736: pourvu qu'ils n'entendent chanter qu'une seule voix, accompagnée de quelques instrumens)): But as for the most curious Part of Music, I mean the Contrast of different Voices, of grave and acute Sounds, Dieses, Fugues, and Syncopes, they are not at all agreeable to their Taste, appearing to them a confused Discord ((1736: une confusion désagréable)).

They have no Musical Notes, nor any Symbols to distinguish the Diversity of Tones, the rising or falling of the Voice, and the other Variations, that constitute Harmony: However they have certain Characters that express the different Tones. The Airs which they sing, or play upon their Instruments, are learned almost wholly by rote, or by the Ear; nevertheless they make new ones from time to time, and the late Emperor *Kang-hi* composed some himself. These Airs well plaid upon their Instruments, or sung by a good Voice, have something in them that will please even an *European* Ear.

Play'd all by Rote, for want of Notes.

The Ease wherewith we are able to take down an Air at only once hearing it, by the Assistance of Notes, extremely surpriz'd that Monarch, who in the Year 1679 sending for P. *Grimaldi* and P. *Pereira* to play upon the Organ and Harpsicord, which they had formerly presented him with, he liked our *European* Airs, and seemed to take great Pleasure in them. Then he ordered his Musicians to play a *Chinese* Air upon one of their Instruments, and play'd himself in a very graceful Manner. In the mean time P. *Pereira* took his Pocket Book ((1736: ses tablettes)), and pricked down all the Tune, while the Musicians were playing ((1736: chantoient)); and when they had made an End, repeated it as perfectly as if he had practised it long before, without missing one Note: This so surprized the Emperor, that he could scarcely believe it. He bestowed great Commendations on the Justness, Harmony and Facility of the *European* Music; But above all admired the Missionary had in so short a time learned an Air which had given him and his Musicians no small Trouble; and that by help of certain Characters he was become so thoroughly Master of it, that it was not possible for him to forget it.

The Emperor surprized at the *European* Manner.

I o be the more sure of this, he made several farther Trials, and sung many different Airs, which the Jesuit pricked ((1736: notoit à mesure)), and repeated immediately after with the greatest Exactness: *It must be owned*, cry'd the Emperor, *the* European *Music is incomparable*, and *this Father*, (speaking of P. Pereira) *has not his Equal in all the Empire*. This Prince afterwards established an Academy for Music, composed of all those who were most skilled in that Science, and committed it to the Care of his third Son, who was a Man of Letters, and had read a great deal. They began by examining all the Authors that had written on this Subject, causing all sorts of Instruments to be made, after the ancient Manner, and according to settled Dimensions. These Instruments appearing faulty, they were corrected by the more

Establishes an Academy for Music.

modern Rules, after which they compiled a Book in four Volumes, with this Title: *The true Doctrine of the* LI HI ((1736: Ly lu)), *written by the Emperor's Order*. To these they added a fifth, containing all the Elements of *European* Music, composed by P. *Pereira*.

Chinese Instruments.

     The *Chinese* have invented eight sorts of Musical Instrument, which they think come nearest of any thing to a human Voice. Some are of Metal like our Bells, others of Stone, and one among the rest has some Resemblance to our Trumpet: Others are made with Skins like our Drums, of which there are several Kinds, and some so heavy, that to fit them for beating on they must be propped with a piece of Wood. They have vast Instruments with Strings, but the Strings are generally of Silk, seldom of Gut, such as the Cymbals, carried about by blind People, and their Violins; each of which kinds has but three Strings, and is played upon with a Bow ((1736: Telles sont leurs Vielles dont jouent les aveugles, & leurs Violons, qui n'ont les uns et les autres que trois cordes que l'on touche avec un archet)). But there is one Instrument with seven Strings, very much esteemed, and not disagreeable when played upon by a skilful Hand. There are others also, but they are made wholly of Wood, being pretty large Tables, which they clap against each other. The Bonzas use a little Board, which they touch with much Art, and in good Time. In short, they have Wind Music: Such are their Flutes, which are of two or three sorts, and an Instrument composed of several Pipes, which has some Resemblance of our Organ, and withal an agreeable Sound, but is very little, being carried in the Hand.

p. 341
The third Journey of Pere GERBILLON *into* Tartary, *in the Year* 1691.

    ....

.....The Emperor reviewed these Troops, by passing along the Ranks; all the Officers great and small standing overagainst their respective Standards. They made no Salute when the Emperor passed, nor did the Kettle-drums ((1736: timbales)) beat, or Trumpets sound. His Majesty then went to a little Eminence, about three Quarters of a Mile distant, where they had set up a great Pavillion and some Tents: As soon as he arrived he order'd the *Kalkas*, who had repair'd thither before, to approach, the *Hyas* being posted on both sides of the Pavillion. Mean while, the Regulos of *Pe-King* came from the Camp in good Order, at the Head of their respective Guards and Officers of the Household. They passed one after another before the Emperor, and posted themselves in Squadrons to the Right of his Majesty; after this they blew four Trumpets, call'd by the *Tartars*, *Lapa*, which have a very dull, disagreeable Sound ((1736: Trompettes fort sourdes)): They are great

Manner of attacking an Enemy.

round Tubes, of Copper, and 8 or 9 Feet long, terminating like our Trumpets ((1736: qui se terminent tant soit peu en cône, comme nos trompettes)). The *Tartars* make use of this Instrument to give the Signal of Battle, and tho' the Sound of it be very deep and hollow ((1736: sourd & désagréable)), it is heard a great way off: But a single Man is not sufficient to manage it, for one must hold it up in the Air, with a sort of Fork, while another blows it. As soon as those Trumpets began to sound, the Troops advanced slowly, and in good Order: When the Trumpets left off, the Troops halted, and did not resume their March till they sounded again. This was done thrice; but at the third time those Instruments being sounded louder than before, all the Troops hasted towards the Eminence where the Emperor was. The Cavalry, who were in both the Wings, extended themselves in Form of a Crescent, as it were to surround the Enemy's Army, which was supposed to be in the Place where we were....

....

Vol. I, p. 351
Of the Furnaces *or* Ovens *for Baking the* China

....

The Workmen do not undertake all the Models that come from Foreign Countries, they have some impracticable given them in *China*, tho' at the same time they perform such surprizing Works as Strangers would think impossible. For Instance, I have seen a large Lanthorn, like that of a Ship, all of one piece of *China*, thro' which one Candle sufficiently enlighten'd a whole Room. This was made seven Years ago at the command of the Hereditary Prince, who also order'd to be made divers Instruments of Music, particularly a Sort of small Organ, call'd *Tseng*, about a Foot high, consisting of fourteen Pipes, whose Harmony is agreeable enough; but they attempted it in vain. They succeeded better in making Flutes ((1736: flûtes douces)), Flagellets, and an Instrument nam'd *Yun-lo*, which is compos'd of divers small round Plates, a little concave, each of a particular Note. They hang nine in a Frame, at different Heights, which they strike like a Dulcimer ((1736: qu'on touche avec des baguettes comme le tympanon)), and it returns a little Tinkling, which agrees in Concert with other Instruments, and the Singers Tone. I concluded they had the Secret of incorporating a little Metal with these Pieces, to diversify the Sound; but I was mistaken, Metal being so incapable of uniting with the *China*, that if a Copper Farthing be put on the Top of one of the Piles in the Furnaces, it would, when it melts, pierce all the Cases and Vessels, so that all the Vessels in the Pile would have a Hole in the Middle. Nothing can give a

Remarkable Pieces of Workmanship.

Lanthorns. Musical Instruments.

Metal incapable of incorporating with China.

better Idea, than this, of the Effect of the Fire on all things in the Oven, which are affirm'd to be in a State of Fluidity.

17 THE EARL OF MACARTNEY'S EMBASSY

This group of extracts consists of observations recorded by members of Lord George Macartney's embassy from the King of England to the Emperor of China in 1793-94. Among the official tasks of the embassy was the obtaining of 'all the information possible about China, not only economic and political, but also military, intellectual, cultural and social as well as information about China's relations with Russia and other countries.'[1] The leader of this first British attempt to establish diplomatic contact with China was born in County Antrim, Ireland, and graduated from the University of Dublin (Trinity College). He was sent in 1764, at the age of twenty-seven, as envoy-extraordinary to the Court of Catherine the Great at St. Petersburg, where he stayed for three years. In 1775 he was made Governor of Grenada, where George Staunton then lived; in 1780 he was appointed Governor of Madras, and took Staunton as his secretary. Macartney's last public position was as Governor of Cape Colony from 1796 to 1798. Staunton was a native of Galway, Ireland, and had studied medicine at Montpellier; in the China embassy he was Secretary and Minister Plenipotentiary, with power to take up Macartney's functions if necessary. John Barrow, a native of Lancashire, was tutor to Staunton's son before the embassy, which he accompanied as Comptroller. He subsequently went to the Cape as Macartney's private secretary, staying there until 1802,[2] and was then for forty years Second Secretary to the Navy. J. C. Hüttner had completed studies in philology at Leipzig in 1787 with a dissertation entitled *De Mythis Platonis*. Staunton engaged him as Greek tutor to his son, in which capacity he was a 'gentleman' of the embassy. Macartney sent him in the brig *Jackall* to reconnoitre the navigation of the Gulf of Peichihli (Chihli), and again four days later sent him in the brig *Endeavour* to discuss the embassy's landing arrangements with the Mandarins. Hüttner also translated into Latin, for the information of the missionaries, documents that were being presented to the Emperor, while the Jesuit missionaries translated Chinese documents into Latin for communication to Macartney. Among the missionaries then in China was Father Jean-Joseph-Marie Amiot, who had been there for some sixty years; Barrow referred to him in the course of his discussion of Chinese music (p.   ). Macartney recorded in his journal that it was Father Amiot who first told him that a letter from the Emperor to the King was being prepared, and also offered his opinion on the reasons why the embassy failed in its chief objects.[3] After the

1. J.L. Cranmer-Byng, *An Embassy to China, Being the journal kept by Lord Macartney during his embassy to the Emperor Ch'ien-lung 1793-1794*, London, 1962, p. 30.
2. See item 19 in this anthology.
3. J.L. Cranmer-Byng, op. cit. p. 151.

embassy Hüttner lived in London, where, when in financial trouble, he was helped by Dr. Charles Burney to obtain a Civil Service post.[1] Aeneas Anderson was personal servant to Macartney, who seems to have foreseen that Anderson might publish his own observations, for he ended a note in his journal with the comment that 'even the memorandums of a *valet de chambre* might be of some value.'[2] William Alexander, a native of Maidstone, Kent, was the embassy's 'draughtsman', in a subsidiary capacity to, and with half the salary of Thomas Hickey, a countryman of Macartney, whose portrait he had painted. Although Hickey was 'painter' to the embassy, he did very little to record its visual side, while Alexander did a great number of depictions. Curiously, neither artist was among those who went with the embassy to the meeting with the Emperor at Jehol.[3] Alexander later became Assistant Keeper of Antiquities at the British Museum, with charge of the collection of prints and drawings.

Yet another member of Macartney's party published an account of his experiences. This was Samuel Holmes, one of the guardsmen, who was described by the contemporary editor of his *Journal* (London, 1798) as a 'worthy, sensible, but unlearned man.' Holmes recorded that as the ambassador's procession entered Jehol, proceeding in slow march, the 'band of music' played *God save the King* (*Journal*, p. 143). Holmes's journal was also published in a German translation (Weimar, 1805).

Macartney's embassy consisted of ninety-five persons who sailed in two ships. Among them was a 'band' of five German musicians (six were engaged, but one deserted at Plymouth) whose leader was John Zupfel. They took with them two violins, a viola, a violoncello, a bassoon, two basset-horns, a clarinet, a German flute and a fife. Their instruments, and all or some of their repertory, were supplied through the agency of Dr. Charles Burney, who noted in his diary that he helped to fit out the embassy with 'whatever belonged to musical matters, whether instruments, compositions, band, or decoration, that might contribute in that line, to its magnificence.' Burney was reimbursed in the sum of £ 76. Is. 4d. as 'balance for musical instruments', and Macartney rewarded him with a 'superb and very costly silver inkstand, of the most beautiful workmanship, upon which he had engraved a Latin motto, flatteringly expressive of his esteem for Dr. Burney.'[4]

Burney had given Macartney, who was a fellow-member of a London 'Literary Club',[5] a list of enquiries which might be made on the

1. Roger Lonsdale, *Dr. Charles Burney*, London, 1965, p. 463.
2. J.L. Cranmer-Byng, op. cit., pp. 199, 343.
3. Ibid., p. 342.
4. J.L. Cranmer-Byng, op. cit., p. 364; Percy A. Scholes, *The Great Dr. Burney*, London, 1948, ii, pp. 115-116.
5. Scholes, op. cit., ii, p. 115.

spot about the nature of Chinese music. With a view to his announced intention, which he did not fulfil, of including a chapter on 'National Music' in his *General History of Music* (London, 4 vols., 1776-1789), Burney had acquired information and music-notations, including material on Chinese music from Dr. James Lind.[1] Burney did, however, write an article on Chinese music for Abraham Rees's *Cyclopaedia* (London, 39 vols., 1802-1820), in which he acknowledged J. C. Hüttner's assistance. In a letter of March 1802 to Hüttner, Burney referred to information about Chinese music that Macartney had given him, in which he understood Hüttner had a part, and said that he had procured in 1777 'from a Gent. who had resided at Canton a Chest of Musical Instruments' and a number of Chinese tunes. In his will, which he made in 1807, Burney mentioned 'my two Gongs and oriental instruments in Chests sent from Canton by Mr. Matthew Raper and two of inferior quality brought by Lord Macartney when he returned from his Chinese embassy.'[2] Raper was presumably the 'English gentleman in Canton' referred to by John Barrow as having collected Chinese instruments and made drawings from which Barrow had engravings made for his book (see p. 193 and Illustrations M and N), and who notated some tunes which Barrow printed.

Although Macartney entered on-the-spot observations in his journal, and also wrote a series of chapters on some specific topics, these were not published in their original form until the edition by J. L. Cranmer-Byng in 1962. The compiling of an 'official' account was assigned to Staunton, who was able to draw on the journal and topic-chapters. He was probably assisted by Barrow, who was Staunton's librarian from 1795 to 1797, and was therefore presumably familiar with the Macartney material when writing his *Travels in China* and his account of the Embassy's voyage there in his *Voyage to Cochinchina*. Hüttner published his account in German, and also sent to the periodical *Journal des Luxus und der Moden*, which was published in Weimar, Karl Kambra's setting of the English poem by 'Hr. Sharp' in which was incorporated the work-song of the oarsmen on the Peyho River in the province of 'Pecheli' (Chihli). It is not precisely known during what years Kambra was in England, where he published sonatas, a collection of country dances and other items. Hüttner referred to 'Sharp' as a medical doctor in Lord Macartney's entourage; this was an error for Scott. Dr. William Scott was surgeon with the embassy, and Dr. Hugh Gillan was its physician and 'natural philosopher' (both were Scotsmen). An anonymous German translation was provided for readers

1. Lonsdale, op. cit., pp. 362, 338, 158; Scholes, op. cit., i, p. 301
2. Ibid., i, p. 301; ii, p. 271.

of the Weimar periodical, in which was also printed the English text. Charles Boettiger, publisher of T.F. Winckler's French translation of Hüttner's book (Paris 1799), added as an appendix some material from the Weimar periodical, including Kambra's setting underlaid with a French translation of the English poem and a translation of Hüttner's comments.

J. L. Cranmer-Byng thought that Aeneas Anderson's account of the embassy contained nothing of value on the diplomatic side, and inferred that it was put together by a ghost writer. He noted, however, that Anderson gave a fuller description of buildings and more details about food and lodging than the writers of other accounts.[1] Anderson's is the only published account that has a description of Henry Eades's funeral. He also made some caustic comments on the ridiculous appearance of those members of the embassy's retinue who went to Jehol in borrowed liveries.[2]

Since William Alexander did not go to Jehol with the embassy, his depiction of the Emperor's entrance (Illustrations L1-3) was not first-hand. It was made from a sketch done on the spot by Lieutenant Henry W. Parish, commander of the embassy's complement of twenty artillerymen and their six brass cannon.

1. Op. cit., 342-344.
2. His *Narrative*, pp. 183-185.

17a JOHN BARROW

John Barrow, *A Voyage to Cochinchina in the years 1792 and 1793*, London, 1806

Chapter VIII: *Batavia*

....

p. 206

....There were not any ladies in the company. Van Weegerman ((a member of the Dutch Council of India)) being a bachelor had no females in his house ((his country-house, a mile beyond the city gate)), except his haram of slaves amounting to about fifty in number, assorted from the different nations of the East, and combining every tinge of complexion from the sickly faded hue of a dried tobacco leaf to the shining polish of black marble. A band of Malay musicians played in the viranda during dinner.

....It was the 8th of March, the anniversary of the birth of the Prince of Orange, and a most magnificent entertainment was prepared on the occasion at the Governor's country-house....In different parts of the Batavian garden were stationed bands of musicians, some of which were Malays, and others Germans belonging to the garrison....

p. 211 ((a ball and supper followed))

....Some of the elder sort sat at table to a late hour, while the younger part returned to the ball-room, where reels and jigs and hornpipes now took place of country dances. A *Scoto- Batavian* officer displayed his raw-boned activity in a saraband, to the great amusement of the native dames, who had seldom witnessed such nimble capering. So fascinating was the entertainment that it was near four in the morning before the company dispersed.

Chapter X: *General sketch of the manners, character, and condition of the natives of Turon* ((in Cochinchina))

....

p. 295

In the farther division of the building a party of comedians was engaged in the midst of an historical drama when we entered; but on our being seated they broke off and, coming forward, made before us that obeisance of nine genuflexions and prostrations, which we had been so very uncivil to omit to the Mandarin and his painted skreen of silk; after which they returned to their labours, keeping up an incessant noise and bustle during our stay. The heat of the day, the thermometer in the shade standing at 81° in the open air, and at least ten degrees higher in the building, the crowds that thronged in to see the strangers, the horrible crash of the gongs, kettle drums, rattles, trumpets, and squalling flutes, were so stunning and oppressive, that nothing but the novelty of the scene could possibly have detained us for a moment. The most entertaining as well as the least noisy part of the theatrical exhibition was a sort of interlude, performed by three young women, for the amusement, it would seem, of the principal actress, who sat as a spectator in the dress and character of some ancient Queen; whilst an old eunuch, very whimsically dressed, played his antic tricks like a scaramouch or buffoon in a Harlequin entertainment. The dialogue in this part differed entirely from the querulous and nearly monotonous recitative of the Chinese, being light and comic, and occasionally interrupted by cheerful airs, which generally concluded with a common chorus. These airs, rude and unpolished as they were, appeared to be regular compositions, and were sung in exactly measured time. One in particular attracted our attention, whose slow melancholy movement breathed that kind of plaintive softness so peculiar to the native airs of the Scotch, to which indeed it bore a very close resemblance. The voices of the women were shrill and warbling, but some of their cadences were not without melody. The instruments at each pause gave a few short flourishes, till gradually overpowered by the swelling and deafening gong. Knowing nothing of the language, we were of course as ignorant of the subject as the majority of an English audience is of an Italian opera. In the shed of Turon, however, as well as in the theatre of the Haymarket, the eye was amused as well as the ear. At each repetition of the chorus the three Cochinchinese graces displayed their fine slender shapes in the mazy dance, in which, however, the feet were the least concerned. By different gestures of the head, body, and arms, they assumed a variety of figures; and all their motions were exactly adapted to the measure of the music. The burden of the chorus was not unpleasing, and was long recollected on the quarter-deck of the Lion, till the novelty which succeeded in China effaced it from the memory. In the latter country, however, we saw no dancing neither by men nor women, which makes it probable that this part of the Cochinchinese entertainment must be an amusement of their own invention, or introduced from the western part of India. A tolerably good notion may be collected of the theatre and the operatic part of the representation from the annexed engraving ((see Illustration K)).

No entrance money is ever expected in the theatres of China or Cochinchina. The actors are either hired to play at private entertainments, at a fixed sum for the day; or they exhibit before the public in a temporary shed, entirely exposed in front. On such occasions, instead of cheering the performers with empty plaudits, the audience throw among them pieces of copper money: for this purpose, the Mandarins brought us some hundred pieces strung on cords, of the same kind as those which are current in China. By the Cochinchinese the regular drama is called *Troien*, or *a relation of histories*. To the operatic interlude of recitative, air and dancing they give the name of *Song-sang*; and a grand chorus accompanied with the *gong*, the kettle drum, castanets, trumpets and other noisy instruments, is called the *Ring-rang*. The Ambassador had ordered his band to attend on shore, where they played a few light airs; but the Cochinchinese had no ear for the soft and harmonious chords of European music. Their *Ring-rang* and their *Song-sang* were infinitely superior in their estimation, and were the more applauded in proportion as they were the more noisy.

17b THE EARL OF MACARTNEY

An Embassy to China, Being the journal kept by Lord Macartney during his embassy to the Emperor Ch'ien-lung 1793-1794, edited with an Introduction and Notes by J.L. Cranmer-Byng, London, 1962[1]

p. 77

Friday, August 9. This morning I dispatched Mr. Proctor ((captain of the brig *Endeavour* of the Bombay Marine, sent by the East India Company to assist the embassy)) in the *Endeavour* from the river. He was obliged to take back with him the two Macao missionaries, Hanna and Lamiot, without their ever coming ashore. We found, indeed, that if they accompanied us to Pekin they would be considered as belonging to the Embassy and obliged to depart with it, whereas their intention is to enter into the Emperor's service and to remain the rest of their lives in China, like the other missionaries.

At noon the gongs or copper drums began to beat with a most deafening noise, and gave the signal for all being ready for departure. In less than an hour our whole fleet was under sail, and we proceeded up the river with a good breeze and flowing tide at the rate of about four miles per hour.

Sunday, August 11. This morning we arrived at the city of Tientsin.... Our yachts stopped almost in the middle of the town before the Viceroy's pavilion. On the opposite quay, close to the water, was erected for this occasion a very spacious and magnificent theatre, adorned and embellished with the usual brilliancy of Chinese decorations and scenery, where a company of actors exhibited a variety of dramas and pantomimes during several hours almost without intermission.

Both sides of the river were lined for near a mile in length with the troops of the garrison, all in uniform, accompanied by innumerable flags, standards, and pennants, and by the clangour of various instruments of war-like music. At noon I disembarked with all the gentlemen of the Embassy and my whole train of servants, musicians, and guards. I was received at my landing by the Viceroy and the Legate, and conducted to their pavilion, where as soon as we were seated the conversation began, and continued for some time in the same general strain of mutual compliments and profession as our former one at Hai-chin miao....

....

1. These extracts are printed by permission of the publishers, Longman Group, Limited, Harlow, Essex, England.

p. 90

Monday, August 19. I went down to the pandals this morning, where I met the Tartar Legate, Wang and Chou, and several other Mandarins, who were assembled there to give orders for the operations of the next day....

.....

....We entertained them with a concert of music, which they appeared to be much pleased with, and when they left us repeated the same flattering expressions and compliments which they had set out with in the beginning of their visit.

    This night died of dysentery after a long illness Henry Eades, a cunning artist in brass and iron, who, hearing of my intention to take with me to China a person in his branch, had strongly importuned both me and Sir George Staunton in London to give him a preference to other candidates....

Tuesday, August 20. Eades was buried this morning, all the servants, musicians, and guard attending his interment; the funeral service was read upon the occasion, and a volley of small arms was fired over his grave. Vast numbers of Chinese were spectators of the ceremony, and seemed to be a good deal affected by its order and solemnity. After it was over our baggage began to move, and a great part of it was dispatched before night.

....

p. 122

Saturday, September 14. This morning at four o'clock a.m. we set out for the Court under the convoy of Wang and Chou, and reached it in little more than an hour, the distance being about three miles from our hotel. I proceeded in great state with all my train of music, guards, etc. Sir George Staunton and I went in palanquins and the officers and gentlemen of the Embassy on horseback. Over a rich embroidered velvet I wore the mantle of the Order of the Bath, with the collar, a diamond badge and a diamond star.

    Sir George Staunton was dressed in a rich embroidered velvet also, and, being a Doctor of Laws in the University of Oxford, wore the habit of his degree, which is of scarlet silk, full and flowing. I mention these little particulars to show the attention I always paid, where a proper opportunity offered, to oriental customs and ideas. We alighted at the park gate, from whence we walked to the Imperial encampment, and were conducted to a large, handsome tent prepared for us on one side of the Emperor's. After waiting there about an hour his approach was announced by drums and music, on which we quitted our tent and came forward upon the green carpet ((see Illustrations L 1-3)).

....

p. 131

Tuesday, September 17. This day being the Emperor's birthday, we set out for the Court at three o'clock a.m., conducted by Wang, Chou and our usual attendants. We reposed ourselves for above two hours in a large saloon at the entrance of the palace enclosure, where fruit, tea, warm milk, and other refreshments were brought to us. At last notice was given that the festival was going to begin, and we immediately descended into the garden, where we found all the great men and Mandarins in their robes of state, drawn up before the Imperial pavilion. The Emperor did not show himself, but remained concealed behind a screen, from whence, I presume, he could see and enjoy the ceremonies without inconvenience or interruption. All eyes were turned towards the place where His Majesty was imagined to be enthroned, and seemed to express an impatience to begin the devotions of the day. Slow, solemn music, muffled drums, and deep-toned bells were heard at a distance. On a sudden the sound ceased and all was still; again it was renewed, and then intermitted with short pauses, during which several persons passed backwards and forwards, in the proscenium or foreground of the tent, as if engaged in preparing some *grand coup de théâtre.*

At length the great band both vocal and instrumental struck up with all their powers of harmony, and instantly the whole Court fell flat upon their faces before this invisible Nebuchadnezzar. 'He in his cloudy tabernacle shrined sojourned the while.' ((Editor's footnote: Milton, *Paradise Lost*, Bk. VII, 247-9)). The music was a sort of birthday ode or state anthem, the burden of which was 'Bow down your heads, all ye dwellers upon earth, bow down your heads before the great Ch'ien-lung, the great Ch'ien-lung'. And then all the dwellers upon China earth there present, except ourselves, bowed down their heads, and prostrated themselves upon the ground at every renewal of the chorus. Indeed, in no religion either ancient or modern, has the Divinity ever been addressed, I believe, with stronger exterior marks of worship and adoration than were this morning paid to the phantom of his Chinese Majesty. Such is the mode of celebrating the Emperor's anniversary festival according to the Court ritual.

....

p. 134

These pagodas, which all adjoin the park, are surrounded by a great wall and each pagoda is in a separate enclosure of its own....They are all buildings of great extent and magnificence, but Potala, which may be considered as the grand cathedral, is infinitely superior to the rest in point of magnitude, splendour and celebrity. It is an immense edifice, and with the offices belonging to it covers a vast deal of ground (not less than twenty-five acres) and contains, I should conceive, a greater quantity of materials than St. Paul's ((London)).....

In the chapel we found all the monks or lamas busily engaged in their devotions, dressed in yellow vestments, with books in their hands and chanting their liturgy in a kind of recitative, not unlike our cathedral service, and not disagreeable to the ear. The paraphernalia of religion displayed here — the altars, images, tabernacles, censers, lamps, candles, and candlesticks — with the sanctimonious deportment of the priests and the solemnity used in the celebration of their mysteries, have no small resemblance to the holy mummeries of the Romish Church as practised in those countries where it is rich and powerful. In the middle of the chapel is a small space railed off and elevated by three steps above the floor, which presents three altars richly adorned, and three colossal statues, one of Fo-hi, one of Fo-hi's wife, and the other of some great Tartar divinity, whose name I forget, all of solid gold....

17c SIR GEORGE STAUNTON

The Earl of Macartney ((from the papers of)), *An Authentic Account of an Embassy from the King of Great Britain to the Emperor of China,* ed. Sir George Staunton, 2 vols[1]., London, 1797

Vol. II, p. 162

Besides the visits which the Embassador received from the missionaries, as well as from the Legate, and Chinese gentlemen who conducted the Embassy, his Excellency was visited every day during his residence in Pekin by mandarines of rank, some engaged to it by the duty of their stations, others allured by curiosity, and not a few by the European band of music, which formed a concert every evening in the Embassador's apartments. Among these visitors was the chief director of the Emperor's orchestra, who constantly attended, and was so much pleased with some of the instruments, that he desired leave to take drawings of them. He declined accepting them as presents; but sent for painters, who spread the floor with sheets of large paper, and, having placed the clarionets, flutes, bassoons, and french horns upon them, traced with their pencils the figures of the instruments, measuring all the apertures, and noting the minutest particulars; and when this operation was completed, they wrote down their remarks, and delivered them to their employer, who said it was his intention to have similar instruments made by Chinese workmen, and to fit to them a scale of his own. A few Chinese had already, it seems, adopted the European violin; but it was not yet in common use. An instrument of their own, bearing a resemblance to it in form, had two strings only. Some Chinese have likewise learned to note their music upon ruled paper ((cp. Cranmer-Byng, p. 104 and n.23, p. 365)).

....

p. 262 ((The Emperor's reception of the embassy at Jehol))

Inhabitants of the different districts of the Emperor's wide domains appeared in separate groups, and in the costume of their respective countries. Whatever was particular in their usual exercises or habits, was here displayed. Several of them danced in a pleasing manner, and with graceful attitudes. There was some singing, and a vast variety of musical instruments. The musicians affected mostly slow and plaintive airs, not unlike those of the Highlanders of Scotland; which they played in exact and measured time. To Mr. Hüttner, a good judge of music, it appeared, that "their gammut was such as Europeans would

---

1. There was also a third volume, of plates, in folio.

call imperfect, their keys being inconsistent; that is, wandering from flats to sharps, and inversely; except when directed by a bell struck to sound the proper notes. Mr. Hüttner farther observed, that the Chinese, in playing on instruments, discovered no knowledge of semi-tones, nor did they seem to have any idea of counterpoint, or parts in music. There was always one melody, however great the number of performers; tho, in a few instances, some of the instruments played in the lower octave, while the rest continued in the upper; and thus approached to harmony". To the musicians, succeeded several hundred persons dressed in an uniform of olive-coloured tunics, who sung and danced in fancied ballets, representing, by the help of lights in transparent lanterns of different hues, such Chinese characters as conveyed great praise of his Imperial Majesty. In the night these ballets would have appeared more brilliant, from contrast; but no amusement could be protracted to that time, as the Emperor, who rises for the most part before the sun, to the dispatch of the affairs of state, and to his devotions, generally retires before it sets.

17d AENEAS ANDERSON

Aeneas Anderson, *A Narrative of the British Embassy to China, in the years 1792, 1793, and 1794; containing the various circumstances of the embassy; with accounts of the customs and manners of the Chinese; and a description of the Country, Towns, Cities, &c., &c.,* 2nd edition, London, 1795

p. 103

1793
August

The sentinels on shore have, each of them, a piece of hollow bamboo, which they strike at regular intervals, with a mallet, to announce that they are awake and vigilant in their respective stations. This custom, as I was informed by the peyings, or soldiers themselves, is universal throughout the Chinese army.

We were awakened at a very early hour by the sound of the gongs, which formed the signal for sailing.

The gong is an instrument of a circular form, made of brass: it resembles, in some degree, the cover of a large stewpan, and is used as bells or trumpets are in Europe, to convey notice, or make signals, from one place to another: when they are struck with a large wooden mallet, which is covered with leather, a sound is produced that may be distinctly heard at the distance of a league.

....

p. 113 ((entering the city of Tyen-sing, i.e., Tientsin))

\ 1793
August

A play was performed on the occasion, as a particular mark of respect and attention to the distinguished visitor. The theatre is a square building built principally of wood, and is erected in the front of the mandarin's palace. The stage, or platform, is surrounded with galleries; and the whole was, on this occasion, decorated with a profusion of ribands, and silken streamers of various colours. The theatrical exhibitions consisted chiefly of warlike representations: such as imaginary battles, with swords, spears, and lances; which weapons the performers managed with an astonishing activity.... The performance was also enlivened by a band of music, which consisted entirely of wind instruments: some of them were very long, and resembled a trumpet; others had the appearance of French-horns and clarinets: the sounds of the latter brought to my recollection that of the Scotch bag-pipe; and their concert, being destitute both of melody and harmony, was of course very disagreeable to our ears, which are accustomed to such perfection in those essential points of music. But we had every reason to be satisfied with the entertainment, as the circumstances of it were replete with novelty and curious amusement.

....

p.119

.... These men have, each of them, a piece of wood, about two feet and a half in length, with a piece of stout cord at each end, by which it is fastened to the ropes attached to the junk; these pieces of wood being thrown over their heads, rest upon their breasts, and by leaning against them the rowers increase the power of their exertions: they are thus harnessed, if I may use the expression, in a strait line, at the distance of about a pace and a half from each other, and when they are all ready, the leader of them gives the signal: they then begin a particular kind of march, the regularity of whose step is essential to the draught of the vessel, and can only be maintained by a sort of chime which they chant on the occasion: this chime, or air, is a kind of brief song; but the words, as far as I could learn, have no more meaning attached to them, than the bawling tones employed by our seamen, as notices to pull at the same moment: they appeared, however, to give the following distinct, articulate sounds, not altogether unlike some of those which we might hear on the Thames, or the Severn. — Hoy-alla-hoya; — which word, for it is delivered as one, was regularly succeeded by the following ones — hoya, hoya, hoy — waudi-hoya. These words are sung in a regular tune; and so universal is this custom among the class of labouring Chinese, that they cannot perform the most ordinary work, where numbers are employed together, without the aid of this vocal accompaniment; which I was disposed to think, had some agreeable notes in it.

.....

p. 133 ((Chinese domestic devotions))

.... When this ceremony is over, an attendant on the altar takes a soft mallet, with which he strikes a bell, that is suspended to it, three times; the persons present then kneel before the images, and bow down their heads three times to the ground, with their hands clasped in each other, which they extend over their heads as they rise.

.....

p. 142

This morning the Ambassador issued regulations for the funeral of Mr. Henry Eades ((one of the mechanics attached to the Embassy)), which, in order to give the Chinese a favourable impression even of our funeral solemnities, was directed to be performed with military honours.

All the servants, mechanics, and musicians, attached to the embassy, were desired to be in readiness on the occasion: Col. Benson also issued orders to the troops to appear with their side arms, except a serjeant and six privates of the royal artillery, who were ordered to be

1793
August
Tuesday 20

armed and accoutered for firing over the grave. As no clergyman accompanied the embassy, I was appointed to read the funeral service of the Church of England on this melancholy occasion.

At nine o'clock the procession began in the following order:
Detachment of the royal artillery, with arms reversed.
The coffin supported on men's shoulders.
Two fifes playing a funeral dirge.
The persons appointed to officiate at the grave.
The mechanics, servants, &c. two and two.
The troops then followed, and closed the whole.

This procession was also accompanied by several of the gentlemen belonging to the embassy.

Thus we proceeded, with all due solemnity, to the burying-ground, which is situated about a quarter of a mile from the Ambassador's residence; and where permission had been granted for the interment of our countryman, with a liberality that would not have been practised in some of the countries of our own enlightened quarter of the globe. Such a ceremonial, as may well be imagined, had excited the curiosity of the city, and we were attended by a concourse of spectators that the most interesting and splendid spectacles would not assemble in the cities of Europe.

17e JOHANN HÜTTNER

J((ohann)) C((hristian)) Hüttner, *Nachricht von der Brittischen Gesandtschaftsreise durch China und einen Theil der Tartarei*, Berlin, 1797

p. 175

Ueber die Musik der Chinesen lässt sich jetzt sehr wenig Neues sagen. Ihre Instrumente sind hinlänglich bekannt, und man weiss auch, dass sie weder Harmonie, noch Ohr dafür, haben. Unsre langsamen Gesänge gefallen ihnen; sie werden, wie mir Vater Grammond in Peking sagte, entzückt durch den Silberklang unserer Klaviere, Flügel und Flöten; aber jede Tertie oder Quinte, so angenehm sie auch unseren Ohren seyn mag, ist für sie ein Missklang. Sie lieben nur Oktaven, und wenn sie auf Saiteninstrumenten spielen, so hat die Samm-jinn (in der Mandarinen-Sprache Sann- jenn, d.i. eine Art Theorbe mit vier Saiten) fast immer die Melodie in der niedrigen Oktave. Die Samm-jinn, die Yutkomm (Mand. Yio-kenn), eine Art von Guitarre, und die R'jenn, ein Instrument mit zwei Saiten, durch welche ein härner Bogen gezogen ist, sind nicht unangenehm; aber die Chinesen machen mit einem sehr grossen Becken, einigen Trommeln und Klappern den abscheulichsten Lärm dazu, und ersticken dadurch alle Wirkung der sanften und klagenden Töne jener Instrumente. Die R'jenn sieht wie ein plumper hölzerner Hammer aus, dessen Kopf zur Resonanz ausgehöhlt ist. Die beiden Saiten dieses Instruments ruhen auf keinem Brette, werden aber dessen ungeachtet, wie die Saiten der Violine, mit den Fingern gegriffen. Der Ton der R'jenn ist etwas heiser, und gewinnt nichts durch das Spielen; denn, anstatt die Uebergänge von einem Accorde zum andern in einfachen Tonfolgen zu machen, schleift man durch alle dazwischen liegende halbe und Vierteltöne, welches Europäischen Ohren bald lästig wird, ob es gleich, seltner angebracht, wie in unsrer Musik, gute Wirkung thun würde. Eben das gilt von ihrem beständigen Beben auf diesem Instrumente. Ihre Bambuflöte, die unsern Querpfeifen gleicht, hat einen melancholischen gedämpften Ton, der den elegischen Tonfolgen ihrer Volksgesänge sehr angemessen ist. Die Chinesen, selbst Knaben, singen fast immer in Falsett, welches ihrer Vocalmusik mehr dem Dudeln, als dem Gesange ähnlich macht, und unsern Ohren nie gefallen kann. Manche vergleichen den Chinesischen Gesang mit dem Mauen der Katzen, und ihr häufiges Trillern erinnert den fremden Zuhörer oft an des Meckern einer Ziege. Es ist übrigens sehr unwahr, dass, wie Viele glauben, kein Zeitmass in der Chinesischen Musik herrsche. Vielleicht ist diese Meinung an sich, ohne das Zeugniss der Erfahrung, ungereimt. Takt, wie man sich leicht überzeugen kann, ist nicht das Werk des Nachdenkens, so wie

unsre Musikzeichen, sondern der natürliche Begleiter jeder Melodie. Es
giebt einzelne Personen, die kein Gefühl für Takt haben; aber sie sind
Ausnahmen, und nie hat man eine ganze Nation von solchen Ausnahmen gefunden. Die Chinesen haben die Schiak-pann-Hölzchen und
die Ssuchu-Trommel ausdrücklich zum Taktgeben, wenn sie bei ihren
Schauspielen singen, und ich kann mich auf das Zeugniss aller Musik-
kenner in der Gesandtschaft berufen, dass wir in Cochinchina, in der
Tartarei und in China, besonders in Canton, die zeitmässigsten Gesänge
gehört haben. In Cochinchina, wo die Sitten, wie man weiss, den Chinesischen fast gleich sind, hörten wir von vier Schauspielerinnen einen
sehr melodischen Wechselgesang, der sich in einen Refrein endigte. Aber
in Canton, wo wir über das vortreffliche Spiel einer Schauspieler-
gesellschaft aus Nanking erstaunten, wurden wir auch durch eine Oper
überrascht, in welcher nicht nur sehr natürliche Recitative, sondern
auch sehr ausdrucksvolle Arien vorkamen, die durchaus mit dem richtig-
sten Zeitmasse gesungen und mit angemessener Instrumentalmusik be-
gleitet wurden.

Die schönste Musik, welche wir hörten, war bei der ersten
Vorstellung des Gesandten in Dschecho. Als der Kaiser auf den Thron
gestiegen war und eine religiöse Stille sich überall verbreitet hatte,
wurden wir aus dem Hintergrunde des grossen Zeltes durch hinreissende
Töne überrascht. Der sanfte Klang, die einfache Melodie, die reine Ton-
folge, der feierliche Fortschritt einer langsamen Hymne gaben wenig-
stens meiner Seele jenen Schwung, der den fühlenden Schwärmer in
unbekannte Regionen versetzt, aber dem kalten Zergliederer der Ursachen nie zu beschreiben ist. Ich blieb lange zweifelhaft, ob ich
Menschenstimmen oder Instrumente hörte, bis letztere von Einigen gesehen wurden. Sie bestanden aus Saiteninstrumenten und aus einer Art
von Bambu-Syrinx. Die Hymne glich den Kirchengesängen der Protes-
tanten, hatte aber keine Mittelstimmen. Die Schiackpann-Hölzchen und
die Ssu-chu-Trommel, welche gemeiniglich in der Chinesischen Musik
den Takt angeben und den Zuhörer betäuben, liess man hier glücklicher
Weise weg; aber zwischen jedem Takte wurde eine metallene Cymbel
gehört, die den Anfang und Ton des folgenden angab, und keine unan-
genehme Wirkung that. Entfernung von den Musikern und Kurzsichtig-
keit verhinderten mich, etwas mehr zu beobachten.

Die Tänzer verschiedener Nationen, die wir bei eben der Gelegenheit sahen, hatten alle ihre eigne Musik; aber sie waren zu entfernt
und zu kurze Zeit auf dem Tanzplatze, als dass ich etwas Genaues hätte
bemerken können, und überdies war ihre Musik selbst durch nichts
anziehend. Was die Chinesen von der Musik urtheilen mochten, die der
Gesandte mit sich gebracht hatte, kann ich nicht gewiss bestimmen, da

ich mich nie ausdrücklich darnach erkundigt habe. Zwar hörte ich, dass die Mandarinen, wenn Andre darüber fragten, zur Antwort gaben: Chau, d.i. gut. Aber da mir unser Dolmetscher sagte, dass sie keinen Gefallen an unsrer Musik fänden, so fürchte ich sehr, dass sie nur aus Höflichkeit, die ihnen so eigen ist, ihren Beifall bezeugten. Ich beobachtete, wenn wir Musik hatten, auch die Miene vornehmer und gemeiner Chinesen und Tartaren, konnte aber nie Merkmahle von dem so unverkennbaren Wohlgefallen an etwas entdecken. Die sonderbare, sinnreiche und durch lange Uebung gelernte Behandlung unsrer musikalischen Instrumente musste übrigens natürlicher Weise ihre Aufmerksamkeit erregen.

Die militärische Musik der Chinesen ist höchst elend, ohne Takt, ohne Melodie und ohne den geringsten Ausdruck. Schalmeien und Hörner fahren über fünf bis sechs Töne hin und her, ohne die geringste Veränderung, und wenn sie auch Stundenlang blasen; mitunter stosst man dazu in eine Art von Zinken, die ein wahres Wolfsgeheul machen. — Ich kann diese Bemerkung über die Chinesische Musik nicht beschliessen, ohne des Flussgesanges der nördlichen Provinzen, besonders Petscheli und Schantong, zu erwähnen, der uns alle so sehr ergötzte.

TRANSLATION

There remains very little new to say about the music of the Chinese. Their instruments are sufficiently well known, and one knows also that they have neither harmony nor any ear for it. Our slow songs please them most; according to what Father Grammond told me in Pekin, they are enchanted by the silvery sounds of our pianofortes, harpsichord and flutes; but a third or a fifth, pleasant as they are to our ears, is to them a discord. They like only octaves, and when they play stringed instruments, the *samm-jinn* (in the mandarin language *sann-jenn*), which is a kind of theorbo with four strings, almost always has the tune in the lower octave. The *samm-jinn*, the *yutkomm* (mandarin: *yio-kenn*), a kind of guitar, and the *r'jenn*, an instrument with two strings, which is played with a horse-hair bow, are not unpleasant; but the Chinese join to them the most horrible noise of a very large cymbal and several drums and rattles, and thereby destroy all the effect of the soft and plaintive sounds of each instrument. The *r'jenn* looks like a rather large wooden mallet, whose head has been hollowed out for resonance. The two strings of this instrument do not have a fingerboard, but are nevertheless stopped with the fingers like the strings of a violin. The timbre of the *r'jenn* is somewhat hoarse, and is no less so in performance, since instead of going from one chord to another by simple scale-steps one slides through all the intervening half- and quarter-tones, which soon becomes tiring to European ears, although if used sparingly, as in our music, it may just as well produce a good effect. The same may be said of their continuous tremolo on this instrument. Their bamboo flute, which resembles our fifes, has a sub-dued and melancholy sound that suits very well the elegiac modes of their folksongs. The Chinese, even children, sing almost always in falset-to, which makes their vocal music more like bagpiping than singing, and cannot be pleasing to our ears. Many people compare Chinese singing to mewing of cats, and their numerous trills often remind the foreign listener of the bleating of a goat. It is by the way quite untrue that, as many believe, Chinese music has no regular beat. Perhaps this opinion is of itself untenable, without the evidence of experience. Musical beat, as one may easily convince oneself, is not the product of reflection, as are our time-signature signs, but the natural concomitant of any tune. There are some people who have no feeling for musical beat, but they are exceptions, and a whole nation of such exceptions has never been discovered. The Chinese have the *schiak-paun*, a small wooden stick, and the *tsou-kou*, a drum, especially to give the beat when they sing in their plays, and I can invoke the witness of all those in the embassy with a knowledge of music that we heard songs sung with a most exact beat in Cochin China, in Tartary and in China, especially in Canton. In Cochin China, where customs, as one knows, are almost the same as among the Chinese, we heard four actresses sing a very tuneful anti-phonal song which ended with a refrain. But in Canton, where we were astonished at the excellent playing of an acting company from Nanking, we were also surprised by an opera in which there was not only very natural recitative, but also very expressive arias, which were sung throughout with a most accurate beat, and were accompanied by ap-propriate instrumental music.

The most beautiful music we heard was at the first presentation of the embassy at Jehol. When the Emperor had ascended the throne and a religious silence had spread over all, we were surprised by the ravishing sounds coming from the background of the great tent. The sweet timbre, the simple tune, the clear mode, the solemn progression of a slow hymn gave, to my soul at least, that vibration which trans-ports susceptible multitudes in unknown regions, but which never can be described by a cold analysis of its reasons. I was uncertain for a long time whether I was hearing human voices or the sound of instruments, until the latter were noticed by some of our party. They consisted of stringed instruments and a kind of bamboo panpipes. The hymn resem-bled the church-tunes of the Protestants, but had no middle voices. The little wooden *schiak-pan* and the *tsou-kou* drum, which usually beat the time in Chinese music and deafen the audience, were fortunately omitted in this instance; but between each beat there was heard a metal cymbal, which gave the beginning and sound-cue of the following beat, and had by no means a disagreeable effect. My distance from the musicians and my short-sightedness prevented me from observing more.

The dancers of the different nations whom we had the opportunity of seeing there ((at Jehol)) all had their particular music; but they were too far away and in the dancing area for too short a time for me to be able to notice anything in more detail, and besides, their music was by no means attractive. What judgement the Chinese formed about the music that the embassy brought with it I could not determine with any certainty, since I have never made express enquiries about this. I certainly heard that the mandarins, when others asked them about it, gave as an answer: *Chau*, that is, good. But since our interpreter told me that they found no pleasure in our music, I am very much afraid that it was only through politeness that they declared their approval of a thing which is so strange to them. When we had music, I observed the expressions of high-ranking and of ordinary Chinese and Tartars, but I could never detect any sign of their having unmistakable pleasure in any of it. However, the particularly clever handling of our musical instruments, learnt by long practice, could not of course but excite their attention.

The military music of the Chinese is extremely poor, without beat, without tune and without the slightest expressiveness. Shawms and horns go back and forth over the same five or six notes, without the smallest variation, even when they are blown for an hour at a time; occasionally they add to these instruments a kind of cornett, which truly makes a sound like the howling of a wolf.– I cannot conclude these remarks on Chinese music without mentioning the river-songs of the northern provinces, especially Chihli and Shantung, which so greatly delighted us all.

17f JOHANN HÜTTNER

The following, from *Journal des Luxus und der Moden*, xi (1796), pp. 36-37, is the relevant part of the editorial matter prefixed to Hüttner's comments on Karl Kambra's song *The Peyho Boatmen*

Herr Hüttner, diess ist der Name unsers achtungswürdigen Landsmannes, fand unter Andern bey den Chinesen alle die Nachrichten bestätigt, die der Vater Amyot und die übrigen Missionaren von der Gesellschaft Jesu in ihren Missionsberichten von den besondern musicalischen Anlagen dieses Volks und ihren sonderbaren Wirkungen gegeben haben. Selbst die Ruder werden nicht nur nach einem gewissen Tacte, sondern auch mit einem eigenen Gesange geschlagen, bey welchem die immer wiederkommende Refrain besonders merkwürdig ist. Er hat Gelegenheit gehabt, diesen Refrain, auf welchem es eigentlich allein ankommt, in Noten zu bringen, und da diese unverständlichen Töne für uns als blosse Töne wenig Interesse haben könnten, und ein Arzt, Hr. Sharp, in Lord Makartneys Gefolge, sogleich ein kleines englisches Lied dazu dichtete; so hat er sowohl dieses Gedicht als auch die Composition eines Teutschen Tonkünstlers in London dazu, als einen Modeartikel aus China den Herausgebern dieses Journals mitgetheilt. Wir glauben unsern Lesern und Leserinnen beym Theetische, in dessen Nachbarschaft ja gewöhnlich ein gutes Clavier oder Fortepiano zu finden ist, eine angenehme Unterhaltung zu verschaffen, wenn sie es versuchen wollen, nach welcher Musik in dem Lande, aus welchem ihre Theekästchen gefüllt werden, dieser Thee selbst auf den Jonken oder Chinesischen Booten, fortgeschafft und in die Faktoreien der Engländer zu Canton abgeliefert wird.

Auch könnte dieses Rudererliedchen noch zu manchen andern Betrachtungen Anlass geben. Die Bemerkung, die Hr. Hüttner bey dieser Gelegenheit über gewisse Aehnlichkeiten der Chinesischen und alten Griechischen Musik, so weit wir durch Muthmassung zu einiger Einsicht in dieselbe gelangen können, in seinem Briefe mittheilt, lässt sich auch auf diess Ruderliedchen anwenden. Auch die Griechischen Ruderer hatten, ausserdem dass sie die Ruder nach einer Mensur schlugen, die ein eigener dazu bestellter Aufseher mit einem Hammer regelmässig angab, auch ihre besondern Ruderrefrains, wohin z. B. das sonderbare oob ob, oob ob rhupapa der Ruderer in den Lustspielen des Aristophanes gehört.[1] Doch wir überlassen diess billig den gelehrten Alterthumsforschern, die sich durch eine Sammlung von alten Schnit-

---

1. Aristophanes, *Frogs*, 1073: "to cry 'rhuppapai' ".

ter-Müller-Spinn- und Schiffer-Liedchen, wovon sich in den Schriften der Griechen noch so manche Spur findet, auch bey den modernen Musik- und Gesang-Freunden, noch immer einen freundlichen Dank erwerben können. Hier sind die eigenen Worte, mit welchen diess Chinesische Tonstück zur Erbauung unsrer Leser uns mitgetheilt wurde.

TRANSLATION

Herr Hüttner, which is the name of our esteemed countryman, found, amongst other things about the Chinese, confirmation of all the information that Father Amyot[1] and the other Jesuit missionaries have given in their mission-reports on the particular musical talents of these people and their special practices. Even the oarsmen made their strokes not merely in a definite tempo but also to a special song, whose ever-recurring refrain is especially remarkable. He took the opportunity of putting this refrain, which is really the only part that matters, into musical notation, and since these unintelligible notes can have little interest for us purely *qua* notes, and Mr. Sharp, a doctor in Lord Macartney's retinue has made a passable little English song-poem to it, Mr. Hüttner has communicated to the editors of this journal this poem and also its setting by a German composer living in London, as a novelty from China. We believe that our readers of both sexes, in whose neighbourhood it is quite usual to find a good clavichord or pianoforte, may obtain a pleasant amusement at their tea-parties if they will try out the music to which, in the country from which their tea-caddy was filled, that tea was actually conveyed in junks, the Chinese boats, and was delivered to the Englishmen's agencies in Canton.

This little song of the oarsmen may also give occasion for many other observations. The remark which on this occasion Mr. Hüttner communicated in his letter about certain similarities between Chinese and ancient Greek music, so far as one can through surmise attain to any insight into the latter, is càpable of being applied also to this little song of the oarsmen. Greek oarsmen, in addition to the fact that they made their oar-strokes at a fixed rate, which a specially appointed overseer regulated with strokes of a hammer, also had their special oarsmen's refrains, to which belongs, for example, that particular *oob ob oob ob rhupapa* of the oarsmen in the comedies of Aristophanes. However, we leave these matters to the learned researchers in antiquity, who incidentally could gain themselves a cordial thank-you from

1. The reference is to *Mémoire sur la musique des Chinois, tant anciens que modernes, Par M. Amiot, Missionaire à Pekin; Avec des Notes, des Observations et une Table de Matières, par M. l'Abbé Roussier, Chanoine d'Ecouis, Correspondant de l'Académie Royale des Inscriptions et Belles-Lettres: Faisant partie du Tome sixième des Mémoires concernant les Chinois*, Paris, 1779. It is planned to reprint soon this often referred to ethnomusicological item.

modern friends of music and song for a collection of ancient reapers', millers', spinners' and oarsmen's songs, of wl ich there exist so many traces in the writings of the Greeks. Here arc the actual words with which this piece of Chinese music was communicated to us for the edification of our readers.

J((ohann)) C((hristian)) Hüttner, 'Ein Ruderliedchen aus China mit Melodie', *Journal des Luxus und der Moden*, xi(1796), pp. 37-40

In den nördlichen Provinzen von China, besonders an den Küsten, pflegen die Schiffer zu den Bewegungen ihrer Ruder einen Gesang anzustimmen, der sehr angenehm und von weitem ungemein auffallend ist. Ich theile ihn Ihnen hier mit. Der Kapitain fangt an, und seine Leute antworten ihm. Diess verhindert Langeweile, unterhält ihre Aufmerksamkeit und befördert die Ebenmässigkeit des Ruderns. Ich erinnere mich mit dem lebhaftesten Vergnügen des Abends, wo wir in einem kleinen Fahrzeuge, von Lord Macartney gesendet, in die Mündung des Paiho-Flusses, in der Provinz Pe-tsche-li zum erstenmale einliefen, und hundert grössern und kleinern Fahrzeugen begegneten, deren jedes mit dem Gesang *Heyo-di-heyo* vor uns vorbey und die Fluth hinab aus dem Hafen liefen. Das Gewimmel auf den Schiffen, die taktmässige Bewegung der zahlreichen Ruder und der Wiederhall dieses von vielen hundert Stimmen auf verschiedenen Seiten angestimmten Gesanges! Wie lebte alles! welch ein Gewühl! London, Liverpool, Venedig und andere Häfen schienen mir nichts dagegen. -- Doch hier ist bloss vom Schiffergesange die Rede. Da man ihn nicht allein singen könnte, und die Bedeutung des Chinesischen Textes niemanden mehr bekannt ist, so schrieb ein Arzt in Lord Macartney's Gefolge einige angemessene Stanzen, die sich mit den Worten des eben angeführten Refrains endigten. Herr Kambra, ein verdienstvoller sächsischer Tonkünstler, der sich jetzt hier in London aufhält, setzte sie mit Beybehaltung des Original-Refrains in Musik, und eine teutsche dem Metrum angepasste Uebersetzung wird diesen Gesang auch für teutsche Musikliebhaber brauchbar machen. Die orientalische Gewohnheit beym Rudern zu singen, bemerkt man fast an allen asiatischen Küsten und Inseln. Ich selbst hörte einen ähnlichen Gesang der Malaier in Batavia und auch in Cochinchina: aber beyde kamen an Melodie dem Chinesischen nicht bey.

TRANSLATION

In the northern provinces of China, especially along the coasts, boatmen have the habit of synchronising the strokes of their oars with a song, which is a very agreeable one and has a surprising effect when heard from a distance. I send it to you herewith. The captain begins and his crewmen respond. This prevents fatigue, keeps up attention and promotes a regular rowing-motion among the oarsmen. I remember with the liveliest pleasure the evening when, sent by Lord Macartney, we entered for the first time in a small boat the estuary of the River Peiho, in the province of Chihli, and met hundreds of large and small boats, each one passing by us with the song *Highodee highau* as they put out from the harbour with the falling tide. The crowd on the boats, the measured movement of the many oarsmen and the repetition of this song by many hundreds of voices striking up on all sides — how full of liveliness, what a tumult! London, Liverpool, Venice and other ports seemed to me to have nothing like it. Here, however, it is purely a question of the oarsmen's song. Since one cannot sing it alone, and the meaning of the Chinese text is now no longer known to anybody, therefore a medical doctor in Lord Macartney's entourage wrote some suitable stanzas which end with the words of the refrain already cited. Mr. Kambra, an experienced Saxon composer who now resides here in London, put them to music retaining the original refrain-music, and a German has made this song usable by German music-lovers by providing a translation in the appropriate metre. The oriental custom of singing by oarsmen is observable around all Asiatic coasts and islands. I myself heard a similar song of the Malayans in Batavia and also in Cochin China, but neither of these came near the tune of the Chinese oarsmen.

17g JOHN BARROW

John Barrow, F.R.S., *Travels in China, containing descriptions, observations, and comparisons, made and collected in the course of a short residence at the imperial palace of Yuen-Min-Yuen, and on a subsequent journey through the country from Pekin to Canton. In which it is attempted to appreciate the rank that this extraordinary empire may be considered to hold in the scale of civilized nations. "Non cuivis homini contingit adire Corinthium". It is the lot of few to go to PEKIN*, 2nd edition, London, 1806

p. 80

......On board the yachts constant mirth and good humour prevailed among the seamen. When the weather was calm, the vessels were generally pushed on by means of two large sculls or oars turning upon pivots that were placed in projecting pieces of wood near the *bow* of the vessel, and not the stern, as is the practice of most other nations. From six to ten men are required to work one of these oars, which, instead of being taken out of the water, as in the act of rowing, are moved backwards and forwards under the surface, in a similar manner to what in England is understood by sculling. To lighten their labour, and assist in keeping time with the strokes, the following rude air was generally sung by the master. to which the whole crew used to join in chorus:

On many a calm still evening, when a dead silence reigned upon the water, have we listened with pleasure to this artless and unpolished air, which was sung, with little alteration, through the whole fleet....

....

p. 313

Of the other two sister arts, painting and music, a more decided opinion may be passed. Of the latter I have little to observe. It does not seem to be cultivated as a science: it is neither learned as an elegant accomplishment, nor practised as an ornament of genteel life, except by those females who are educated for sale, or by such as hire themselves out for the entertainment of those who may be inclined to purchase their favours. And as the Chinese differ in their ideas from all other nations, these women play generally upon wind instruments, such as small pipes and flutes; whilst the favourite instrument of the men is the guittar or something not very unlike it, some of which have two strings, some four, and others seven. Eunuchs, and the lowest class of persons, are hired to play; and the merit of a performance should seem to consist in the intenseness of the noise brought out of the different instruments.

The gong, or, as they call it, the *loo*, is admirably adapted for this purpose. This instrument is a sort of shallow kettle, or rather the lid of a kettle, which they strike with a wooden mallet covered with leather. The composition is said to be copper, tin, and bismuth. They have also a kind of clarinet, three or four different sorts of trumpets, and a stringed instrument not unlike a violoncello. Their *sing* is a combination of uneven reeds of bamboo, not unlike the pipe of Pan; the tones are far from being disagreeable, but its construction is so wild and irregular, that it does not appear to be reducible to any kind of scale. Their kettle drums are generally shaped like barrels; and these, as well as different-sized bells fixed in a frame, constitute parts in their sacred music. They have also an instrument of music which consists of stones, cut into the shape of a carpenter's square, each stone suspended by the corner in a wooden frame. Those which I saw appeared to belong to that species of the silicious genus usually called Gneiss, a sort of slaty granite. In the Keswick museum are musical stones of the same kind, which were picked up in a rivulet at the foot of Skiddaw mountain; but these seem to contain small pieces of black shorl or tourmaline It is indeed the boast of their historians, that the whole empire of nature has been laid under comtribution in order to complete their system of music: that the skins of animals, the fibres of plants, metals, stones, and baked earths, have all been employed in the production of sounds. Their instruments, it is true, are sufficiently varied, both as to shape and materials, but I know of none that is even tolerable to an European ear. An English gentleman in Canton took some pains to collect the various instruments of the country, of which the annexed plate is a representation, but his catalogue is not complete ((see Illustrations M and N)).

A Chinese band generally plays, or endeavours to play, in unison, and sometimes an instrument takes the octave; but they never attempt to play in separate parts, confining their art to the melody only, if I may venture to apply a name of so much sweetness to an aggregation of harsh sounds. They have not the least notion of counterpoint, or playing in parts: an invention indeed to which the elegant Greeks had not arrived, and which seems to have been unknown in Europe as well as Asia, until the monkish ages.

I never heard but one single Chinese who could be said to sing with feeling or plaintiveness. Accompanied with a kind of guittar, he sung the following air in praise of the flower *Moo-lee*, which it seems is one of the most popular songs in the whole country. The simple melody was taken down by Mr. Hittner, and I understand has been published in London, with head and tail-pieces, accompaniments, and all the refined arts of European music; so that it ceases to be a specimen of the plain melody of China. I have therefore given it in its unadorned state, as sung and played by the Chinese, together with the words of the first stanza, and their literal translation.

I have not thought it amiss to subjoin a few other airs of the popular kind, which were written by the same gentleman at Canton, who made the drawings of their musical instruments.

They have no other notion of noting down music than that of employing a character expressing the name of every note in the scale; and even this imperfect way they learned from Pereira the Jesuit[1]. They affected to dislike the Embassador's band, which they pretended to say produced no music, but a confusion of noises; yet the Emperor's chief musician gave himself a great deal of trouble in tracing out the several instruments on large sheets of paper, each of its particular size, marking the places of the holes, screws, strings, and other parts, which they conceived necessary to enable them to make others of a similar construction.

It would be difficult to assign the motive that induced father Amiot to observe, that "the Chinese, in order to obtain their scale of notes or gamut perfect, were not afraid of submitting to the most laborious operations of geometry, and to the most tedious and disgusting calculations in the science of numbers;" as he must have known, that they were altogether ignorant of geometry, and that their arithmetic extended not beyond their *Swau-pan* ((he has earlier explained and illustrated this, which, he says, "has been compared, how justly I cannot pretend to say, to the Roman *abacus*)). Of the same nature is the bold and unfounded assertion of another of the Jesuits, "that the musical system of the Chinese was borrowed from them by the Greeks and Egyptians, anterior to the time of Hermes or Orpheus! "

1. See the account by J.-B. Du Halde.

18 MUNGO PARK

Mungo Park (1771-1806) qualified as a doctor at Edinburgh University, and in 1792-3 went to Sumatra as a ship's medical officer. At the instance of Sir Joseph Banks, president of the Royal Society, he was invited by the African Association to lead an expedition in search of the Niger. In the course of his travels, which began in May, 1795, he was held prisoner by a Moorish (i.e., non-negro Muslim)) chief, escaped after nearly three months, and experienced the adventure reprinted here. During his return journey from Silla, on the Niger, which he was the first modern European to reach, he was attacked and robbed, and was ill at Kamalia for seven months. He arrived back at Falmouth in December, 1797.

The first edition of Park's *Travels* was published in 1798, the second edition in the following year. He gave in the Preface the following account of its writing:

The following Journal, drawn up from original minutes and notices made at the proper moment and preserved with great difficulty ((some in the crown of his hat, which with his shirt and trousers were all that survived the robbery)), is now offered to the Public by the direction of my noble and honourable employers, the Members of the African Association. I regret that it is so little commensurate to the patronage I have received. As a composition, it has nothing to recommend it, but *truth*.....

Immediately after my return from Africa, the acting Committee of the Association, taking notice of the time it would require to prepare an account in detail, as it now appears.....determined that an epitome, or abridgment of my travels, should be forthwith prepared from such materials and oral communications as I could furnish, and printed for the use of the Association. A memoir, thus supplied and improved, was accordingly drawn up in two parts.....the first part consisting of a narrative, in abstract, of my travels, by Bryan Edwards, Esq; the second, of Geographical Illustrations of my progress, by Major James Rennell, F. R. S.....

. . . .Mr. Edwards has kindly permitted me to incorporate, as occasion offered, the whole of his narrative into different parts of my work.....

The "Negro Song", with words incorporating those in Park's account, and music by G. G. Ferrari, is not included in the reprint of the *Travels* in the *Everyman's Library* series. Though its ethnomusicological value is limited by lack of evidence of any musical connection with the tune used by the African young women, it has some interest as a period piece. Its composer, Gotifredo Jacopo Ferrari (b. Rovereto,

1763; d. London, 1842), settled in London in 1792, where he composed stage works and songs, wrote singing tutors and taught singing to socially elevated people. The list of his works in G. Barblan's informative article in *Die Musik in Geschichte und Gegenwart* (iv, 1955, cols. 75-77) does not include the present song, which was also printed separately in London about 1810. Another setting of the words, with slight differences, under the title *The AFRICAN'S pity on the WHITE MAN,* by François Hippolyte Barthélemon (1741-1808) was also printed in London.

Mungo Park, *Travels in the Interior Districts of Africa......in the years 1795, 1796, and 1797*, London, 1799

p. 197

((Near Sego, the capital of Bambarra, Niger, July 20th, 1796; Park was sent out of town by a message from Mansong, the King, that he should await further instructions about how to conduct himself.))
.....This was very discouraging. However, as there was no remedy, I set off for the village; where I found, to my great mortification, that no person would admit me into his house. I was regarded with astonishment and fear, and was obliged to sit all day without victuals, in the shade of a tree; and the night threatened to be very uncomfortable, for the wind rose, and there was great appearance of a heavy rain; and the wild beasts are so very numerous in the neighbourhood, that I should have been under the necessity of climbing up the tree, and resting amongst the branches. About sunset, however, as I was preparing to pass the night in this manner, and had turned my horse loose, that he might graze at liberty, a woman, returning from the labours of the field, stopped to observe me, and perceiving that I was weary and dejected, inquired into my situation, which I briefly explained to her; whereupon, with looks of great compassion, she took up my saddle and bridle, and told me to follow her. Having conducted me into her hut, she lighted up a lamp, spread a mat on the floor, and told me I might remain there for the night. Finding that I was very hungry, she said she would procure me something to eat. She accordingly went out, and returned in a short time with a very fine fish; which, having caused to be half broiled upon some embers, she gave me for supper. The rites of hospitality being thus performed towards a stranger in distress, my worthy benefactress (pointing to the mat, and telling me I might sleep there without apprehension) called to the female part of her family, who had stood gazing on me all the while in fixed astonishment, to resume their task of spinning cotton; in which they continued to employ themselves great part of the night. They lightened their labour

by songs, one of which was composed extempore; for I was myself the subject of it. It was sung by one of the young women, the rest joining in a sort of chorus. The air was sweet and plaintive, and the words, literally translated, were these.— "The winds roared, and the rain fell.— The poor white man, faint and weary, came and sat under our tree.— He has no mother to bring him milk; no wife to grind his corn. *Chorus.* Let us pity the white man; no mother has he, &c, &c." Trifling as this recital may appear to the reader, to a person in my situation, the circumstance was affecting in the highest degree. I was oppressed by such unexpected kindness; and sleep fled from my eyes. In the morning I presented my compassionate landlady with two of the four brass buttons which remained on my waistcoat; the only recompence I could make her.

....

p. 278

Of their ((the Negroes')) music and dances, some account has incidentally been given in different parts of my Journal. On the first of these heads, I have now to add a list of their musical instruments, the principal of which are, — the *koonting*, a sort of guitar with three strings; — the *korro*, a large harp, with eighteen strings; — the *simbing*, a small harp, with seven strings; — the *balafou*, an instrument composed of twenty pieces of hard wood of different lengths, with the shells of gourds hung underneath, to increase the sound; — the *tangtang*, a drum, open at the lower end; and lastly, the *tabala*, a large drum, commonly used to spread an alarm through the country. Besides these, they make use of small flutes, bowstrings, elephants' teeth, and bells; and at all their dances and concerts, *clapping of hands* appears to constitute a necessary part of the chorus.

With the love of music is naturally connected a taste for poetry; and, fortunately for the poets of Africa, they are in a great measure exempted from that neglect and indigence, which in more polished countries commonly attend the votaries of the Muses. They consist of two classes; the most numerous are the *singing men*, called *Jilli kea*, mentioned in a former part of my narrative. One or more of these may be found in every town. They sing extempore songs, in honour of their chief men, or any other persons who are willing to give "solid pudding for empty praise." But a nobler part of their office is to recite the historical events of their country: hence, in war, they accompany the soldiers to the field; in order, by reciting the great actions of their ancestors, to awaken in them a spirit of glorious emulation. The other class are devotees of the Mahomedan faith, who travel about the country, singing devout hymns, and performing religious ceremonies, to conciliate the favour of the Almighty; either in averting calamity, or insuring success to any enterprize. Both descriptions of these itinerant bards are much employed and respected by the people, and very liberal contributions are made for them.

Postscript

The incident of the Negro Song, related in the 15th Chapter of this work (p. 198), having been communicated to a Lady, who is not more distinguished for her rank, than for her beauty and accomplishments; she was pleased to think so highly of this simple and unpremeditated effusion, as to make a version of it with her own pen; and cause it to be set to music by an eminent Composer. With this elegant production, in both parts of which the plaintive simplicity of the original is preserved and improved, the Author thinks himself highly honoured in being permitted to adorn his book; and he laments only that he had not an opportunity of inserting it in its proper place in the body of the work.

19 JOHN BARROW

John Barrow,[1] *An Account of travels into the interior of Southern Africa in 1797 and 1798*, London, 1806

p. 97

It has frequently been observed that a savage who dances and sings must be happy. With him these operations can only be the effects of pleasurable sensations floating in his mind: in a civilized state, they are arts acquired by study, followed by fashion, and practised at appointed times, without having any reference to the passions. If dancing and singing were the tests by which the happiness of a Hottentot was to be tried, he would be found among the most miserable of all human beings; I mean those Hottentots living with the farmers of Graaff Reynet in a state of bondage. It is rare to observe the muscles of his face relaxed into a smile. A depressed melancholy and deep gloom constantly overspread his countenance. A Ghonaqua man and a young Hottentot girl from Sneuwberg, both of them in the service of one of the farmers who crossed the desert with us, were the only two I had hitherto met with who seemed to have any taste for music. They had different instruments; one was a kind of guittar with three strings stretched over a piece of hollow wood with a long handle; it was called in their language *gabowie*. The other instrument was extremely simple: it consisted of a piece of sinew or intestine twisted into a small cord, and fastened to a hollow stick about three feet in length, at one end to a small peg, which, by turning, brings the string to the proper degree of tension, and at the other to a piece of quill fixed into the stick. The tones of this instrument are produced by applying the mouth to the quill, and are varied according as the vibratory motion is given to the quill and string by inspiration or expiration. It sounds like the faint murmurs of distant music that "comes o'er the ear", without any distinct note being made out by that organ. This instrument was called the *gowra*.

1. See the introduction to item 17.

MUSIC-NOTATIONS

I

♩ = original minim in transcriptions a-f

a) Canidé-iouue, canidé-iouue, heuraouech

b) Pira ouassou aoueh Kamouroupouy - ouassou a oueh &c.

c) He he he he he he he he he he

d) Heu, heuraiire, heiira, heiiraiire, heiira, heiira, ouch

e) (1585) He, he, hua, he, hua, hua, hua

(1586) He, he, hua, he, hua, he, hua, hua

Trois Chansons des Ameriquains (Mersenne, 1636)

f) **I** Canide iouue. **II** He he he he.

III Heu heura heura ouccbi

Chanson des Sauvages du Canada (Rousseau, 1768)

g) Ca ni de jou - ve, ca ni de jou - ve. He he he he he heu..

. . . . ra heu - ra on ce bé.

1. Two tones higher, with c-clef on first line and B-flat signature, in other prints; 1605 has a minim *f'* between last two notes.
2. 1585 has flat on second space, as in (a).
3. Two tones higher in the other prints; with F-flat signature in 1586; with B-flat signature in 1593 and 1605.
4. These two notes appear to be semiminims in 1585, 1593, minims in 1586, 1605, 1625.
5. First two notes missing in 1585; second note is *g'* in 1605, third note *e'* in 1625.
6. This note is *a'* in 1953, *f'* in 1605, 1625.

NB. Notations a-e and the variants noted here may be compared with the transcriptions in Luiz Heitor Corrêa de Azevedo, "Tupynambá Melodies in Jean de Léry's *Histoire d'un voyage faict en la terre du Brésil*" in *Papers of the American Musicological Society: Annual Meeting, 1941* (Richmond, 1946), pp. 85-96. Azevedo and some other sources give Geneva as the place of publication of the 1585 print; however, this is given as La Rochelle in *Biographie Universelle*, s.v. Jean de Léry.

II

III

Ma - ri - a, to - do es Ma - ri - a,   *Mary, all is Mary,*

Ma - ri - a, to - do es à vos: *Mary, all is yours:*

To - da la no - che y el di - a   *All the Day and Night*

Se me voi pen - sar en vos.[3]   *I think on nothing but you.*

<table>
<tr><td>

2.

Toda vos resplandeceis
Con soberano arrebol,
Y vuestra casa en el *Sol*
Dice David que teneis.

</td><td>

2.

You are all glittering
With Sovereign Light,
And *David* says
Your House is in the Sun.

</td></tr>
<tr><td>

3.

Vuestro calçado[4] es la Luna,
Vuestra vestidura el Sol,
Manto bordado de Estrellas,
Por corona el mismo Dios.

</td><td>

3.

The Moon is your Footstool,
The Sun your Garment,
Your Veil embroider'd with Stars,
God himself your Crown.

</td></tr>
<tr><td>

4.

Aunque le pese al Demonio,
Y reviente Satanas,
Alabemos[5] à Maria
Sin pecado original.

</td><td>

4.

Tho' it fret the Devil,
And Satan burst for Rage,
Let us praise *Mary*
Conceiv'd without original Sin.

</td></tr>
<tr><td>

5.

El Demonio esta muy mal,
Y no tiene mejoria,
Porque no puede estorbar[6]
La devocion de Maria.

</td><td>

5.

The Devil is very ill,
And not likely to mend,
Because he cannot obstruct
The Devotion to *Mary*.

</td></tr>
</table>

1. The sharp-sign undoubtedly applies to all three notes in the measure; this was not an uncommon practice in seventeeth-century European notations.
2. The sharp-signs precede the previous note in each case in original French print.
3. Text as in original French print; the print of the English translation has *Se me vai enpensar en vos*.
4. English translation print: *calgado*
5. French print: *Alabemus*
6. French print: *desturbar*

IV

ZAPATEO, *a Dance in* Peru *and* Chili

1. *a'* in the French print.

V

CHINESE AIRS

1. The clef is G on the first line throughout.
2. English edition *c"*; original edition *d"*.
3. These are eighth-notes in both editions.
4. English edition *c"*; original edition *d"*.
5. This is a quarter-note in both editions.
6. This is an eighth-note in the original edition.

The following music-notation was given in George Soulié de Morant and André Gailhard, *Théâtre et musique modernes en Chine* (Paris, 1926), p. 124; compare No. [II] above.

Joie, plaisir, boisson. y yènn y pann (yuann pann)

VI

AIR

Solo by the Master
Hai - yo hai-yau   hai-yo hai-yau

Chorus by the Crew
Hai - yo hai-yau   hai-yo

hai-wha de ____   hai-yau hai-yau

hai-yau   hai-yo hai-yau

VII

MOO - LEE - WHA

I

Hau ye-to sien wha
1 2 3 4 5
Yeu tchau yeu jie lo tsai go kia
6 7 8 9 10 11 12 13
Go pun tai, poo tchoo mun
14 15 16 17 18 19
Twee tcho sien wha ul lo.
20 21 22 23 24 25

II

Hau ye to Moo-lee wha
1 2 3 4 5 6
Man yuen wha kai soy poo quee ta
7 8 9 10 11 12 13 14
Go pun tai tsai ye ta
15 16 17 18 19 20
Tai you kung kan wha jin ma.
21 22 23 24 25 26 27

Literal Translation

I

How delightful this branch of fresh flowers
1 2 3 4 5
One morning one day it was dropped in my house
6 7 8 9 10 11 12 13
I the owner will wear it not out of doors
14 15 16 17 18 19
But I will hold the fresh flower and be happy.
20 21 22 23 24 25

II

How delightful this branch of the *Moo-lee* flower
1 2 3 4 5 6
In the full plot of flowers blowing freely none excels it
7 8 9 10 11 12 13 14
I the owner will wear this gathered branch
15 16 17 18 19 20
Wear it yet fear, the flower seen, men will envy.
21 22 23 25 24 25* 27

*Sic in print.

CHINESE POPULAR AIRS

No. I.

No. II.

No. III.

No. IV.

This is identical with Du Halde's No. II.

No. V.

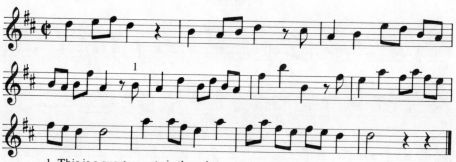

1. This is a quarter-note in the print.

No. VI.

This is identical with Du Halde's No. I.

No. VII.

This is identical with Barrow's No. IV above, and with Du Halde's No. II.

No. VIII.

This is identical with Du Halde's No. III.

No. IX.

This is identical with Du Halde's No. V.

VIII

[Title-page] Two Original Chinese Songs Moo-Lee-Chwa & Higho Highau for the Piano Forte or Harpsichord. Published & Humbly Dedicated to the Right Honble The Countess of Macartney and to Lady Staunton, by K. Kambra London Printed for the Author to be had, No 26 Greek Street Soho, & at all the Music Shops

[Music-heading] The following Chinese Songs were brought to England by a Gentleman of the late Embassy to China, who took them down upon the Spot. Their Originality, therefore, may be depended on, and Mr. KAMBRA, in offering them to the Public, with the addition of a Bass, flatters himself to have rendered them more agreeable to the English Ear.

MOO - LEE - CHWA

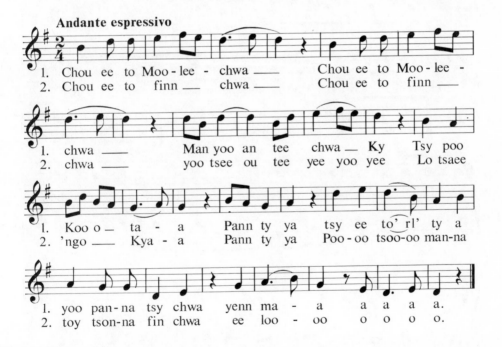

Andante espressivo

1. Chou ee to Moo - lee - chwa ___ Chou ee to Moo - lee -
2. Chou ee to finn ___ chwa ___ Chou ee to finn ___

1. chwa ___ Man yoo an tee chwa ___ Ky Tsy poo
2. chwa ___ yoo tsee ou tee yee yoo yee Lo tsaee

1. Koo o - ta - a Pann ty ya tsy ee to' rl' ty a
2. 'ngo ___ Kya - a Pann ty ya Poo - oo tsoo - oo man-na

1. yoo pan-na tsy chwa yenn ma - a a a a.
2. toy tson-na fin chwa ee loo - oo o o o o.

N.B. The vowel â to be pronounced as in Italian.
    Engrav'd by S. Straight. No. 4. Green Street, Leicester Square.

CANZONETTA CHINESE
or MOO-LEE-CHWA

The Original Words translated into English verse by Dr. SCOTT,
second Physician to the late Embassy to China.

Andante espressivo

Hail match-less flow'r mild Moo-lee-chwa, love li-est of the gay par-terre. how shall I strive thy charms to draw, Thy bal-my sweet-ness fills the Air. Fain would I pluck thee peer-less flow'r, and place thee on my panting breast, lest some one feel-ing too thy pow'r, should snatch thy bloom to make him blest.

2

Let others range the Garden round
And cull the sweets of ev'ry Clime;
Tho' some more splendid may be found,
Yet soon their fragrance yields to time.
Thy varied beauties long I'll prize
As spring still follows nature's law:
No other flow'r shall charm mine eyes,
Their Joy is plac'd in Moo-lee-chwa.

CHORUS

This Chorus is sung by the Boatmen all over the Northern and Eastern provinces of China, and those that have heard it there, mention is as having a very striking effect at a distance. Yet, as it loses its effect upon the Piano Forte, Mr. KAMBRA has composed, and adapted it to, the following Song.

The PEYHO BOATMEN
or Higho highau

The Words by Dr. Scott.

Allegretto

The Sil - ver wa - ters gent - ly __ flow, a - midst thy wind - ing Banks PEY - HO, the state - ly Junks are __ mov'd a - long.

While Boat - men with their lof - ty __ Poles and

cheer - ful Toil, soon clear the shoals, re-sound-ing

to their Jo - cund song, re-sound-ing ___ to ___ their

Jo-cund Song. Hig - ho hig-hau hig-ho

hig-hau hig-ho dee hig-hau. As

Dal Segno

2

As on they trace thy Mazy bounds,
Where gaily smile the cultur'd grounds,
The Village Nymphs, that shun the throng,
With cautions [*sic*] step oft slyly meet,
Or lightly trip on Fairy feet,
To listen to the Boatmen's song.
    Higho Highau &c.

In the version of *The Peyho Boatmen* that Hüttner sent to the *Journal des Luxus und der Moden* the keyboard introduction is an octave higher and the ending differs. The following is the German text printed there:

Der Peyho Schiffer

Da wo des Peyho Silberfluth
In Chinas grünen Armen ruht,
Da wimmelt es den Fluss entlang
Von Schiffchen, prächtig ausgeziert,
Die vogelschnell der Rudrer führt,
Und alles schallt im frohen Sang:
   Heiho, heihau, heiho, heihau!
   Heihodie, heihau, hiehau, heihau!

Und wenn nun Jonken, gelb und grün,
Längs schöneblümter Ufer ziehn,
Seht, wie da manches Nymfchen springt,
Wie sie das kleine Füsschen dreht
Und trippelnd an dem Ufer steht,
Und lauscht, wie alles jubelnd singt:
   Heiho, heihau, heiho, heihau!
   Heihodie, heihau, hiehau, heihau!

The following French translation was printed in *Voyage à la Chine par J. C. Hüttner, gentilhomme d'ambassade. Traduit de l'allemand* [par T. F. Winckler]; avec une carte de la Chine gravée par [J.B.P.] TARDIEU, et de la Musique chinoise, Paris, an VII [1799]:

Chanson des Rameurs Chinois

Tu déroules a longs replis,
O Peiho! ton cristal liquide.
La Jonque suit tes bords fleuris,
Docile au Rameur qui la guide,
Et qui, courbé sur l'aviron,
Apprend à l'écho sa chanson:
   Heiho, heihaou, heiho, heihaou!
   Heihodi, heihaou, heihaou, heihaou!

Ralentis le cours de tes eaux
A l'aspect de ces champs fertiles:
Vois se glisser dans tes roseaux
Cet essaim de Nymphes agiles,
Qui suit d'un pied leste et mignon
Et le Rameur et la chanson:
   Heiho, heihaou, heiho, heihaou!
   Heihodi, heihaou, heihaou, heihaou!

IX
SONG

from Mr. Park's Travels
The Words by the Dutchess of Devonshire
The Music by G. G. Ferrari

Adagio

The loud wind roar'd, the rain fell fast, the White Man yiel - ded to the blast! he sat him down be-neath our tree, for wear-y sad and faint was he, and ah! no wife or moth-er's care, for him the

milk or corn pre-pare; for him the milk or corn pre-pare.

CHORUS

The White Man shall our pit-y share; a-las! no wife or moth-er's care, the milk or corn for him pre-pare; the milk or corn for him pre-pare.

a Negro Song
from Mr. Park's Travels

The loud wind roar'd, the rain fell fast,
The White Man yielded to the blast!
He sat him down beneath our tree,
For weary, sad, and faint was he;
And ah! no wife or mother's care
For him the milk or corn prepare.

CHORUS

The White Man shall our pity share;
Alas! no wife or mother's care
The milk or corn for him prepare.

The storm is o'er; the tempest past;
And Mercy's voice has hushed the blast.
The wind is heard in whispers low;
The White Man, far away must go;
But ever in his heart will bear
Remembrance of the Negro's care.

CHORUS

Go, White Man, go; but with thee bear
The Negro's wish, the Negro's prayer;
Remembrance of the Negro's care.

ILLUSTRATIONS

A. Maraca-player and dancer, from no. 1

umbs Geld zu zeigen. Daß ihre Bärendäntzer   Wallfarths Andacht ertråncken. An solch ei=
haben auch solche Comödianten bey sich/ die un=   nem Tage hat sichs begeben/daß ein volles Weib
ter andern alsbald einen Possen (oder Klücht   aus dem Kruge gekommen/ auff dem Wege nie=
(wie es die Holländer nennen) mit Bopven agi=   der gefallen und eingeschlaffen. Indem ein an=

B. Psaltery (gusle) and fiddle in Russia, from the 1696 German
edition of the original of no. 5

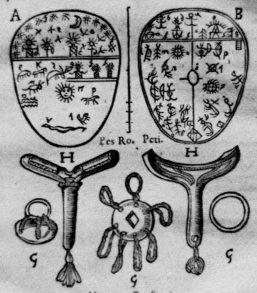

*pingunt res terrenas, & animantia varia, ut ursos, lupos, rangiferos, lu-
tras, vulpes, serpentes, tum paludes, lacus, fluvios & id genus. Et hoc quidem tympanum, quemadmodum describit Samuel Rheen, cujus
quoque istam dedit picturam.*

Notarum Explicatio.

In Tympano *A. a.* Thor. *b.* famulus ejus. *c.* Stoorjunkare.
d. famulus ejus. *e.* aves. *f.* stellæ. *g.* Christus. *h.* Apostoli ejus.
i. ursus. *k.* Lupus. *l.* rangifer. *m.* bos. *n.* sol. *o.* lacus. *p.* vulpes,
q. sciurus. *r.* serpens.   Q 3   in

C. 1-6 Lappish drums, from no. 6

quasdam forte prorsus immutari. Quod ut rectius intelligatur,
ecce tibi duo alia delineata , quorum utrumque accepi ex Musæo
Illustrissimi Regni Cancellarii.

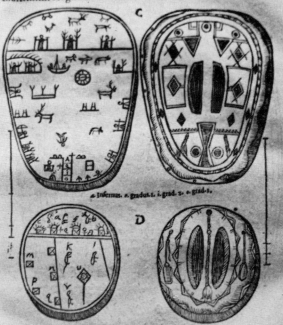

a. Infernus. *o.* gradus. 1. *i.* grad. 2. *e.* grad. 3.

a. notat aves. *b.* vulpes nigras. *c.* Tiuur, deum. *d.* Thoor, deum.
e. malleum Thoronis. *f.* Stoorjunkare, *g.* idolum ligneum. *h.* fa-
mulum. *i.* stellam. *k.* bovem. *l.* hircum. *m.* stellam. *n.* lunam. *o.* So-
lam, *p.* stellam. *q.* itidem. *r.* lupum. *s.* Norias fiord. *i. c.*

E

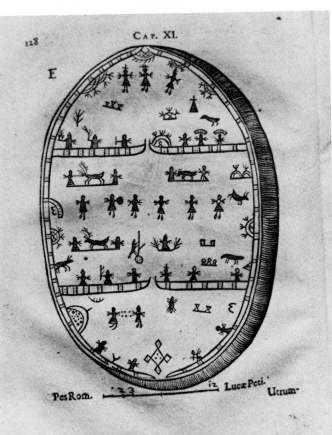

PesRom.   3 3   iz Lucæ Peti.   Utrum-

Utrumque exhibet adversam faciem non magis, quam aversam. Utrumque præfert non signa magis, quam eorum explicatiónem, sicut quidem est ad me perlata.   Qualis & in tympano B est adjecta.

Facies adversa tympani

Pes Romanus Lucæ Peti.

R

Nec

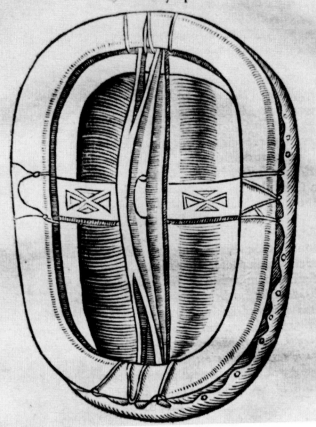

The Explication of the Figures.

In the Drum A. a markes *Thor.* b *Thors Servant.* c *Storjunkare.* d *his Servant.* e *Birds.* f *Stars.* g *Christ.* h *his Apostles.* i *a Bear.* k *a Wolf.* l *a Rain-deer.* m *an Ox.* n *the Sun.* o *a Lake.* p *a Fox.* q *a Squeril.* r *a Serpent.*

In the Drum B. a denotes *God the Father.* b *Jesus Christ.* c *the Holy Ghost.* d *S.John.* e *Death.* f *a Goat.* g *a Squeril.* h *Heaven.* i *the Sun.* l *a Wolf.* m *the fish Siik.* n *a Cock.* o *Friendship with the wild Rain-deer.* p *Anundus Eerici (*whose drum this was*) killing a Wolf.* q *Gifts.* r *an Otter.* s *the friendship of other Lapps.* t *a Swan.* u *a sign to try the condition of others, and whether a disease be incurable.* x *a Bear.* y *a Hog* β *a Fish.* ᴠ *one carrying a Soul to Hell.*

(In the Drum C. a denotes *Hell.* e *its first stage.* i *second stage.* o *third stage*). (Shown in Latin under this drum; not shown in the English translation).

In the Drum C (correctly D). a denotes *Birds.* b *black Foxes.* c. *Tinur, a God.* d *Thor, a God.* e *Thors hammer.* f *Storjunkare.* g *a wooden Idol.* h *his Servant.* i *a Star.* k *an Ox.* l *a Goat.* m *a Star.* n *the Moon,* o *the Sun.* p *a Star.* q *another Star.* r *a Wolf.*

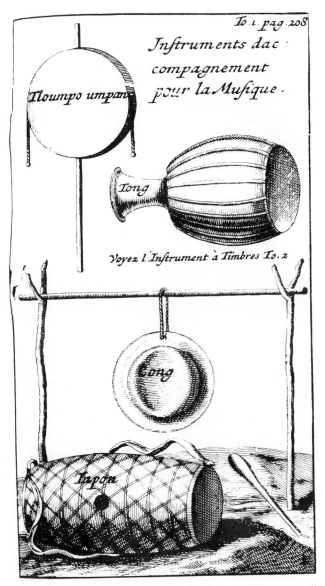

D. 1-3 Siamese instruments and song, from no. 8

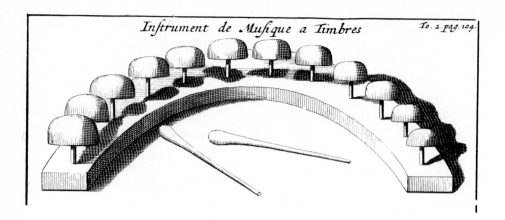

Instrument de Musique a Timbres

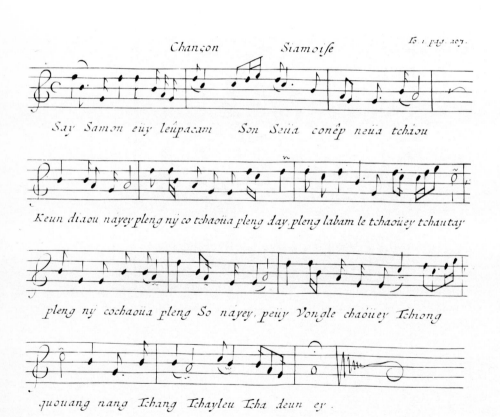

Chançon   Siamoise

Say Samon euy leüpacam   Son Seüa conép neüa tchaou

Keun diaou nayey pleng ny co tchaoüa pleng day, pleng labam le tchaoüey tchautay

pleng ny cochaoüa pleng So nayey, peüy Yongle chaoüey Tchong

quouang nang Tchang Tchayleu Tcha deun ey.

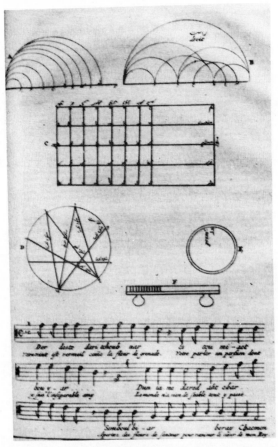

E. Persian music-diagrams, instrument and
song, from no. 12

G. Japanese instruments, from no. 14

The hall of hundred mats, where the Princes of the Empire and the Dutch Ambassadors are admitted to an audience of the Emperor... A,B,C,D,E,G,H,I,K,L, M,N,O, are the organs, violins bells, flutes, trumpets, drums and other musical Instruments of the Japanese, as I found them represented in their own books. Many of these they have in common with other Indian Nations. The description of the musical instruments of the Persians, as given p. 740 & *seq.* of the *Amoenitates Exoticae,* may serve, in good measure, to explain these.

Planche.IX.pag.59.

A. *jndien du Chili en Macuñ jouant a la Sueca, jeu de croce*
B. *jndienne en Choñi .* C. *Cahouin touhan ou fête des jndiens*
D. *Gardes Espagnoles pour empecher le desordre .* E. *Pivellea ou Sifflet*
F. *Paquecha ou tasse a bec.* G. *Coulthun ou tambour .* H. *Thouthouca ou trompette*

H. South American instruments, from no. 15

(At foot of Plate, from Monsieur Frézier, *A Voyage to the South-Sea):*

Plate IX, *p.* 62, *explain'd in* English.

A. *An* Indian *of* Chili, *in the Posture of Playing at* La Sueca, *a Sort of Bandy.*
B: *An* Indian *Woman holding the Liquor for her Husband.*
C. Cahouin touhan, *or an* Indian *Festival or Rejoycing.*
D. Spanish *Guards appointed to prevent Disorders.*
E. Pivellea, *A Whistle, or Pipe.*
F. Paquecha, *A Drinking-Dish with a long Beak.*
G. Coulthun, *A Drum.*
H. Thouthouca, *A Trumpet.*

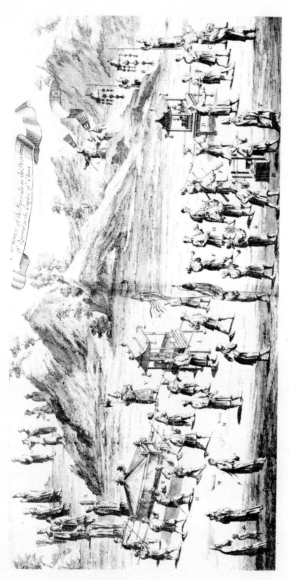

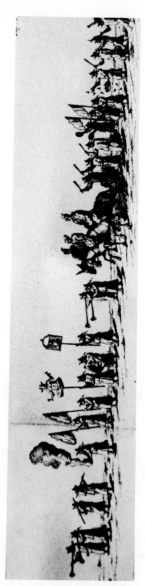

J. 1 Chinese **funeral** procession, **from**
Dr. John Francis Gemelli Careri,
A Voyage round the World, in A.
and J. Churchill, *A Collection of
Voyages*, IV, London, 1704 (the
voyage was made in 1693-1699)

J. 2 Chinese fertility
procession, from
the same

K. An opera in Cochinchina, from no. 17a

L. 1-3 William Alexander's water-colour, made from a sketch by Lieutenant Henry Parish, of the arrival of the Emperor Ch'ien-lung at the Imperial audience tent at Jehol on September 14th, 1793, with details of music-groups, from the original in the British Museum, Department of Prints and Drawings

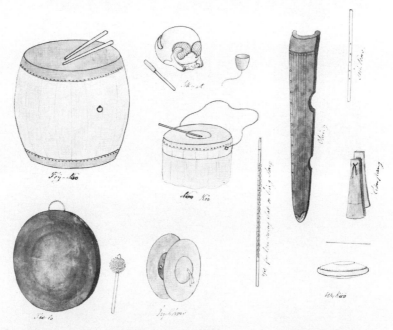

M. Chinese instruments, probably drawn by Matthew Raper, from the British Museum manuscript Additional 33,931

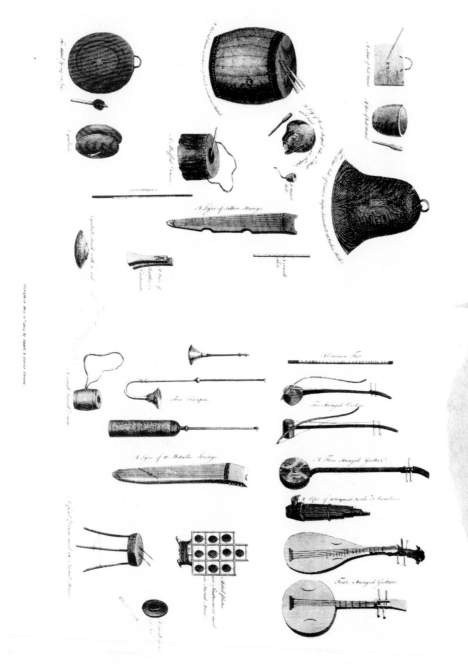

N. Chinese instruments, from no. 17g

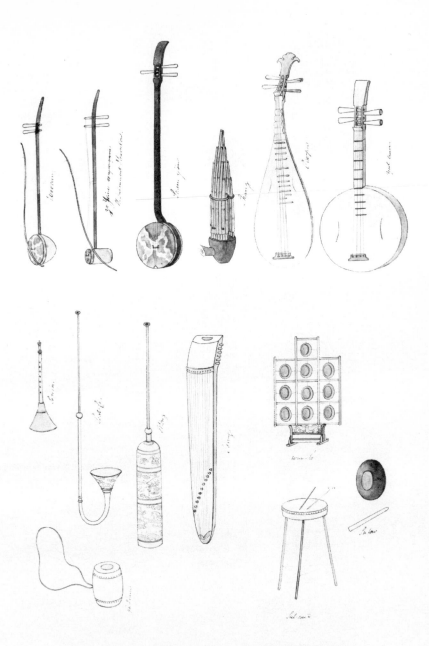